MANAGEMENT
DECISIONS
BY OBJECTIVES

George S. Odiorne

Prentice-Hall, Inc. *Englewood Cliffs, N. J.*

PRENTICE-HALL INTERNATIONAL, INC., *London*
PRENTICE-HALL OF AUSTRALIA, PTY. LTD., *Sydney*
PRENTICE-HALL OF CANADA, LTD., *Toronto*
PRENTICE-HALL OF INDIA PRIVATE LTD., *New Delhi*
PRENTICE-HALL OF JAPAN, INC., *Tokyo*

Reward Edition 1982

PRINTED IN THE UNITED STATES OF AMERICA
B & P

HOW THIS BOOK WILL HELP MANAGERS MAKE BETTER DECISIONS

This book is mainly for operating managers, staff department heads and other people in management who have to solve problems and make decisions. In recent years experts have studied decision making most intensively, and have brought some startling new insights to the process. In so doing however they have often left the work-a-day executive behind. They speak two languages which are often unintelligible to those not especially trained in their field. The first language is mathematics, and the second is the jargon of the behavioral sciences. This book is based upon an intensive review of these specialized works, and converts them into practical terminology. It also draws on the findings and observations of successful executives who have tried to lay out in intuitive fashion what they do when they make good decisions.

This book will help managers improve their decision making ability:

(1) By explaining how to define a problem in very specific form. The definition of a problem is simple and hard nosed. "A problem is the difference between the *present condition* and the *desired condition*" (or objective). So, you see, if you know where you are, and you set an objective you have defined the limits of the problem.

(2) By making it clear that to get a problem solved somebody has to make a *commitment* to somebody else whose opinion is important, that he will change something to bring the actual condition closer to the objective. (That's why the book is called *Management Decisions by Objectives*.) The committed man has to choose and decide among alternative solutions and moves. The uncommitted man can delay, put it off, and not get things done.

(3) By using some *analytical tools* which strap the facts and goals into a model for decision. The alternative to such tools is emotion or intuition,

which will not be entirely eliminated, but which can be managed and organized better if there is a system.

(4) By explaining how to *screen options* to find the best one, which is the heart of the decision process. Much of the mathematical study of decision making has centered on this problem, but the basic process is a logical one, not purely mathematical. The manager who understands the basic logic of the process can use it even if he isn't mathematically trained. This book explains the underlying system, and also goes into some simple illustrations of how these apply to decision making.

(5) By transferring these *decisions into action* to make things happen, and by applying them to the actual problems the executive faces in his job.

The best way to use this book is to read through it completely from start to finish. If you're an engineer or use mathematics in your work, the mathematical segments will seem simple. If you are less adept at math you can read the text, and, if the math seems esoteric, simply read right past it and come back at your leisure to study it in more depth. The last segment of the book is a summary of the mathematical tools with illustrations out of everyday life in the plant, office, or home.

The company training director who wishes to use this as a supplement to a supervisory or management development course in managerial problem solving and decision making can assign chapters for reading, to be supplemented by action training exercises such as games, case studies, or as the writer has done, with small group discussions using actual problems presented by the members of the group.

It comprises an advanced reading text for a Management by Objectives program, where the company has installed a goal program, and wants to sharpen the skills of the managers on those special problem-solving objectives which emerge once the regular objectives are under control.

The purpose of this book is to teach. As a result of studying it the manager should be better able to define his problems, and make the decisions necessary to solve them. If you learn, you should change your behavior, be more effective, achieve more of your objectives, and make more things happen.

GEORGE S. ODIORNE

ACKNOWLEDGEMENTS

I would like to express my thanks and acknowledgement to the following publishers for their courtesy in permitting quotations from the following copyrighted works:

To John Wiley and Sons, Inc., for permission to quote from J. Von Neumann and O. Morgenstern, *Theory of Games and Economic Behavior* and from R. F. Norman and John J. Hayes, *Creative Management*.

To Appleton-Century-Crofts, Inc. for permission to quote from B. F. Skinner, *The Behavior of Organisms*.

To the *Saturday Review* to quote from an article by J. W. Krutch, "Man Is Not a Fact."

To McGraw-Hill Book Company, Inc. for permission to quote from Rensis Likert, *New Patterns of Management*.

To Richard D. Irwin, Inc. for permission to quote from D. W. Fiske and S. R. Maddi, *The Functions of Varied Experience*.

To St. Martin's Press, Inc. for permission to quote from J. M. Keynes, *Treatise on Probability*.

CONTENTS

xi

Part II. DECISION MAKING ON THE RUN

Part III. THE TOOLS OF DECISION MAKING

Part I

Decision Making
by Objectives

Despite some limitations as a complete explanation of decision making, the rational methods of decision making found in systems engineering, operations research, and applied mathematics are an essential ingredient in making choices as a manager. Good decision making (making choices) today demands a mastery of the underlying ideas behind decision theory.

In this part of the book we'll examine the stages of decision which lend themselves to rational treatment, survey those rational methods, and show how they relate to the decision theories of the social psychologist.

The specific details of the mathematical and theoretical tools employed will be picked out and comprise a final section of the book for those who wish to study them in more detail.

chapter 1

YOU CAN
LEARN TO DECIDE

*There are things that are never realized but
remain only able to be so.*
                    —ARISTOTLE—*(Logic)*

The world of "might have been" is an imaginary utopia. It's filled with
happy marriages that might have taken place if somebody could have made
up his or her mind. It's full of businesses that could have been started. Its
stock portfolios are crammed with winners. Its factories are models of
efficiency filled with good ideas that were promptly used. The reason it's
all a dream is that somebody didn't make up his mind.

More time is lost, success forfeited, careers stymied, and frustrations
confronted from this inability to make a good decision than can be
estimated.

Wrong decisions make more mischief than a thousand devils working
their fiendish schemes. The hasty and ill-thought-through action leads to
opposition, conflict, confusion and hesitancy.

Many of our moral crises are actually crises of decision making. Albert
Camus put it: "All systems of morality are based on the idea that an
action has consequences that legitimize it or cancel it." Looking for the
good guys and bad guys may be actually a process of identifying people
who can make right decisions as contrasted with those who make wrong
ones.

Using a system for making up your mind

A lot of excellent decision makers make up their mind by intuition. They have learned from experience, hunch and imitation how to make up their minds and to have the decisions right more often than they are wrong. We shouldn't overlook nor downgrade such decision making.

Other people didn't have anybody around to imitate who could teach them good decision making. Or perhaps they never had the good luck to be placed in a position where they had to learn by hunch and experience. If this is the case, perhaps a conscious *system* for making decisions is what you need.

Even if you are already a pretty good decision maker, having a system is better than not having one. For one thing you can improve what you are doing. For another, you'll be able to change parts of the system without scrapping it all. For a final point, if you want to teach other people how to make better decisions you'll have to teach them by some kind of system.

Some systems are complex and mathematical in nature. They employ such techniques as operations research, linear programming, matrix algebra and the like. This book won't do more than touch on the theory underlying such systems, since it's written for non-mathematical readers. Some of the meanings which these more esoteric systems use we'll adopt (convert into English) since they are useful, especially terms like certainty, uncertainty and risk.

Some of the best decisions, on the other hand, are really based on folklore and hunch. They are rooted more in cracker barrel philosophies and old wives' tales. We'll try to grasp what underlies the reasons for success of these. The old rule for deciding whether or not to carry an umbrella according to the saying "red sky at morning sailor take warning, red sky at night sailor's delight" isn't an especially reliable system. Better perhaps to turn on the radio or TV and get some current information from the weather bureau which has received radar and observer reports over the wire, and run them through a computer to predict the weather.

A system doesn't do your thinking for you. It merely helps to organize the facts, get the cobwebs out of your mind, and help you define where you want to go. It leads to a point in decision making where you finally take your decision and put it into action and make it work. At this stage the "logic of practice" takes over. We'll look at this logic of practice and see how it relates to theories of decisions based on more scientific methods.

. . . But I don't have a decisive personality!

Many persons who have trouble making up their mind throw up their hands at the idea of doing better in this respect. They may note how others do it and attribute this skill to inner qualities with which the person was born. These genetic factors certainly affect your behavior in making decisions and carrying them out. They aren't the only influence however. Let's look at how this would look in a diagram:

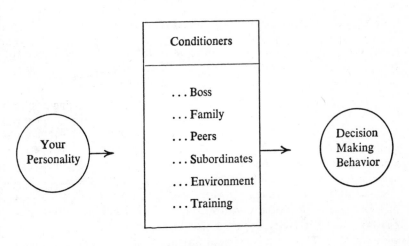

Figure 1-1

Your personality is composed of those innate capacities which you inherited from your parents (and other ancestors) as sandpapered by life. It means that left to your natural devices—without any obstructing influences—you might tend toward a certain kind of behavior.

Nobody is wholly guided by his personality. If he were we would return to the jungle. Civilization means that our instincts and traits are channeled into social paths. We have institutions such as marriage, the family, home, government and laws which help us survive against some natural pressures that could destroy us if left unhampered. Our natural instinct is tempered by what we have *learned,* as well as the other people who surround us.

Having arrived at voting age, we are hard put to isolate those things about our behavior which can be attributed to our genetic make-up and which we have learned. The only thing that's certain is the behavior which we see. People choose one kind of behavior over another; they go to the ball game instead of the opera. They stick with their first wife or they philander about. They sell a million dollars' worth of insurance, or they operate a machine in a factory. Behavior is what people *do.* You can see it and measure it.

Decision making is treated in this book as a kind of behavior (making choices) which can be learned. Thus if you make decisions in one manner now, you are probably doing so because of certain influences in the past.

You can change the future if you can learn how.

When you are done people may say that you are "more decisive." This will probably be because they see different behavior than before. They may conclude that you are *different* inside.

. . . So you need a system for decision making

Starting with the kind of personality you have (and there's not much you can do about that), and the kind of people who surround you, you can still make up your mind and make *better* decisions. Stop worrying about your personality, and concentrate for awhile with me on a system for decision making.

A system isn't anything strange; you're surrounded by them. The thermostat which controls the temperature is part of a system (a temperature control system). Your children attend a school system. Your light bill is calculated by an accounting system. The electricity you get, for what you paid, is part of the electrical system. If you vote, get married, get arrested, or write a letter to your congressman, you are touching a system (of government). It's pretty apparent that you are familiar with systems in your daily life. This book is going to propose a system for decision making (and problem solving, which is considered the same thing) which will serve the same purposes in making up your mind that the political, economic, or engineering systems previously mentioned serve the managers of such systems to get things done. As we'll note, a system isn't an insurance policy. A system should serve you in these ways:

1. It should tell you what you should probably do *first* in order to get something done. This means you always start at the point where things go in. We'll talk about these as *inputs*. (In this book they are objectives.)

2. It should have some kind of machinery, tools or *processes* it goes through in working over the inputs. In this book these processes are tools of *logic* and *acceptance* in decision making.

3. It should help you see what is coming out of your efforts in such a way that you can measure how well you did. These end products are the outputs (the results).

4. It should allow you to compare the *inputs* and the *outputs* to see if they are equal. If they are it was worthwhile, and will also show you where you can improve next time. This is the process of feedback (which simply means you feed back to the input point the information on how big the output was).

Let's see how these four ingredients look when we make a diagram of a system.

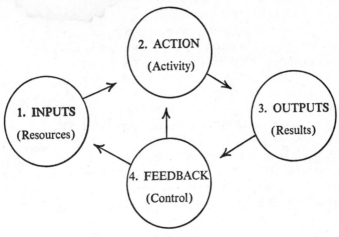

Figure 1-2

For example, the *inputs* in your heating system are coal, oil, gas wood or electricity and perhaps water.

Your furnace is the engine that *processes* these *inputs* and converts them into something else you want.

The *outputs* are heat, measured in BTU's or degrees of temperature, and humidity.

The *feedback* is done at the thermostat. This is a two-part switch which measures the temperature in the room constantly, reports the result to a switch. If it gets over a fixed temperature it feeds back notice to the input stage to stop putting in the ingredients that are processed. The furnace goes off and stays off until the temperature drops. When it falls below a certain temperature it sends an impulse feedback to the inputs to start working and the furnace starts up again.

What has all of this got to do with decision making? You can use a system for making up your mind. You'll need to identify what the parts of the system are and try them out a few times. Your system won't work perfectly the first time you try it. Even your plumber has to putter with the furnace to get it operating properly, and it may go out of kilter and have to be adjusted. Despite this, a temperature control system is better than running up and down the stairs every time you think the temperature is too high or too low.

It's certainly better than freezing or roasting, crying all the while that your personality must be wrong, or you wouldn't be so cold- or warm-blooded. What is a system for decision making? What good is it?

You might control your budget.

You might run your office better.

You can become a better salesman.

You can get better grades in school.

You can learn better from your own experience.

You can teach it to others and help them avoid mistakes.

You can correct your own decisions before it's too late.

You can get off the dime of indecision by knowing where to *begin*.

You'll make better use of your time.

You'll see more results from your efforts.

You'll avoid some of the crises which seem inescapable.

The quality of your work will improve.

You won't have to do things over as often.

A panacea? Of course not. Using a system doesn't make life perfect, nor make you a superman. It does improve your chances of getting where you want to go. It helps you live more fully in the time you have.

Why decision making by objectives?

The system of management known as management by objectives has been dealt with in greater depth elsewhere. In its essence it presumes that management of our affairs on a continuing basis requires that we define objectives before we release energy or resources to achieve them. If you aren't clear where you are going then the road too must be unclear, and if you aim for nothing, that's what you will achieve.

The term "management by objectives" is similar to the language of navigation—we navigate by a star, or by the sun. When we manage by objectives we mean simply that we will fix our ultimate purpose in mind before we start our journey. This objective then becomes a target, a goal, a desired outcome, and along the route becomes a criterion for measuring progress. Finally, when we have spent our time and energies, we are able to evaluate the degree of success by measuring it against the objective.

The system of decision making described here is "by objectives," which means that the first step in solving a problem or making a decision is to clarify your objectives.

Management by objectives also requires a *commitment*. If you are committed to an objective to somebody else whose opinion is important to you, you are practically obliged to do something about it. If you work in an organization and have a boss, he might comprise such an important person, since he appraises your performance for purposes of promotion, pay raises, coaching, personnel records, and subsequent assignment.

In the kinds of objectives which we can make to our boss there is an ascending hierarchy of objectives.

1. Regular or routine   —measured by exceptions from standards
   objectives

2. Problem solving —measured by solutions and time established as objectives.

3. Innovative goals —measured by productive changes sought and achieved in time.

In all three kinds of objectives time is an important ingredient, and it is the time element which makes a commitment important.

This book deals almost wholly with the second kind of managerial objective—the problem-solving and decision-making objectives.

In the next chapter we'll run quickly through the entire system, then deal with the specific parts in some detail in the remainder of the book.

chapter 2

THE STAGES OF DECISION MAKING

—He likes to see objectives concretely defined. He abhors the thought that there is only one way of doing things; he is intensely interested in alternatives.
—WILLIAM W. KAUFMAN
The McNamara Strategy

One way we learn to do things properly is to imitate somebody who does it well. Another way is to know the underlying principles, and follow them. With this in mind, we'll look in this chapter at a system for making up your mind. We'll also look at the plan used by some of the notable decision theorists.

Robert McNamara, the former Secretary of Defense, former president of the giant Ford Motor Company, for example, brought a new style of decision making to the most complex decision-making job in the world, the secretaryship of the Department of Defense. His visible success wasn't always accompanied by applause from those who were adversely affected by his decisions, but by those who saw need for clear decision making in the Pentagon he was widely admired.

Naturally we won't describe in detail the complex man who was the Secretary of Defense. In tune with the rest of this book, a decision-making process which has much in common with systematic decision making as it is used by many people, will be presented in simplified form—only the essentials which might help you make up *your* mind.

In its briefest form the decision-making system described here is one which has been used by good decision makers everywhere. (See Figure 2-1.)

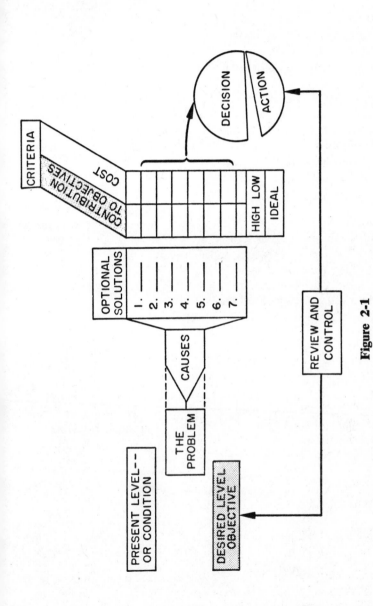

Figure 2-1

A MODEL FOR PROBLEM SOLVING AND DECISION MAKING BY OBJECTIVES

- Have an *objective* in mind before you start.
- Collect and organize all of the pertinent facts.
- Identify the problem (the difference between what actually exists now and your objectives), and its causes.
- Work out your solution and some options to it.
- Screen these options through some decision criteria.
- Set up some insurance actions to prevent failure in the form of controls.

Since this book isn't intended to be a technical treatise we'll stick with the bare essentials. Our point here is that the best decision makers in management are agreed to be precise thinkers, and certainly know how to make up their minds. If you'd like to acquire some of that skill, understanding a method might help.

Have an objective in mind

You can't really solve a problem or make a decision unless you have some idea why you want to solve it, or what an ideal outcome would be. Secretary McNamara used one called "cost effectiveness" by which he meant getting the most defense for the country for the least amount of dollars spent. Others use profit. You need to know what *your* objectives are before you can make good decisions.

You aren't running the Defense Department, but merely your own department or your own firm. You still need some objective to judge whether or not your decision is OK once you've made it. What is your goal? To raise sales volume by $1 million? To cut costs by $100,000? Or it may be that you are simply trying to make up your mind about your daughter's suitor? In the latter case you should clearly identify your objective before judging John Smith, who has been dropping around regularly and to whom she seems attracted. You might have one of the following objectives:

- To have her marry a young man of good moral character.
- To have her marry a rich young man.
- To get her off your hands as soon as possible.
- To have her marry anybody as long as she loves him.

Your decision-making processes will be affected by your objectives. Once you have these goals clearly spelled out, you are then ready to move to the rest of the plan. You'll want to get more information (facts) upon which to make up your mind.

Then get the facts about what exists now

Immersing yourself in the situation at hand seems to be a good guide. Get all of the data, the relationships between people, the numbers, the examples. One good way of getting at the facts is to list them chronologically, as if it were a diary kept on the situation. Sometimes by seeing how events occurred one after another we can find a better way of getting out of a bad situation.

Another way of pulling the facts together is to draw some kind of sketch showing graphically how the facts lie in relation to one another.

Still another way would be to make a chart or graph of the facts. By arranging them in this visual or charted form you see them in relationships that point up the true nature of the problem you are trying to solve. We'll look at some useful tools for fact gathering in some detail later on.

One of the pitfalls to be avoided in fact gathering is that you avoid treating things as facts when there is no evidence that they are true. Let's illustrate these points with a homely example:

The case of the embattled marriage

Each evening before returning home Mr. Smith enters a bar and consumes four martinis. By the time he gets home he is quite inebriated. He no sooner enters into his front door than Mrs. Smith begins berating him loudly for his condition. She continues this on into the evening, during which he often consumes several more drinks.

Upon being interviewed, Mr. Smith reports that the reason he drinks so heavily is because his wife "is a nag." Mrs. Smith, upon being interviewed, states that she wouldn't nag if Mr. Smith would come home sober.

What are the facts in this case?

1. It is not a *fact* that poor Smith is married to a shrew. (That is a conclusion arrived at by Smith and his friends.)

2. It is not a *fact* that poor Mrs. Smith is married to a hopeless lush. (That is merely the opinion of Mrs. Smith and her friends.)

The facts are that he drinks and she nags and that they each perform these acts simultaneously.

What harm is done if you conclude as their respective friends have done? If you conclude that opinion is fact you start out with no common ground of arriving at a decision which can be implemented.

Facts should be verifiable and agreed-upon data. They should be backed up by some evidence to which all can agree. It's a fact if you can see it or measure it or perhaps smell it; hear it, taste it, or otherwise check it with your senses.

Much decision making goes wrong because we won't treat facts objectively. We try to garb other things such as opinions, biases, hunches, or conclusions as if they were facts. Having jumped ahead thus, we may then overlook something important because it means that we have barred other possible solutions.

Here's a small test of your grasp of this idea:

> Young John Smith was arrested last night while driving on Jackson Road by Officer Harrison of the local sheriff's office. He was held for driving without a license, and for the possession of liquor.

Write F beside those statements which represent fact in the foregoing case:

...... 1. Smith's parents should be blamed as well as John.

. . 2. John was probably drunk.

.... 3. John Smith was arrested and put in jail.

.... 4. Officer Harrison is of the local sheriff's office.

. . 5. John had forgotten his license.

. 6. Driver education in the schools doesn't do any good.

The only fact in this list is (4), and the rest is speculation, opinion and gossip. If you fell into the trap of assuming that one of the others was fact you went beyond your evidence.

We'll spend the entire fifth chapter on ways you can improve your fact-gathering abilities.

What makes a problem a problem?

The mere existence of a shocking fact doesn't of itself comprise a problem. Let's say, for example, that John Smith, who was arrested by Officer Harrison, was a stranger. The news item becomes a piece of idle information. There may be a serious problem for young Smith, or his parents, or his family, but not for you.

Add this factual bit of information about the arrest to another fact that the same John Smith has been seeing quite a bit of your daughter lately. It may not be a problem then until you tie these facts to your objectives regarding your daughter's marriage choice. Now you may indeed think you have a problem. Let's suppose the following two circumstances were the case:

(1) *Your objective*: You wish to have your daughter marry a moral young man who will make her happy.

(2) *Your facts*: Young Smith, whom she has been seeing often, was arrested last night, as reported in the paper.

(3) *Your problem?* It's basically the difference between what you want to achieve and the facts that indicate a serious or important difference exists. Can your daughter meet your marital objectives in a choice of mate if she continues to see John Smith? If Smith behaves this way is he the suitable one? The problem is in this case more potential (it lies ahead) rather than existing at present.

She isn't married yet. You induce the probability that she won't achieve the best objective by continuing her relationship with Smith as he presently appears to you.

The point of all this isn't that Dear Abby should be more scientific, nor is it intended to teach you how to run your children's social life. Even if you make the logical decision your daughter may not accept your decision.

The point is that *a problem is the difference between what we see factually to be the present situation and what we would like to see to meet our objective. The problem is the difference.*

For example, if we had read or heard instead that John had won a National Merit Scholarship, or been elected deacon of his church, or elected to his class presidency, we wouldn't see a problem. What we want (our objective) seems to be consistent with what we are getting. Result? No problem.

To define a problem takes two ingredients; an objective and some facts about present conditions that would show differences. Before you condemn young Smith and start working over your daughter with the sharp edge of your tongue it might be better to get all the facts on young Smith. Was he really drunk? Were there extenuating circumstances? Does the news story refer to the same John Smith?

It's also wise to spell out your objective and match it against the factual situation. Do you really want her to marry a moral young man, even if he bores her to death? What if Smith is the son of a millionaire? Suppose she loves the ne'er-do-well? What do you really want her to marry for? What would you settle for? (You may have minimum and maximum objectives.)

With these guidelines you can pinpoint the problem.

Once you've clarified the problem you can start thinking about some possible solutions.

Let's look at a few more examples, not tied to a domestic problem.

● You would like to manage your sales force in a way which would produce a million-dollar volume, but reach only $600,000. You aren't producing the desired volume, and note that your salesmen don't make more than one call a day, are indifferent to customers' expressions of interest. Your *problem* is low sales by $400,000 and the facts point to some possible causes of the problem.

● You would like to be promoted to a corporate officer rank in your firm and stand three levels below that position now. You also note the facts that all of those above you in rank are younger than you, are doing a good job, and like their jobs. Your *problem* is that your aspirations to high rank are blocked and the circumstances won't be eased in the foreseeable future.

Try defining a few of your own actual problems in these terms of (1) your objective; and (2) the facts which point up (3) the difference. Now you're ready to turn to a more creative and imaginative kind of activity.

Developing solutions and decisions

While we'll be looking at the various ways of developing sound options in a later chapter, suffice it to say at this point that from the problem you move to listing possible solutions. Note that we're pressing at this point for alternative solutions, one of which may prove to be best. It's at this stage that McNamara dug deep in what he called "the search for options." Your solution may be better if you have a wide range of options from which to make your final choice. You might prepare this set of options as a simple listing of alternatives. For example, take some possible optional solutions to your daughter's problem.

1. You might send her on a trip to Europe (fly now, pay later).
2. You might privately warn Smith to buzz off for good.
3. You might talk to your daughter.
4. You could ignore the whole thing.
5. You could introduce her to several nice young men and hope she'll find one more attractive.
6. You might give her direct orders to avoid him, and so on.

Screening the optional solutions

Once you've listed all the options you can think of, and perhaps you have had others help you think, you now need a filter of some kind to eliminate the worst ones and clearly label the best option. This screen is already at hand in your objectives and some variations of it. You make a simple decision-screening grid.

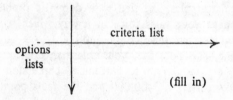

Let's come back to that hypothetical daughter of yours.

list the various options here	list your criteria for choosing one option across here. For example:		
	contribution to objective	cost	feasibility (will it work)
1. trip to Europe	medium	high	high
2. scare Smith off	high	low	low
3. talk to her	uncertain	low	low
4. ignore it	low	low	high
5. introduce others	uncertain	low	medium
6. issue orders	uncertain	low	low
DESIRED OUTCOME	HIGH	LOW	HIGH

Figure 2-2

The actual estimates of the correct wording to use in filling in the boxes must be based on your judgment in each frame. Presuming that you have accurately estimated your daughter's temperament, your relations with her, and the degree of influence you have, you now have structured the information in a way to make the decision easier.

1. It seems that only two feasible options exist. Either send her on a trip to Europe (which she would like very much) or ignore the whole thing.

2. If cost is a major consideration (you aren't well to do and have heavy expenses already), you ignore it. If on the other hand you are comfortably well off, you decide that sending her to Europe is the best option.

Controlling the effects of your decisions

The array of solutions doesn't really solve your problem nor comprise more than a first (logical) pass at devising a satisfactory solution. A sound search for options should also entail some follow-up, *if-then* calculations as a guide to making the action effective.

If you send her on a European trip

> *then* she might forget him
> *or* she might find that absence makes the heart grow fonder
> *or* she might meet somebody else
>> who proves to be perfectly satisfactory
>> *or* who proves to be a worse heel than Smith.

Such calculations for each of the various solutions (options) can be tested by the use of probability guides or decision criteria. For example, if the chances of her forgetting him rather than growing more ardent by being away are 50-50 (one chance in two), you must then press on and study the chances of her meeting somebody else, which is likely to occur in any meaningful way only if she has forgotten Smith back home. Say the chances of finding another man are also 50-50 (one chance in two), then we must multiply the odds so that the probability of the event (she'll go to Europe, forget Smith and find another man) are one in four. Now you must face the chances of her meeting a foreign ne'er-do-well. You calculate them at 50-50 (one in two). This ratio must be applied to the one-in-four possibility previously arrived at. This means that the chances are only *one in eight* that she will find a suitable European husband. The chances are also *one in eight* that she'll meet a poor choice in Europe. This puts a new perspective on using Europe as a site for finding a good substitute for Smith. On the other hand, the chances are one out of two that she will forget Smith and be left unattached from her European trip. You still won't have achieved your objective; you'll merely have prevented its being barred by the Smith alliance.

If you decide to try the European trip as a solution then, it's time to move to the next step in your decision-making process. Set up some controls to make the decision work better.

Since the chances are one out of two that the trip will lead to her forgetting Smith, your controls should do these things.

1. You should plan the trip to be so interesting that her mind won't keep wandering back home. Boredom, and reminders of Smith should be prevented.

2. Since the chances of finding a good European are the same as finding a bad one, and both are meager, she shouldn't be overly exposed to young European men.

Your final decision then is shaped to fit these criteria:

● She is to take a trip to Europe accompanied by a vivacious young matron aunt who can fend off the ardent Europeans, won't join in any escapades she might be tempted into entering, but won't be boring. (This excludes your old Aunt Martha, a notable bore.)

● She tours constantly, perhaps in a rented car, and doesn't light in any one place too long where she might be exposed to a phony count or a handsome ski-bum for long periods of time.

● The whole idea must be acceptable to her.

SUMMARY

The point of all this example, of course, hasn't a thing to do with your daughter. It's merely been a familiar example to illustrate a model for decision making. You've gone through a process which in review follows this pattern:

● Have an objective in mind before making up your mind.
● Get all of the relevant facts.
● Identify the problem (and its causes).
● Develop some solution, with options.
● Predict the effects and screen your option through criteria.
● Set up some controls to assure that your decision will work.
● Get acceptance of your decision.

If you've been impatient with this simplified example, we'd suggest that right here you should practice the method of making up your mind on a real problem of your own. It may be a business problem, a professional decision, a domestic problem, or a career choice. Put the book down and try it. Then come back for more details on each of these major steps in making up your mind.

chapter 3

SETTING OBJECTIVES

If you don't know where you are going, any road will get you there.

—THE KORAN

Systematic decision making means we apply the systems approach. Having a system not only suggests what you do, but what you do *first*.

The first step in decision making and problem solving systematically is to *define your objectives*.

● If you don't have objectives you won't know whether your actions were effective when you took them.

● Unity of effort is possible where objectives exist and are made known to the people who must effect them.

● Objectives comprise criteria for judging results.

In systems we find the three ingredients of INPUT, PROCESS, and OUTPUT lend themselves to systemization of decisions and problem solving.

● Objectives are statements of *expected outputs*.

● Objectives are defined before inputs are released.

● Objectives determine which activities and processes to use, and what inputs will be required.

● In problem solving by objectives we treat the desired outcome (the solution) as the achievement of the objective. Hence no objective—no problem.

• Objectives should be set with their subsequent use as criteria in mind, and should meet the requirements of good criteria.

Organizations in which the performance of the organization is measured are differently operated than organizations in which no such measurement occurs. The measurement of machine performance, human performance, the performance of investment capital, the level of achievement of the various tools and organizational units is a vital part of the management of the organization. Without objectives nobody knows where he is going, whether he has lost the way, whether he is indeed headed in the right direction. The common questions "How am I doing? What is expected of me? What's wrong here? How could we do better?" have meaning only within a context of known objectives.

The three classes of objectives

Simply listing rosters of goals in helter-skelter fashion can encompass all of the organization's goals if the writer sticks with his task long enough. Perhaps a better way would be to classify the goals into useful categories. Furthermore, each of these major categories should be stated in terms which are measurable, and upon which decisions can be made. The concern of this chapter, then, will be to set forth three categories of goals. This will be followed by some guides to make objectives measurable.

1. *Regular or routine objectives.* The necessary statements of objectives for any organization are definitions of the regular, ordinary requirements which are necessary for the survival of the firm. Often covered by job description, such routine objectives may be further defined by stating the average requirements which are needed to keep the organization stable. Literally millions of such regular tasks will exist in the large firm. To illustrate but a few of these:

> Paymasters must issue regular paychecks.
> Machine operators must produce at standard rates of output.
> Accountants must produce monthly reports.
> The tax manager must file yearly tax statements.
> Maintenance men must grease the machines at regular intervals.

When any of these regular chores are undone, or done at less than required times and amounts the organization begins to decline. The systems of the company are often geared toward the maintenance of such regular work levels. Whenever less than the regular amount of work is being done or routine objectives are not being met, we can clearly note that danger to the organization in some degree exists, and a *problem* has been created. The problem? To bring the actual level back up to the desired level.

The end result of all of the regular objectives being achieved is that the organization maintains the status quo. It doesn't move ahead, and if its competitors are doing more than it is, or are improving their regular objectives steadily, the organization may even be falling behind its competitors.

2. *Problem-solving objectives.* In addition to the routine duties are those which are often performed by staff department groups. Industrial engineers, cost accountants, quality control men, plant engineers, production planners, and systems men find most of their objectives in the areas of problem solving. Problems may be created by the natural tendency of matters to get worse if left alone. Individual supervisors and managers can demonstrate their skill in managing precisely in this area of their job: they see problems and solve them when they occur. Usually such problems solved on the plant floor are the intermittent problems which crop up daily due to changes in some facet of the work. The work of the industrial engineer and other staff people is more likely to deal with continuing problems which defy simple solution, or which require the mustering of resources and skills cutting across several departments. Objectives in this category call for managerial and rational problem-solving skills of a higher order than the routine objectives and their maintenance. They might include such problem-solving objectives as these:

> uncovering causes of defective work
> product contamination reduction
> falling off of sales performance
> decline in share of market
> lowering of morale in the organization
> high turnover among personnel

The treatment of such problems as objectives means that they are to be specified with some precision, the causes of the variance from standards determined, and solution developed and applied.

3. *Innovative or improvement objectives.* The highest order of objectives, quite different in character from those which maintain the status quo, are the objectives which "make things happen." To make decisions on such objectives is a quite different matter from problem-solving kinds of decisions. The latter are problem-centered, and are designed to maintain things as good as they were. The innovative category of objective starts with the assumption that even the perfect completion of routine objectives isn't good enough. It assumes that problem solving is merely a necessary step in keeping that regular level of objective at the regular level. The level of decision-making objective at this third level might include such objectives as these:

We will become bigger than competitor X by 1968.
We will become a billion-dollar corporation by 1970.
We will capture 20 per cent of the market by 1966.
We will introduce a computer into clerical operations this year.

Operations research will be started in this firm by January 30.
Our quality control will be converted to statistical quality control.
We will initiate and conduct management development programs.

These are quantum breakthroughs rather than restoration decisions. Usually they can be made only by persons having substantial managerial authority. They are not *intrinsic* (centered in a study of the present results being obtained), but are just as often *extrinsic* (centered in new ideas from outside the firm which occur in the mind of some manager).

The third category differs from the first two in being *action* decisions rather than *reaction* decisions. Somebody decides that something should happen. He may have opposition, or be faced with apathy, scoffing, or conflicting interests. His general decision to proceed may not follow the specific details of the plan which he originally thought he would follow. The only remnant of the original decision to move ahead is the statement of the objective itself. It is a visionary objective, which often can be clearly seen only by its originator. His task is to convince others of its suitability, and persuade them to accept it as their own objective, in whole or in part.

Of the three sorts of objectives outlined here, the third is the most essential to company growth. It is of a higher order than the others since it is rarest in occurrence. This hierarchy of objectives has considerable leverage in management for one reason:

> *Having a hierarchy of objectives places the greatest premium on managerial decision making which moves the organization to greater growth and achievement.*

● It presumes that people who do routine work are worth less to the organization than people who can see problems and solve them.

● It presumes that regular or problem-solving work is worth less to the corporation than work which innovates and causes the organization to move ahead.

Thus, in salary administration the raises go to persons who do more than their regular job. The problem solver who, in addition to meeting the regular objectives of his job, also sees and solves problems, is more promotable than the routine worker who doesn't see and solve problems as they occur. The person who applies certain problem-solving skills to alleviate chronic conditions that are lowering regular standards is less valuable to the firm than the superior performer who can be described as *the manager who does all of his regular duties, solves his ordinary problems, and in addition adds new and novel ideas through innovative or improvement objectives.*

This hierarchy of objectives serves in parallel fashion as a hierarchy of decision making. The contribution of the person who by his choices and decisions is able to maintain the status quo is worth less than that of the decision maker who can analyze problems and make decisions on causes, alternatives and action that remedy flaws in the process, eradicate excessive costs, or eliminate trouble. The highest order of decision maker is the kind who decides in favor of realistic visions. This higher order of decision-making skill finds its high value in its scarcity. It is sometimes identified as the entrepreneurial function, or the managerial function. Clearly it is not wholly rational. What kind of rationality would lead a Westinghouse to think of forming a firm to manufacture air brakes, or a James Ford Bell to pool the country's flour mills into a complex such as General Mills? Such decisions are rooted in the imagination and spirit of the originator. These decisions in turn are followed by exhaustive applications of common sense, intense application of science and logic, and hard work. Yet, it is not the rationality alone which accounts for the breakthrough. Even when logic has apparently failed and every avenue of a logical nature seems blocked, he persists because the visionary core of his objective remains intact.

OBJECTIVES MUST BE MATCHED BY METHODS OF MEASUREMENT

Simply having an objective doesn't lead to sound decisions. The objective must be stated in terms which lend themselves to measurement of results. When all of the effort has been expended, the logic applied, the measures of results expected provide the only means of specifying a route for the accomplishment of the decision.

One certain way to avoid disappointment is never to expect anything. A certain way to avoid making decisions is to avoid having high standards of performance for yourself, your associates, or your organization. No matter what happens, then, you can look the other way. Of course, you might also note sadly that you have gone broke, your business has failed, or your competitors have outstripped you. Setting some tough but attainable goals is part of the betterment process through decision making.

HOW TO DEFINE MEASUREMENTS FOR OBJECTIVES

When you set a goal you define the conditions that will exist when your problem is solved. A large corporation which has 20 per cent of the market by some means, logical or emotional, sets a goal to garner 30 per cent of the market within five years. The management of the corporation now has a problem—the difference between the present 20 and the desired 30 per cent. The area where decisions must be made is the 10 per cent difference. Some decisions are called for.

● This means you must identify the present level or state you find yourself in. This may sound obvious but it is hard to do, since emotional barriers, obstinacy, and unwillingness to face the truth are widespread among mortals. Take the case of the large steel mill in which various superintendents complained incessantly that the intraplant shipments of metal often arrived late. Such grumbling and squabbling occurred chronically for years. One day the general manager asked the question: "Exactly what per cent of our shipments run behind schedule?" Everyone ventured an opinion ranging from 10 to 100 per cent. "Let's find out exactly," the boss ordered. Following a detailed study, the actual level was determined to be 60 per cent of the shipments arrived late. Further analysis of the reasons showed them to stem from four or five basic causes. After developing a remedial program plan, a new lower estimate was made that incorporated two ingredients:

1. The predicted new lower level of late shipments.
2. The time when this expected new low level of shipment could be expected.

This became a guide to those charged with remedying the defects in method, and spurred their energies to focus their attention toward achieving the goal. Hard decisions which had been deferred were shaped up and executed.

The reason for establishing an objective is to permit its use in measurement later on. While the discussion of measurement is often deferred until later when criteria are being discussed, it is important that we have a measurement of results in mind when we are defining goals. It's equally important when we are defining the present condition. This is of added significance when we note that objectives are an important part of criteria in evaluating choice, and in measuring final effect.

Objectives must be specific, measurable, tangible, and under the effective control or influence of those setting the goals. To some, these limits bar the establishment of objectives, for at first glance many areas seem to be incapable of being precisely defined. (See Figure 3–1.)

HOW TO MEASURE THE UNMEASURABLE

When the future is certain, estimation of goals and time commitments is easier than when uncertainty is present. These decisions in the face of uncertainties comprise the hard decisions, and discourage many from even trying to set goals. "You can't predict such things as weather, taxes, accidents, business conditions or illness." So goes the reason for not trying to improve the decision-making process through setting sound objectives for shaping decisions. Yet, experts in decision making have defined five useful categories which you can use to sharpen your own objectives when your goals are being set in the face of uncertainty. Let's look briefly at each criterion. You should note that we will be making some judgments about *probabilities* or the chances of something happening when we're defining objectives for the uncertain.

1. *You might assume that all chances are equally true.* For example, you might be setting the date for the country club outing next year. You need to define your objectives in terms of budget dollars. We'll ignore the social consequences for now. It is well known that rain tends to dampen attendance at picnics and outings. Low attendance might break your club treasury. You would naturally like to have sunny weather. An indoor picnic would kill the attendance, fray nerves, and probably cost the sponsor a lot of money. You jot down the three possible outcomes:

a) It might be a sunny, beautiful day, or with scattered clouds.
b) It might be cloudy with showers.
c) It might rain cats and dogs all day.

If you assumed that all three outcomes were exactly equal in their likelihood of happening you calculate the outcome accordingly. Each has a probability of .333 of happening. A first calculation of the budget plan for the outing uses this criterion.

possible weather outcome	budget consequences of that outcome
1. Sunny	surplus of $500
2. Cloudy with showers	break even
3. Heavy rain	lose $350

We now add the consequences of these three possible outcomes which we have assumed are all equally probable. The total of the three comes to a predicted consequence of a $150 surplus ($500 plus $0 minus $350). A certain amount of grumbling may also be expected if it rains. This is the predictable outcome of running an outing if you assume that the chances of weather are all equally probable.

It may be possible then, to do better. For example, we may be a little more accurate in our estimate of the chances for good or bad weather by calling the weather bureau. We can ask them what the weather has been in June for the last five years. If they tell you that only three days have been rainy in June in the last five years, you now have *some* basis for moving away from the equal probability assumption. If you are going to use probability at all, you should use the best estimate of the probability. The chances of three outcomes being equally probable is itself highly improbable and perhaps you should keep digging until you get some leads which provide you a basis for an estimate that weights one more than the other.

2. *You might set a goal which counts on the most likely outcome.* Under such a goal-setting plan you make your decision based on the assumption that the most likely thing is the one which will happen. You simply ignore the possibility of other options happening. For example, in choosing the outing date you learn from the weather bureau that it rained only three days in June in each of the last five years. You conclude that it will rain 10 per cent of the day at the picnic. You therefore boldly decide to schedule

SETTING GOALS TO MEASURE THE UNMEASURABLE

1. It is often necessary to devise measurements of present levels in order to be able to estimate or calculate change from this level.

2. The most reliable measures are the real time or raw data in which the physical objects involved comprise the measures to be used (dollars of sales, tons of output, number of home runs hit).

3. When raw data can't be used, an index or ratio is the next most accurate measure. This is a batting average, a per cent, a fraction or a ratio.

4. If neither of the above two can be used, a *scale* may be constructed. Such scales may be "rate from one to ten," a nominal rating against a checklist of adjectives such as "excellent, fair, poor," or one which described "better than" or "worse than" some arbitrary scale. (These are useful but are far less precise than the above.)

5. Verbal scales are the least precise but can be extremely useful in identifying present levels and noting real change. *Verbs* such as "directs," "checks" and "reports" are indicative of actions to be taken.

6. General descriptions are the least useful, but still have value in establishing benchmarks for change. "A clear, cloudless fall day" is obviously not the same as a "cloudy, foggy, misty day" and the two descriptions could be used to state conditions as they exist and conditions as they should be.

7. The statements of measurement should be directed more toward *results* than toward *activity*. (Much activity may prove impossible to state in specific terms, whereas results of that activity can be stated.)

8. In stating results sought or in defining present levels, effort should be made to find indicative, tangible levels and convert verbal or general descriptions into such tangible scales, ratios or raw measures where possible.

9. If you can't count it, measure it, or describe it, you probably don't know what you want and often can forget it as a goal.

Figure 3-1

it for a date late in the month and plan for two hours of rain exactly. You schedule an indoor movie. When somebody querulously inquires, "But what if it rains all day?" you may even state with vast assurance, "Statistically it *never* rains all day in that month," or perhaps other statements which indicate that you are treating the most likely outcome figured on probability as though it were really certain. In common parlance, most of what we use "certain" to define should actually be "pretty sure" or most probable outcome. Since it ignores the consequences of other outcomes, it may lead the decision maker to set his goals without establishment of controls or provision for alternatives in the event the improbable outcome occurs. No "rainy all day" plan would be ready on a standby basis if such an assumption were made.

3. *You set goals based on the highest possible imaginary outcome.* Not a very sensible process, it assumes that everything that could go right will go right. It ignores possible losses, delays, and other adverse events. Called *maximax* by the experts, this is the game in which every play works, every stratagem succeeds, and no untoward events enter into the outcome to keep it from being the hole-in-one on every shot. In the event of our outing plan, the likelihood isn't so remote as touring the golf course in 18 strokes, but rather would have the same characteristic, since it would never admit the possibility of failure, nor recognize that success and failure may be a ratio rather than totally one or the other. Humorist Ogden Nash once described a golfer who, playing winter rules, teeing up in the traps, and with ten conceded putts, shot an 89. Henceforth afterward this became his normal score toward which he always aimed. Naturally he spent the rest of his life a frustrated man.

In the case of our steel mill manager it would have been *maximax* to state his goal as *no* (zero) late trains delivering materials. Quality control managers often profess to produce perfect work. Sales managers who aim at capturing 100 per cent of a potential market, or the student who promises his folks 100 per cent in every subject all the time, are making a maximax assumption. It makes the goal setter seem ambitious when in truth he is more likely to be acting in a foolhardy manner.

4. *Goals may be stated to reduce losses or raise the lowest possible level.* Here is a kind of criterion for goal setters which aims at keeping the losses to the least possible amount. It may also aim at raising the lowest possible gains. For example, with our outing we would presume that it will rain cats and dogs, and design all of our plans around reducing the losses. Obviously the most sensible thing to do here is to cancel the outing, a conclusion which this kind of criterion often leads to. Called *minimax,* it has some uses when taken as one assumption and is useful in making safeguards. To raise the lowest level of gain we might decide to run the whole outing in a hall. This would cut attendance, especially if the weather proved good outside, but it might be possible to run one that broke even or even showed

a slight surplus in the budget. It could hardly be considered a smashing success socially however, since the number of persons attending is cut by the decision not to take a chance on any loss due to rain.

In the event of the late steel deliveries, the manager might set a goal so easy that anybody could achieve it. This might be such a bland goal as "we won't get any more than 2 per cent worse," or it might be "2 per cent improvement." This would be the businessman who decides to act along the lines "we couldn't possibly make less than . . ." or "we couldn't possibly lose more than . . ."

Such goals often result in maintenance of the status quo and seldom provide much motivation to change or move forward.

5. *Bayes Rule: Figure out the largest expected value and choose in favor of that.* The "expected value" is more than simply the single item of budget outcome in our outing example. It means also that we figure out the probability of each outcome and weigh the financial results according to the likelihood of its happening. In this case we would take the dollars of surplus for each kind of weather and multiply it by the probability that each of the possible outcomes will occur.

ACTION CHOICE		POSSIBLE OUTCOMES		
		ALL DAY RAIN	SHOWERS	SUNNY
PROBABILITIES		.10	.20	.70
1.	COMMIT TO ALL DAY OUTDOORS	-$350	$300	$500
	EXPECTED VALUE	-$35	$60	$350 $375
2.	PLAN OUTDOORS, BUT ARRANGE EMERGENCY COVER	$0.00	$450	$450
	EXPECTED VALUE	$0.00	$90	$315 $405
3.	PLAN FOR INSIDE OUTING	-$100	-$100	-$150
	EXPECTED VALUE	-$10	-$20	-$105 $-135

Figure 3-2

Figure 3–2 shows how this calculation works. Down the left margin you list the three choices of decision which you might make for your club outing. You might assume (1) that it will be sunny all day, and cheerily ignore the possibility of even a shower. You might plan (2) for an all-day outing but also rent a large tent and arrange the movie for emergency shower entertainment. You might play it very cagey (3) and run the whole outing inside, rain or shine.

Across the top you list the three possible outcomes for the weather on the day of the outing. For each of these outcomes (all-day rain, showers, and sunny) you get the best information you can from the weather bureau and your favorite weather prophet at home or your bunions, and post these at the head of each of these columns of possible outcomes.

The next stage is to post into the respective squares the financial consequences of each decision under each possible outcome.

It would be possible to make the decision here without figuring expected value, based on common sense. You'd take the second choice because it gives you a chance to make $450, without any risk of losing anything out of the treasury. Some decisions won't be this transparent to the glance however, so we'll figure our expected values for illustrative purposes.

As the arrows on the table indicate, you multiply the probability of the outcome by the dollar consequence, and post the product in the lower right of the square. Having done this for all squares, add the expected values for each decision *across* the column. This sum of the horizontal row of expected values comprises the total expected value of that decision. Now your decision is made: *Choose in favor of the highest expected value.* In this case it is the second choice, which has an expected value of $405. This indicates that for budgetary purposes the best choice for the picnic would be to have an emergency cover available in the event of showers.

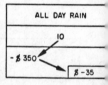

One word of caution lies in choice of a zero value. You may recall that including a zero value where multiplication is involved results in a zero in all subsequent multiplication. In this simple case the effect is not significant. In very complex applications it might wipe out the mission.

Of course we should also note that this illustration deals only with the budget consequence. In complete decision making you might need to weigh dollars against social acceptance, aspirations for the club presidency, or other factors. In such cases you might need to add further calculations which reduce these unlike variables (money and social acceptance) to a common measuring instrument called utility. In a later example we'll show how this is done. We'll also find that this table of expected values is used in other kinds of modern decision tools such as the decision tree.

Our point here isn't on how to run outings, because we all know more about outings than this chart tells us. The point is to show how Bayes rule works without getting ensnarled in detail.

Using tools like the expected value can help you because it clarifies something that isn't obvious. It doesn't actually remove judgment from your decisions, (you've got to judge or figure probability), but it patterns this judgment, and ties it to the things you know for sure (the costs of the various outcomes) and in so doing reduces the mistakes to their minimum possible level.

Figuring utility as a basis for goal setting

At this point you may rightly be impatient that we have treated such a splendid social event as an outing only in terms of budget. After all, man doesn't live by bread alone, and all of our values aren't going to be estimated by their money worth.

> The idea of utility is a useful way of setting measurement on goals for yourself or your organization. It is useful because it includes more than money, and takes in all of the things that cause us to prefer one thing to another.

To get the most from the idea of *utility* in stating your goals you should use a suitable measurement scale for your utilities. "Utility is a common yardstick created to measure the unmeasurable." There are several types of measurement methods for your utilities. All are designed to find a common yardstick for unlike phenomena.

● *Cardinal measures are a common and familiar measurement.* It is customary to use rulers, yardsticks, and cardinal measures for those measurements which can be stated in units such as pounds, ounces, feet, inches, IQ, and the like. It helps us compare and measure by referring to a common number for each characteristic we want to measure. This is the kind of measure the steel mill managers used when they stated the late deliveries in terms of per cent of late deliveries to total deliveries.

Many *indices* such as Mickey Mantle's batting average are cardinal measures. If Mantle "hit .310" in a particular year we mean that he got 31 hits for every 100 times he was at bat. One of the parts of the decision-making and problem-solving processes often entails developing indices in order that you can note progress, or in order to set meaningful goals at all.

● *Measurement by ordinal scales* is another way of using utilities in the goal-setting process. This means you set out to beat somebody else, "to be better than the Joneses," or to be more than something which you have selected as a goal. "I'm going to be earning $10,000 a year by the time I'm thirty." The ordinal scale is no more than a determination of whether or not the outcome is *more* or *less* than other objects—using last year's results as a goal, for example.

Ordinal scales are really riskless choices, since they entail only the relationship of the actual outcome to a certain chosen point. It doesn't equate gains with favorable outcomes or losses with unfavorable outcomes. Sometimes it may have a possibility of gain without the risk of loss, as in a footrace run for a medal. The losers didn't "lose" the medal; they never had it to start with, and if they have a medal previously won, they keep it (this of course doesn't include side bets or pari-mutuel arrangements as a side condition to the actual race).

● *Figuring your utilities by a nominal scale.* When setting goals, you may pick them from a scale which you have constructed, using *adjectives* such as "tired" or "fresh." It may be a rating of positive or negative from a fixed rating point chosen in advance and would illustrate nominal scales. A nominal scale will help you set goals and measure progress from one point to another. Let's illustrate this:

Suppose you were to be surveyed at this point on how well you like this book. After some cogitation between publisher and author it was decided that the important features of a book like this are that it should be: (1) of value to the reader (it meets his needs) and (2) it is interesting (it is easy to read). We could construct a scale here of a simple bar type as in Figure 3-3.

REGARDING THIS BOOK SO FAR CHECK YOUR REACTIONS ON EACH OF THE FOLLOWING SCALES. (√)

Value to me

none   utmost

Interest

none   utmost

Figure 3-3

Ignoring for the moment the very likely condition that ratings on the lower extreme of the scale would be absent (if it were that dull and useless you would have quit reading before now), how could such a scale be used in goal setting?

First: The author might try it out in manuscript form, and if ratings were below the 4.0 divider he might rewrite sections or even scrap the whole thing. He thus makes it his objective to write a book which would be rated 4.0 or better on the scale.

Second: For specific classes of readers he might be able to determine how effectively he had achieved his goal with each class.

Again, the purpose of this illustration is to show how the measurement system can be constructed, not actually to measure your reactions. Still another kind of scale would be a survey questionnaire like the following:

> My opinion of the book so far is best described by the following sentence: (check (√) one.)
>
> —— Very valuable and interesting
> —— Fairly valuable and interesting
> —— Useful but dull
> —— Interesting but not too useful to me
> —— Boring and useless

This too is presented as an illustration of a nominal scale. Other examples might include a taxonomy, statement of a physical unit or condition in varying amounts, or polar opposite conditions.

Some common assumptions which we can believe

In the goal setting process there are a few ordinary assumptions which seem to work with most ordinary people.

1. Preferences are usually transitive, that is, if we prefer apples over pears and pears over pineapples, we ordinarily would be expected to prefer apples over pineapples.

2. We prefer things that bring us the most satisfaction and are easier to get over things that are unsatisfying and hard to get. (It's better to be rich and healthy than poor and sick.)

3. Some things which could be chosen as goals will be preferred and this implies others that are not preferred.

4. There are many alternatives for which we have no preferences and to which we are indifferent.

5. Many of our preferences are not of our own choosing, but are derived from other people's preferences. If our bosses, our wives, or our families prefer something, we may overcome our indifference.

SUMMARY

Decision theorists often gloss over the objectives-setting stage by merely stating "objectives must be set." This misses an important point about objectives.

- Objectives create the problem and define it.
- Objectives are criteria by which final outcome must be measured.
- Objectives cannot always be stated in raw data, but must be stated in terms of gains, risks, expected values, utility, or other criteria which will indicate change, or indicate the degree to which action has been effective.
- Objectives are guided by a *principle of summarization* in dealing with

problems which exist in an organizational setting. The *objectives* for the boss becomes *activity* when he subdivides them for his subordinates. To put it another way, the subordinates' objectives may be considered activity for the boss. For this reason we must build criteria into objectives when we delegate them, or when we make commitments to achieve them. Without criteria a breakdown in the relationship between the superior and the subordinate is possible.

● No single objective can cover all of the requirements of a position or its encumbent. He is always dealing with a competing set of objectives, which requires that he *trade off* accomplishment in one responsibility in order to achieve satisfactory results in another.

● Stating objectives as *result ranges* is a practical method for placing the subordinate under self-control, without losing vital contact with his results. Take the foreman on the production line for example. He has responsibility for production, quality, the size crew employed, scrap and the like. His objectives might look like Figure 3-4.

AREA OF RESPONSIBILITY	RESULT RANGE (OBJECTIVES)		
	LOWEST ACCEPTABLE	AVERAGE EXPECTED	HIGHEST PROBABLE
1. PRODUCTION IN UNITS DAILY	6800	7000	7900
2. QUALITY-PERCENT REJECTED	.08	.025	.001
3. CREW SIZE USED NUMBER OF MEN	73	70	65

(TRADE-OFFS)

Figure 3-4

Delegation consists of defining the result ranges permitted. Unless the supervisor hears to the contrary he assumes that the outputs are at average or above. The foreman knows that if he goes below the "lowest acceptable" level or approaches it, he should notify his superior that something has gone wrong. An indicator gone wrong becomes a "problem."

It should be noted again that decision theory would ordinarily treat many of the matters discussed in this chapter under the subject of "criteria." When decision-making and problem-solving become a method of managing an organization, and reality is involved, plus the commitment of subordinates to achieve objectives, the setting of objectives is also the calculation of criteria for their measurement at some future time.

chapter 4

HOW TO GATHER FACTS

> Not long ago Printers Ink *innocently asked
> a group of human guinea pigs to name the
> magazines read regularly and an aston
> ishing 8 per cent of the responses named
> Colliers—which had suspended publication
> several years before* . . .
>
> —J. W. KRUTCH

What is a fact?

The chemist, physicist or astronomer assumes a fact to be something which is everlasting, unchanging and demonstrated by proof. In making up our minds however, we run into the additional consideration of people's opinions, biases, hunches, and emotions which will alter the acceptance of the solution once we make it.

It's probably better, then, for us to use this definition of facts:

A fact is a condition which evidence indicates is true.

Clearly such a definition won't do in the hard sciences, but it will prove far more practical and satisfactory in decision making.

HOW TO GATHER FACTS TO HELP YOU MAKE UP YOUR MIND

Using this definition of a fact, how do you go about pulling together the facts in the case you are confronted with? Eight guides may be of some assistance when you are conducting the preliminary investigation which will lead to an important decision. Of course you won't use all eight in every instance (if the decision isn't very important, or the consequences of a bad solution are trivial). In the big decisions you might want to apply

36

every one of them.

1. *You might simply list the facts as you know them.* This is probably the best first step. You take a note pad and jot down all of the facts as they come to mind. This has the advantage of giving you an *array* of the material, a mental and written form of line-up for inspection. You can see them visibly and edit them to be sure you have not omitted anything which is known, nor included anything which should be excluded. One tangible aid here would be a list in the form of a fact sheet (Figure 4-1).

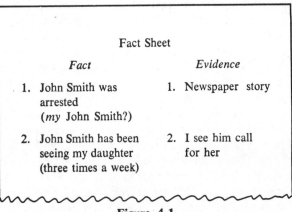

Fact Sheet

Fact	Evidence
1. John Smith was arrested (*my* John Smith?)	1. Newspaper story
2. John Smith has been seeing my daughter (three times a week)	2. I see him call for her

Figure 4-1

This fact sheet offers you a chance to ask yourself several important questions which will improve the quality of your decision and to increase its acceptance later when you come to the crucial point of making up your mind.

● You can note *evidence* that it really is a fact which you have noted.

● You can check these facts against your *objectives* and possibly find some new areas where facts are needed for making up your mind.

● You can see in tangible form whether you have included your own *biases* and *hunches,* and so mark them.

● You can rank the facts in order of certainty by noting how hard the evidence is.

2. *You might classify the facts by major categories.* From the original fact sheet construct a second which breaks them down into major categories. You might classify business facts into such areas as "financial facts," "personnel facts," marketing, and the opinions of different persons who might be important in getting acceptance of the final solution.

The major advantage in such classifying of facts is the improvement of your analysis. Once you have established a category of facts you are better able to go back through the raw information and find new insights and facts you might have missed in simply listing them.

This classification of facts is a great aid in conducting further investigations. You are not simply storing up facts like a squirrel collecting nuts, piling one on top of the other. You have some clearly defined fact areas which must be investigated. You may find, for example, that you have fallen into one of the two major errors which can occur in fact gathering.

● You might have noted all the positive and negative *opinions* of people involved, at the expense of paying proper attention to the hard logical evidence. If some important person is emotional about the situation, you may let this fact override all other factual information. The most vocal person may have undue influence on the final outcome if you fall into this pit.

● On the other hand, you may be so obsessed with *data*, real facts, tangible evidence and measurable phenomena that you omit the feelings of people, the position of the union, of subordinates, the boss, your husband, or some other persons whose feelings or opinions could upset the whole applecart if you made the decision ahead without concern for them.

One convenient way of assuring that you have taken into consideration facts both "human" and "non-human" would be to establish these two major divisions of facts. These notes may have an important bearing in deciding whether or not to call all of the interested persons together for a discussion of the issues and resolution of the problem. At this stage, however, they are merely a means for establishing as clearly as possible what you really know for certain. If you should decide to confer with all of the affected parties, you'll be farther ahead if you have all of the available facts well in hand before you start. We'll spend some time later discussing the advan-

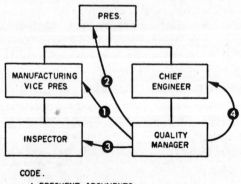

CODE.
 1. FREQUENT ARGUMENTS
 2. JUMPS CHAIN OF COMMAND
 3. TECHNICAL ADVICE
 4. OFFICIALLY HIS SUBORDINATE

Figure 4-2

tages and disadvantages of this conference method of making group decisions and how to make it work when you try it.

3. *You might make visual charts of facts to point up relationships.* It often clarifies the facts to display them visually in some form of simple diagram, scheme or picture (some call it a "sociogram"). In some business problems the organization chart is a good starting place for such diagrams, since it shows formal relationships of the people. In other cases you chart the informal organizational relationships.

For example, take the case of the quality manager in a manufacturing plant who was having some problems .in achieving high quality. The sketch of his factual relationships with other members of the management team looked something like Figure 4-2.

Such charting can clarify and depict the facts more clearly than a verbal statement and by constructing the chart may lead us to ask questions which would complete the chart. For example, in the chart shown, "What is the relationship between the chief engineer and the manufacturing vice president? What is the relationship between the president and each of his immediate subordinates?" Such information, if not known, might be obtained or even estimated, thereby throwing more light onto the situation. The quality of the decision may be improved and the possibility of acceptance of the decision can be planned with greater likelihood of success.

4. *You might construct a relationship grid to contain the facts in the case.* Using a grid can help you overcome the shortcomings of presenting facts in one or two dimensions, which is wrong when you are confronted with a situation which has several dimensions. Let's take the case of the work committee which wasn't getting anything done in a voluntary organization. The chairman is perturbed by the committee's lack of effec-

Committee Behavior Chart			
Member	1st meeting	2nd meeting	3rd meeting
1. Peter George	Talked whole meeting	Talked about absentees	Talked whole meeting
2. M. Hastings	Argued	Absent	Silent
3. J. Post	Absent	Absent	Argued with George
4. L. Solo	Said nothing	Was sympathetic	Silent

Figure 4-3

tiveness. Rather than leaping into action without first identifying the problem, he constructs a fact-grid like Figure 4-3.

The hardest part in constructing this chart would be for Peter George to be objective and factual about his own behavior as chairman of the meeting. If he were able to do so, however, he would gain some valuable insights into the nature of the problem based on the display of factual evidence before him on the grid. If this were true he might ask others in the group to assist him in reconstructing the facts for the grid, and perhaps the evidence so developed would make solution easier.

5. *You might polarize the facts in the situation.* The underlying nature of the facts are sometimes clarified when they are divided into two categories, or polar opposite positions. This works well when the facts appear to cluster around two major themes, ideas or positions. Some of the kinds of polar classifications which have worked well for decision makers, especially the computer man, include these:

a) Facts of the "before-after" polarities. Take the case of an engineering research group which was working well together as a team until a new man joined the group. Following his entry into the group their teamwork slipped badly. The leader constructed a chart on operating methods of he team as follows:

Before Fester	*After Fester's Arrival*
1.	1.
2.	2.

b) Polarities of the "Is vs. Is Not" type. Take the case of the gasoline retail manager who found that customer complaints were rising, and business was falling off. His first impulse was to call a general meeting of all of the concerned parties and raise cain. Instead he constructed a two-column table in which he listed stations where the complaints and lost business were occurring and where they *were not.* It looked something like the before-after table, except that the headings included those where complaints "are rising" and those where they "aren't rising." In the process he found areas where his attention should be focused and those places which he could leave alone. This saved him time and energy. Some instances of places where this clustering of facts into polar opposite positions could be useful might include employee tardiness (which department is, and which isn't characterized by lateness), union grievances, safety violations, rising spoilage, children not doing their chores (if you have several). It averts the general campaign which assumes that everyone is equally responsible.

c) Polarities of the "for vs. against" type. In dealing with human problems in which decisions are needed, it's sometimes wise to note in advance what evidence exists that certain people are in favor of one position and which are against it. Politicians use this in deciding where to concentrate their campaigning efforts and funds. The first step is to classify those territories which are clearly "for," apart from those which are "against." In some instances this leads to a useful by-product; those classes which fit neither category. This could be a third category called "undecided," and often represents the area of greatest productive effort. The political strategist, for example, may simply write off those wards which have always been in the opponent's camp. He might also not devote excessive energy and time to those which he can win anyhow. His campaigning is devoted to the undecided voters to swing them to the favorable side at elections.

Such analysis, it should be noted, is only possible after the polar opposite positions have been established. The middle ground category is a by-product of polarizing the facts.

6. *You might feed in some commonly held information.* No decision-making situation is independent of some kind of surrounding environment. Every case is wrapped up in the laws, the values, the customs, and the mores of the society which surrounds it. Where certain of these environmental facts have some relevance you might include them in your array of facts. In laying out the facts in a case where your employees are being approached by a union seeking to organize them into a local in your plant or office, you might well note that the law of the land stipulates that the company "must bargain in good faith over wages, hours and conditions of work with duly recognized representatives of the majority of employees in the appropriate unit." This doesn't mean you give up your opposition if that is the course you have set as an objective, but merely to note that the laws of collective bargaining covering representation are hard facts in the case. This shouldn't be stretched to imply that you should *add facts* where there is no evidence. It is reasonable to assume that a fresh egg which has been thrown on a cement floor was smashed (even if you didn't actually see the messy end-result yourself). The addition of assumptions is risky, however, and overly quick assumption beyond that of "where there's smoke there's fire" may lead to weaker solutions.

7. *You may treat inescapable conclusions as facts.* If the facts are clear that one of the parties in the case is the father of two boys and two girls you may conclude that they add to a total of four children. If you know that he has four children and know for sure that two are boys, you may safely state that he has two children whose sex is undetermined (by you at least).

The key to making conclusions is that they are defensible conclusions from the hard facts at hand.

● If A is larger than B, and B is larger than C, then A is larger than C.
● You avoid concluding the improbable or implausible unless the preponderance of evidence points in that direction.

8. *Your facts should be both material and human facts.* If you are

collecting information upon which to base your decision you should always keep in mind that the *logical* exactness of the decision is to be tempered by its *acceptance* by people who may have to live with the outcome, make it work, or execute its details. These guides to fact gathering have attempted to present both such considerations. They can't be treated separately, but must be considered simultaneously.

Research evidence in groups of executives has shown the author that time spent in gathering facts, both human and non-human, will not only increase the likehood of a decision's being right, but of its being accepted as well.

9. *You can never get all of the facts.* If decisions were to await getting all of the facts or even most of them, nothing would ever be done in this world. The simplest case is comprised of millions of bits of information. This requires some abstraction by the decision maker, in which he seeks out and finds the important facts, or sorts out the existing ones according to relevance.

In many cases where the facts don't exist, systematic search for relevant facts is possible through the proper use of sampling. This uses the laws of statistcs to seek out small parts of the whole population. If these samples are random and representative of the total population, the fact gatherer has available a tool of great power and usefulness. By studying the sample carefully, he may then generalize from the characteristics of the sample which he knows in detail to the larger population which he doesn't know.

The use of systematic research in human areas, although fraught with possible errors, when carefully constructed and professionally executed, may elicit facts in selected areas of opinion, interest and desires of a large group of people.

The specific mechanics of sampling will be discussed a little more fully in a separate section of this book under *tools,* but the key principle here is that sampling or simply casual inspection is useful, for no decision can ever be made on complete facts. The best we can do is be sure we have obtained all of the facts available within the limits of time and resources before we decide.

OBTAINING FACTS FROM OTHER PEOPLE

Much of the foregoing has assumed that the evidence which lies beneath the collection and arrangement of facts is as available and visible as would be present for a scientist in his laboratory. Yet, in practice the information needed may not be present in documentary or recorded form and must be obtained by seeking it actively from individuals who possess it.

We have pointed out some of the ways in which questionnaires of a sampling nature might be used for obtaining opinions from aggregates of people. Often, however, the information which might comprise the evidence that we cluster into a generalization for factual evidence, must be obtained one individual at a time, or perhaps wholly from one person. Under such circumstances, the method of obtaining such information is often the face-to-face conversational method commonly known as the interview.

Two extreme kinds of interviews are available. The first is the patterned or structured interview. The interviewer has a prepared line of questioning which he presents one item at a time to the subject and notes the responses. The second is the non-directive or depth interview in which the emphasis is upon letting the person being interviewed respond very freely. Although the two methods may be mixed in a single interview—for example, starting out with a structured interview and letting it become non-directive at crucial points—the two are distinct forms of interview. One of the skills of the fact gatherer is to be skilled in both and practice them apart before combining them

Non-directive interviewing

What is the non-directive interview? It is a form of counseling and active listening which uses non-directive techniques. In this form of interviewing, the major point is to establish rapport with the person being interviewed. It has two major goals. The first is to provide a psychological structure through words and actions that get the other person to talk freely. The second is to get the person to solve his own problems or to divulge information that he has but perhaps has blocked for one reason or another.

Setting the stage. Physical factors are quite important in establishing rapport. The meeting should be on neutral ground, which is to say that the meeting should not be conducted in a form of interrogation chamber and should avoid any aspect of the individual's being "called on the rug." The seating should be such that there is no formidable barrier between the two people that might create a social distance. These things have an importance in establishing a climate for the other person to talk.

Stages in non-directive counseling

1. *Catharsis*—The point in catharsis is that the person being interviewed is able to talk to somebody and get things off his chest. He has been bottling up some information, has a problem, or has some feelings that are running quite high and has been barred for one reason or another from expressing them freely.

2. *Insight*—At this stage, after the person has gotten things off his chest and has had an opportunity to ventilate, he arrives at the next stage, which is "Now I see my problem."

3. *Decision*—At this stage, the person having gotten things off his chest and having some insight into his problem, works out an action plan, maps it out in general detail and has chosen what his course of action will be.

4. *Action*—This is a stage where the person is in movement following his plan.

5. *How to do it.*

a) Rephrase the feelings expressed—This is done by such phrases as "you feel that you—" or "as I understand it you are saying this."

b) Simple acceptance—Express neither approval nor disapproval of what is heard, since either of these alternatives would result in the other person heightening his emotional situation and would have an effect on what was said that might be blocking to the non-directive process. Such phrases as "uh huh, tell me more, yes?" are all forms of simple acceptance as long as they are done without any emotional coloration, sarcasm, or editorial pressure on the individual.

c) Redirect the question—If the individual asks you a direct question such as, "Do you think that I ought to take this upstairs to the boss?," you redirect the question by saying, "As I understand it, you wonder whether you should take this upstairs to the boss?"

d) Answer the question—Once the interview has progressed to a point where all of the emotional steam has been taken out of the situation and you are on an extremely rational basis, you might then proceed with your own answer to the question if it is appropriate. If it is discovered that this merely rearouses antagonism or causes an emotional block, it should revert back to the non-directive passive acceptance and earlier stages of the interview. It is important here that you not use "conversation stoppers" by putting pressure on the other individual, probing too hard, or expressing horror, regret or other value judgments of his particular emotional problem.

The structured interview

The structured interview presumes that the person being interviewed has information or facts which he will divulge to the interviewer through the process of his being asked questions. Its use depends upon the assumption that the person will tell the truth as he knows it, and the inaccuracy of answers will be caused by genuine misinformation believed true by the respondent, or lies on his part for reasons not easily known to the interviewer. These two judgments upon the part of the interviewer become part of the validity judgment which must be made about the data so collected. Does he really know the truth? Will he tell me the truth? He might be concealing part of the truth to cover up his own interests, or to protect others who might be damaged by the truth.

With these major limitations in mind, the interviewer plans the progress of the interview by preparing his general question pattern in advance. For example:

Question: "By what method do you validate your inventories?"
Answer: "By physical inspection of the inventories, which are checked against the tickets made by the tally clerk."
Question: "Do you re-count every item?"
Answer: "No, we random sample."

At this point the interviewer might expect that he will amplify his original question with other questions developed on the spot during the interview to clarify or amplify the answer. The questions asked during the interview then will fall into two categories: (1) The major questions which deal with the general topic to be covered as the interview progresses. (2) Clarification or expansion questions which amplify or expand upon the original response to develop more details. Some further guides to eliciting facts by structured interviews might include the following techniques:

1. Prepare for the interview. Go over all the areas in which you need facts which the person being interviewed might be able to supply. He may not realize all he has to offer, and you must plan your questions for key areas in advance to cover all of the fact areas you need to obtain information about.

2. Set up the right environment. The interview should be free of distraction, the setting comfortable and the subject put at ease. Explain the reasons for the interview and tell him some reasons why it would be to his advantage as well as yours to present complete factual answers.

3. Take adequate time. When you have obtained an especially useful piece of new information the temptation to cut the interview short and rush out to make your decision should be resisted. There may be much more useful bits of data forthcoming.

4. Use a conversational manner. Don't become stilted or adopt the manner of a reporter or TV announcer. Reword your question if the subject appears to miss the full meaning.

5. Take notes of his answers during the interview. Most subjects will not be offended nor suspicious, but will be flattered by note taking of his words. Beyond this, you will find that your records will be more accurate and complete.

6. Dig for facts. Stress facts, and when inconsistencies appear, simply point them out for clarification. Check dates, weights, distances, times, sequences and relationships.

chapter 5

SPECIFYING THE PROBLEM

*No pleasure is comparable to the standing
upon the vantage ground of truth.*
—FRANCIS BACON

The act of specifying the problem is to answer the question, "What decision(s) must be made here?" It is usually to be found by setting forth clear and tangible objectives, classified as either routine objectives, problem-solving objectives, or innovative objectives. These objectives are matched against the facts which have been uncovered.

The difference between what you have and what you would like to have comprises the problem.

Assuming that all of the regular ordinary functions of the firm are being achieved, the only remaining function for maintenance of the *status quo* is to recognize problems as they occur—or even in advance of their occurrence—and their solution through logical methods. Problems which are not created by something gone wrong, but are created in the mind of the decision maker, are of a different character. We'll deal with each as a separate matter.

PROBLEMS OF RESTORING EQUILIBRIUM

In a large can factory a sudden rash of complaints from customers came back from the field regarding corrosion around the base of the nozzles of some one-quart oblong cans. The nozzles were soldered onto the container by machine, using wire solder and flux. Immediately the quality control people recognized that they must uncover the cause and correct it. In specifying the problem they defined the normal or routine condition as being "corrosion-free nozzles." The fact-gathering procedure produced these facts:

1. Recently the company had changed to a new oleic acid flux for soldering nozzles.

2. The oleic acid flux had been tested for corrosion and had been found non-corrosive.

Apparently at an impasse, they dug into several other details of the case. They found that the materials from which the nozzles were made consisted of several different thicknesses on tin coating, specifically .25, .50 and 1.25 pounds of tin per hundred pounds of steel. The resistance of tin to corrosion is greater as the amount of tin coating increases. Going back to the testing lab they inquired as to the specific thickness which had been used in making the corrosion tests. The laboratory couldn't state with accuracy. "We took the nozzles right off the production line."

"On what day did you take the nozzles off the line for the tests?"

"On Wednesday afternoon, the thirteenth," was the reply.

A quick check of the production schedule revealed that the line had been running 1.25 thickness nozzles that day. A new test was conducted and this time .25 and .50 thickness were used in the test. Immediately corrosion appeared on the test nozzles. The problem was identified:

> Corrosion will occur if you run oleic acid flux in soldering nozzles onto oblong cans with tin coating on the nozzles of .25 or .50, but not on nozzles with a tin coating of 1.25.

The decision here was to change back to the older rosin alcohol flux, or, in the event that oleic acid were used, to limit it to those jobs running with 1.25 tin coating on the nozzles.

The decision also included provision for using up the available stocks of oleic acid flux, then discontinuing its use.

What does such a case illustrate? It is a good example of how the method of problem solving, logic and the scientific method of analysis can be used to restore the status quo. The sequence can be sketched as shown in Figure 5-1.

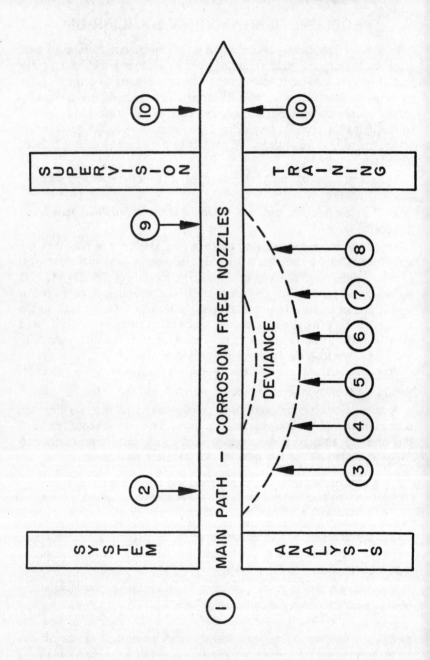

Figure 5-1

48

1. The objective was to produce corrosion-free cans.

2. The change to oleic acid occurred after tests.

3. Corrosion followed.

4. Quality control, keenly sensitive to the objective, obtained all of the facts possible. It polarized the facts into a "before-after" division. The polarity of "is—is not" was applied to the tin coatings which were being used.

5. Confronted with an apparent impasse the investigators generated more facts. They found that the lab had taken nozzles "right off the line." Seemingly a practical and sensible approach, it proved in fact to be an unscientific short cut that caused a problem.

6. They found that the nozzles had been taken from the line on Wednesday, at which time the heavier tin coating had been in production.

7. This led to the conclusion that the tests *had not* proved the suitability of oleic acid for the other two thickness of tin coating. The other two thicknesses were *lighter* (known to be more susceptible to corrosion) than the 1.25 thickness.

8. This led to the possible conclusion that oleic acid would corrode the two lighter coatings, at the same time it would be satisfactory with the thicker coating.

9. This conclusion was tested in the laboratory, using oleic acid on all three thicknesses. New facts were *created* in order to uncover the solution and set guides for decision and action. The tests showed that oleic acid corroded the lighter metals.

10. The cause having been isolated, the decisions remaining to be made included:

• How to communicate the new specifications to all interested parties to prevent a recurrence (a training problem).

• Develop a proceduce so that the newly learned facts about the performance characteristics of the fluxes would be used to prevent a recurrence (a systems problem).

• Arrange with the department head to use up the remaining oleic acid on the 1.25 nozzles, but not on the other two thinner coatings. When all of the oleic acid flux was used, to return to rosin alcohol flux on all nozzles (this is a supervision problem).

A close analysis of the process employed to restore equilibrium shows that several distinct groups of persons were involved in the decision-making process. The problem would have been impossible to state clearly without the collection of data from persons or groups having unique functions (nor would the problem have been caused without such joint and several behavior of different persons). Problem definition then can be aided by noting which kind of problem it is.

SYSTEMS PROBLEMS

The most common problem which lends itself to the kind of logical analysis illustrated in the case of the corroded nozzles is one in which a system, designed for control and uniformity, has gone astray. Such systems would include industrial engineering, accounting, manufacturing processes, quality control, production control, preventive maintenance, office system, personnel procedures, organizational plans, sales systems, customer complaint procedures, and the other formal and technical processes in an organization.

Such a system requires that uniformity be maintained, and in itself is a breeder of problems, since perfect uniformity and consistency are impossible to achieve. This creates problems, for when a change in the system occurs, or its operation deviates from the stipulated pattern, the results predicted for the system are likely to veer from the expected results.

These kinds of problems must be identified separately from training or supervision problems, which entail human behavior and communication. To attempt to treat a systems problem as if it were a human relations problem might lead to numerous diversions, wasted effort and inefficiency. Many managers, under the impress of the modern emphasis upon human relations, often gravitate to human-centered explanations of all problems.

Had this been done in the case of the corroded nozzles, much time might have been wasted in scouting around for villains and weaklings in the organization. The assumption of incompetence in the organization (curable by tighter supervision or intensive training) is fruitless, if it is indeed the system which is at fault.

SUPERVISION PROBLEMS

Distinct from systems problems are those in which the deviation from the desired norm or system originates with the behavior of people who simply aren't doing as well as they know how. They may be well trained, may have done well in the past, but the managerial or supervisory direction they have received or are receiving now doesn't control their behavior. The supervisor, as the person who immediately directs the work force, has fewer systems responsibilities in modern industry than in the past. His responsibility has enlarged, however, in the areas of control and human relations. Essentially today's foreman or first line supervisor has the major burden for the checking, correcting and teaching of work to workers, and of presenting an amiable face of proprietorship to the employees. His organization is most likely established by a staff person or executive. His production layout is established by engineers, the methods of workers, the flow of work, and the payment system for employees are calculated by industrial engineers. Machine scheduling and production planning are the responsibility of a service group in production control.

What remains is an important role. It means that he watches other work, asks questions and answers them, talks to individuals and observes the operation of machines and materials. As he checks he also corrects. This must be done in a human manner, showing that he (and the company) holds the worker in high regard and wishes him to succeed. He may permit some variance in minor details, but for the most part his function in supervision is to make the system work, not to modify it nor encourage others to do so. The specific details may be tightly prescribed by the system, or they may permit much individual discretion. The machinist, stock man, or inspector, for example, is prescribed in terms of results and in many methods required, but also has some latitude of specific means of achieving them. Machine operators in a mass production or highly engineering plant have little discretion other than to do the job as it has been defined in the system or not to accept the job.

Where the facts show a deviation from the norm provided for in the system, the possibility of improper supervision is one real alternative. As a general approach, however, in seeking causes for variance it is probably more sensible to start with a study of the system and a search for changes that have occurred in the inputs into the system before assuming that supervision is at fault.

In the case of the corroded nozzles, the system proved to be the cause, but in one aspect of the final brace of decisions, supervision of the use of the remaining oleic acid was a supervisory (control) problem. It required that the supervisor check each scheduled job and when the schedule called for 1.25 coating on the nozzles, to direct, check and control the work of those in charge of setting up the line to use up the remaining supply until it was all consumed. He would also be required to exercise supervisory control over the flux to assure that oleic acid was not used for the other kinds of nozzles.

TRAINING PROBLEMS

In order to obtain a more precise definition of training for purposes of problem solving and decision making, training is defined as "planned changing of behavior." Behavior is the specific activity of people which can be seen or measured. Behavior may change for a variety of reasons. The system may affect behavior, supervision may affect behavior. When it is a planned course of coaching, classes, or guided experience, originated and designed for the specific purpose of changing behavior, it is a training problem. How can you determine when you have a training problem?

● You have a problem—something has deviated from the norm.

● You have eliminated the possibility that it is a systems problem.

● You have found that supervisory control is breaking down and obtain further evidence that control by the supervisor is impossible because the people involved simply can't behave in a suitable fashion because they don't know how.

● There have probably been changes in people occupying certain positions, or the people are the same but the job has changed in a way that required new behavior of which they are not capable nor aware.

Training problems fitting these criteria often have generated a series of further decisions which need to be made before a suitable action can be taken.

● *Can the problem be solved by a systems change, thereby averting the necessity for training?* This alternative is based on the knowledge that training is often more time-consuming, resistant of success, and costly than systems changes.

It may be better to redesign the sales reporting form to make it easier to fill out, than to attempt to train the salesmen to fill out an extremely complex form. The likelihood of getting better results is increased. The purpose is to get the information, not to harness salesmen.

The system may itself be a shaper of behavior if it presents stimuli which make the desired behavior more likely. It may likewise remove stimuli which are encouraging undesirable behavior.

> The commander of a small army post found that the incidence of unauthorized wall-jumping after hours was extremely high. One of his commanders proposed that the guards around the post perimeter be armed with live ammunition and instructed to "put a final halt" to the unauthorized nocturnal excursions. Others suggested a tighter bed-check. Still another proposed a stepping up of lectures on discipline and reading the regulations. Another proposed some stiff courts-martial. The commander sought more facts and found that the major attraction was a string of beer joints just off the post. After some consideration he authorized the post exchange to sell beer on the post, and a small beer garden was constructed in the rear. Beer was sold at low cost (without tax) and canteen checks issued by the orderly room permitted a form of credit. The unauthorized wall-jumping dropped to negligible proportions.

● *Can the training be done within the supervisory framework?* Often the word training means "classes." Such forms of training have a purpose but may run the risk of being unreal, tangential to the real problem, or even diametrically opposed to the purposes for which it was initiated. For these reasons the best kinds of training are those which are done on the job, by the supervisor of the worker. It averts the possibility that the training class may teach a kind of behavior which the supervisor back on the job may not permit nor endorse when the newly trained worker returns. It is related to usefulness in the eyes of the trainee; he sees that it works because he is learning it in the work environment by doing the thing that he is learning. This often entails the training of the supervisor in methods of job instruction. During World War II when millions of new workers were required to man defense jobs, thousands of their supervisors were taught how to be effective instructors on the job through a process known as J.I.T. —Job Instruction Training. It required that the supervisor first construct a detailed description of the job as it should be performed (the system), and that he teach the job in stages which included:

- prepare the learner and the workplace;
- present the behavior sought one step at a time;
- performance tryout—let the worker do the job, answer his questions and correct errors;
- follow up supervision later on to assure continued behavior.

Training courses and classes should be considered last. The conduct of classes is probably most effective when the behavior sought is written or verbal behavior. This would include courses whose objectives are the transmission of knowledge, such as shop math, computer programming, atomic energy, or physics. The end product is that the student knows something he didn't know before, and may be required to demonstrate it in exams which he writes or gives orally.

In other cases the classes may involve learning specific behavior which is pertinent on the job and which is needed to solve the problem at hand. Under such circumstances it becomes important that methods other than lectures be used. Action training is most useful here. The ingredients of action training include:

1. The trainee engages in action in the classroom which simulates the requirements of job behavior.

2. The action resembles the behavior which is sought back on the job.

3. The trainee receives feedback on the effectiveness or success of his actions in the training, or the lack thereof.

All of these specifications of problems aim at decision making which will be similar to the thermostat; they restore the desired level when it has changed due to some outside influence, or some new input into the system. Specifying the problem in the kind of case where the objective is to make a major change, introducing a wholly new idea, or making an innovative leap forward, calls for different kinds of action by the decision maker.

SPECIFYING A PROBLEM OF INNOVATION

The major distinction between homeostasis (keeping things on an even keel) and innovation (breaking through to new levels of achievement) is in the objectives which are set. In setting such goals the manager has to be stimulated by competition, by past successes from innovation, or simply an inward restlessness with the status quo.

Shortly after an innovative problem is assumed, voluntarily or otherwise, it becomes apparent that innovative problem solving is not like the kind discussed earlier in this chapter, and in many of the present books on decision making and problem solving. For one thing it almost never comes from heroic action by a single individual with a monopoly on logic. The possibility of a "one-man gang" as Joseph Juran has called him, making a major breakthrough into new heights or levels of achievement is pretty slim in a modern organization. The innovator today works through organization. He must use adroit specialists for analysis of the problem and for digging out facts. He must consult with the people who must live with the change to gain their acceptance. He would be wise to consult with users of the ideas for the purpose of getting their insights into methods as well, simply because they may have some information or ideas which would improve the quality of the program.

How the innovation problem begins

Some firms seem to move naturally toward growth and innovation. Others have the stultified, dull-gray look of mediocrity and over-obsession with administrative control. Reports flow up and vetoes flow down. There are few eruptions, and quiet and order are valued highly. How is such a static environment altered to one in which change, innovation and improvement are typical?

● It often grows out of competition. The need for survival often places a premium upon new products, new methods, new markets and new ideas. Where the industry is peopled by such firms, the one which stands still may expire.

● Technological obsolescence. Products which are today's breadwinners may not be worthwhile tomorrow. The constant question is how to foresee tomorrow's breadwinner and make choices and decisions which will have it ready in time.

● Human obsolescence. Engineers twenty years out of school without retraining are more than 50 per cent obsolete, based on changes in curriculum alone. This human obsolescence attacks every profession, and requires clear identification of problems that are created out of the environment in the mind of a few top managers.

● It distinguishes between reactive thinking and action thinking and treats the objectives developed under each as different problems.

● It calls for organized effort rather than individual reflection for its solution. The president or general manager may conceive a goal, but it is not he alone who will carry the objective through to solution.

Decision-making machinery

In innovative decision making, no single individual using the tools of mathematics or of problem-solving conferences in a charismatic or manipulative fashion will achieve the quality and acceptance of decision which must be made in order to turn objective into reality.

● It involves organization which is established for the specific purpose of *raising* the present level of achievement rather than *restoring* it when something changes for the worse.

● New positions are often created to achieve such organization form. Such titles as commercial development manager, economist, market information specialist, market researcher, director of research, personnel researcher, organization planner, management development specialist and, sometimes, financial analyst fall into this new category.

● Simultaneously with the creation of the positions, objectives of an innovative nature must be stated for the whole firm. This statement of long-run plans for growth and improvement covers the major objectives for each of the innovative departments or units.

● Special skills such as knowledge of mathematics, behavioral science, statistics, economics and marketing are thus brought to bear upon the objectives initiated and guided by the top management of the firm. These tools have much in common with the logical skill of the problem-solver who applies them to restore present levels. They are applied to less tangible but not less important problems.

Research decisions

Research is a typical example of how unclear specification of objectives can blunt the effectiveness of the innovative problem specification. What should a firm expect from a research department? What are the possible outcomes?

1. *It can obtain monopolies.* By pressing into the state of the art in a field of science, a research effort might produce new combinations of existing knowledge, and produce new knowledge. Where this process produces unique ideas they can provide the parent firm sponsoring the research a monopoly and exclusive right to the manufacture and sale of the new product or process. Patent laws and basic research team together to solve a clear problem of obtaining trade advantages in the market.

All too often, however, the purposes of basic research are not thus clearly defined by its sponsors and initiators, and are left open to domination by the scientists who manage the actual conduct of the research.

2. *It can achieve cost reductions.* Other products of research are modification in the process or product which result in its being made less expen-

sive to manufacture, or which enlarge its market attractiveness. The latter will increase volume in distribution and thus reduce costs. Research of this kind is often referred to as development, and in many instances is more in the category of problem solving of a restoration level. Major equipment breakthroughs, such as occur in automation and mechanization of a major degree, are of course innovative.

3. *It can provide technical service.* When the production or marketing organization runs into variances or problems it tends to call immediately for research talent to be brought to bear upon the variation. This is reasonable action from the viewpoint of the requesting departments, but may be crippling to the rest of the research effort. As one research director reported:

> We never would have dreamed of setting up such a wonderful research laboratory simply to provide technical service to the rest of the organization. It just seems that once we were here it was thrust upon us, and we are now treated like a fire department. Whenever everybody has a problem they can't figure out for themselves or something goes wrong, they call us. Over 30 per cent of our time goes into this fire-fighting kind of problem solving.

The tendency to push research into the third category is nothing more than a variation of the desire to solve the problems which are inescapable, and are centered around control and maintenance of the status quo. In part this tendency to divert research from innovating stems in suspicion of research in the lay manager's mind. It is also compounded by the vexing nature of practical problems in keeping present systems on an even keel, and the knowledge that the scientific method—in which researchers are trained—may be a method of arriving at a rapid solution and restoration of normal.

While this division of research objectives is all too often unobserved by managers—even those who initiated the research program to begin with—the existence of even a small segment of the research team finding time to work on innovations can lead to new knowledge of a useful nature. Nor is the division of research objectives outlined for physical scientific research limited to such activity. It extends to personnel research, market research and economic research.

Thus the clear statement of the problem where the objective is innovation has a far poorer record of achievement than statements of problems which point toward restoration of the status quo.

Whichever type of problem has been stated, alternative solutions and option routes to alleviating the problem or achieving the innovation must be developed. This is the subject of the following chapters.

chapter 6

THE SEARCH FOR OPTIONAL SOLUTIONS

And while I at length debate and beate the bush, here shall steppe in other men and catch the burdes.

—JOHN HEYWOOD

A brief review

Lest we get lost in the various steps entailed in making up our minds, we should orient ourselves in the process once more.

● We start by making it clear that making up your mind is an important influence in your total effectiveness as a person. This process is one which can be studied systematically and improved by study and practice.

● The system suggested here leans very heavily on the use of probability, and the search for certainty. Some basic ideas about certainty and its application are given in Part III. These are some basic principles you'll run across again and again in the pages to follow.

● The system itself, in its bare-bones format, consists of taking six major steps:.

1. Define your objectives or ideal outcome.
2. Get the facts, material and human.
3. Treat the difference between the two as the problem which needs solving. Isolate significant causes.
4. Figure out some options or alternative solutions to get from where you are to your goal.
5. Screen the options through criteria.
6. Take action with controls to prevent deviation.

Since it would be too simple to leave it at this six-part statement, we're developing each subject in enough detail so that you'll be able to apply and test your skills in each.

In this chapter we'll be dealing with developing alternative solutions or options for alleviating the condition, correcting the problem, or achieving the objective.

HOW TO DEVELOP ALTERNATIVE SOLUTIONS

Psychologists argue among themselves about the true nature of creativity. What happens inside the brain of the creative individual is pretty much a mystery. Some suggest that it is a magic and mysterious process which can never be identified. Others declare that psychological tests can identify the creative person and distinguish him from the non-creative person. Psychologist Robert McMurry says that creativity means that the person has created something—in other words, it is past behavior which you can predict will continue in the future. Others say that it consists of manipulating memories. Since we can't wait for the resolution of debates to get on with solving our problems and making up our minds, we'll take the most useful of the methods which have been tried and apply them to developing options in solving our problems. The methods suggested here will assist you in uncovering basic causes, and show you where to start a developing alternative solution to the problem you've identified. They consist of eight possible actions.

● Make a hard specification of the problem.
● State the problem in terms of end results, intervening variables and root causes.
● Separate the fixed from the conditional causes.
● Separate the vital few from the trivial many causes.
● Follow the three stages of innovation in developing new ideas.
● If germane, use problem-solving conferences.

Since this is but a simple listing of the possible ways of developing options which might solve the problem and help you make up your mind, we'll look at each item on this list in some detail.

(1) *Make a hard specification of the problem.* The difference between a hard and soft specification of the problem is best identified as the difference between a tangible, measurable problem and one which is vaguely labeled. In business and in personal life we have more skill in labeling our problems than in specifying them. We are more likely to label a problem as a "morale problem" or a "motivation problem" than to be specific about the end result which we hope to see achieved. While verbalizations place problems in a suitable category, they are useless when it comes to developing solutions and taking action. As a starter, it may do no harm to state the "charge" against the situation. This should be accompanied by a

"specification of the charge" or the charge is meaningless. In the military discipline system this is used in courts-martial for GIs who get into hot water with military codes of conduct. The specific offender may be charged with "insubordination," but unless the prosecuting officer can demonstrate some specific behavior such as "on May 12 at 11:30 P.M. Private Jones willfully refused a legal order from Captain Smith to return to his post," the whole case is thrown out of court.

The example fits with your problem solving and making up your mind on options which can solve the problem. You may state that you have a "discipline problem" with your daughter, but unless you specify it in more tangible actions which represent the difference between what you want and what you are getting, you may as well throw out the whole matter. You must have a tangible statement of difference between what you want and what you are getting before you have labeled your problem with sufficient rigor to do anything about it.

(2) *Identify end result, intervening variables, and root causes.* The end result involves matching the final objectives against the desired objectives. Take the following chart which a general manager of a retail store constructed from reports (Figure 6-1).

Operating End Results	Results This Month	Same Month Results Last Year
Customer complaints	150	30
Inventory investment	200	170

Figure 6-1

It is obvious to him that the store should be operating as well this year as it was last year, since there has been no decline in retail sales generally in the city nor the economy at large. If he were to stop here he might find himself treating symptoms. These symptoms will always be more evident than the causes of the problems, and attacking the symptoms may merely suppress them and cause trouble elsewhere.

Accordingly he must press back into the problem and find the cause-effect chain which is producing the undesired end results. This cause-effect chain often looks like Figure 6-2.

END RESULT	INTERVENING VARIABLES	ROOT CAUSE

Figure 6-2

The end result in this case sent the manager back into the organization to investigate what was causing the poor results. A study of the customer complaints showed that 90 per cent of the complaints were due to delivery being slow, or to the wrong place. A lady bought an item and asked delivery, but she either received the wrong goods, or delivery was very slow, or to the wrong address. An investigation of the second end-result which was troubling the manager showed that the excessive inventory investment was due to surpluses of items still in the hands of the company, many of them after they had already been sold.

Connecting the two problems, he pressed back further to uncover the causes of the intervening variables. He discovered that most of the delivery problem was caused by improperly filled out sales slips. Failure by sales personnel to complete addresses legibly and fully was causing a great log jam of undelivered orders in the packing and delivery department. These backlogged goods made up most of the surplus inventory. The manager then was able to identify the key problem as one of sales personnel behavior in completing sales slips and reports.

In identifying his problem, this manager was now working two levels back of the end result. In some cases he might be working back five, six or seven levels before he found the root cause. The key to pressing into end results and intervening variables is to ask *why* the results observed exist. Having discovered the basic *why* in this case, the manager ordered an immediate training program using programmed instruction and coaching by sales supervisors to teach the sales persons the correct manner of filling out sales slips. This was coupled with a program of control, and the eventual modification of the induction training of all new sales persons to prevent a recurrence.

This pressing into the facts of results with questions as to reasons is difficult for many because the results so often can be traced back to the individual who is most concerned. The manager in this case had permitted an expansion of the store to occur without having allowed enough time or budgeted funds for adequate training of personnel when they first joined the staff. Parents often fail to press fully into the *why* of their children's behavior because it leads back to themselves.

At the same time there is a danger in tracing down the *why* of an existing condition. That danger is that the history of the problem will be fully aired, and in uncovering the history of the problem the problem-solver can become so intrigued with this history that he forgets that he must turn once more to the future and answer for himself, "What must be done now and in the future to correct the situation and prevent its recurrence?" This is the "IF THEN" morass which ensnarls so many decision makers.

If the retail manager, in our example, had become entangled in the IF THEN morass he would have dwelt at great length on the folly of the past, his own shortcomings and perhaps have mentally run through the old song, "if I knew then what I know now," which is an interesting pastime, but fatal to getting on with making up one's mind.

This trap can be pictured by the following addition to the result- (intervening variable)-root cause chain in identifying problems and developing options (Figure 6-3).

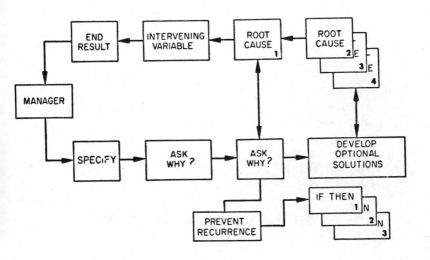

Figure 6-3

The decision maker who permits himself to be overly diverted into this bypass faces a peril that he may never get back to developing answers to the question: "What must I do, do differently, or stop doing to remedy the situation?" While exercises in academic logic would make such an excursion perfectly suitable, for people with decisions to make such byways are snares.

One value can come from such findings. It may be a guide to future action to prevent a recurrence of an identical outcome if an identical or similar kind of situation arose again. Thus the manager in the retail case might make a mental note to himself that the next time an expansion occurs or in future hiring, the training will be different for the new sales personnel:

> Finding root causes helps solve immediate problems by pointing up the spot for immediate action. Playing the IF THEN game may be valuable in long-run prevention of the problem in the future.

(3) *Some causes of problems are conditional causes.* In searching for options which can alleviate the condition, a habit of overgeneralizing to particular conditions can be harmful. Take the case of the firm which could report the following problems in terms of end results:

> Credit losses in animal feeds rose from 5 to 23 per cent. Plant efficiency rose by 11 per cent.

What appeared on the surface to be one problem and one result which didn't comprise a problem actually were conditional one upon the other. The sales department eased its credit to customers to a point where many risky credit sales were made, resulting in losses due to weak credit customers not paying for the goods purchased. Meanwhile back in the plant they had operated two shifts, and at maximum capacity in order to fill the needs. This lowered the unit costs of manufacturing. The improved plant efficiency was conditional upon the laxity of the sales in establishing credit and bred some false figures which might indicate that things were better than they were. Here are some conditional causes that might be used to illustrate how conditions can affect results and may be useful in tracing backward into identifying root causes as the problem.

- Training courses which change behavior are conditional upon top management support of the behavior change taught by the training department once the trainee has returned to the job.
- Sales managers who exhort salesmen to push a particular line may find that increased sales are conditional upon changing the commissions to pay more for the sale of that product.
- Parents who wish to have their children behave in accordance with the dictates of Emily Post should realize that such behavior is conditional upon their behaving in the desired way themselves.

The search for WHY can be assisted by seeking out the conditional forces working upon the end result.

(4) *Separate the vital few from the trivial many causes.* Once you've uncovered the root causes you are in a better position to take effective action. Your options must meet the same criteria however, as they did for defining the end result problem. Let's see how this would look in the case of our retail store manager.

a) He started out by identifying two result areas as problems:

	actual	desired	problem
customer complaints	150	30	reduce by 120
inventory investment	200	170	reduce by 30

b) In tracking back into causes he uncovers these kinds of figures with regard to clerical errors:

Result Area	*Actual Rate*
clerical errors on sales slips	75 errors per 1,000 slips

He uncovers this through an investigation in which sales slips for all personnel are audited for three consecutive days according to a plan devised by his systems man. Yet, he doesn't have past experiences to give him a firm standard of what comprises a satisfactory level of error (a normal amount). Under these circumstances he is faced with several options.

● He might retrain everyone and hope to eliminate all of the errors by an overall coverage of the whole workforce.

● He might set his objective as "zero errors" on sales slips. This, of course, is highly laudable as a goal, but it may be unrealistic for humans working under pressure.

How then can he set a reasonable objective and what options are available to him in correcting the sales slip-error situation in a way which will improve his end operational results?

One principle which will work wonders here is the principle of the vital few and the trivial many. This principle (Pareto's Law) applies a mathematical principle which goes something like this:

> In cause and effect, the majority of the effects can be attributed to the minority of the causes.

This has been stated as a rule of 20/80, which has shown that on the average 80 per cent of the results in a situation can be attributed to 20 per cent of the possible causes. For example:

- 20 per cent of the drivers cause 80 per cent of the accidents on the road.
- 80 per cent of the grievances are filed by 20 per cent of the union members eligible to file grievances.
- 20 per cent of the auto dealers sell 80 per cent of the cars.

This principle can be applied wherever cause and effect have been identified as numerical figures.

Our retail manager can apply this very quickly.

"20 per cent of the sales personnel are causing 80 per cent of the errors in the sales slips."

The question for the retail manager is not whether the principle works in his case (it does), but *which 20 per cent of his sales force?* Once he knows that the maldistribution between errors and numbers of sales persons occurs, he is armed to uncover them with greater speed. Let's suppose that he investigates and finds that the majority of errors are occurring among newly hired employees and that this group comprises 20 per cent of the total sales force. If he could improve them by training he could eliminate 80 per cent of the 150 complaints, which equals 120 (nearly his objective). Accordingly he orders, not a general training program for all, but a specific intensive retraining program in sales slip procedure for all newly hired sales persons. What has been the advantage of using this law of the vital few?

● He has uncovered an optional action program which will get at the root causes rather than merely treating symptoms.

● Training 20 per cent rather than 100 per cent will save great amounts of time, money and trouble.

● It will not rouse antagonism among the old hands who were already doing their job satisfactorily by implying that they don't know their job.

● It helps him set a realistic objective for his program of improvement based on a scientific principle rather than establishing an unrealistic goal of zero errors and then being disappointed when he doesn't get what he asks for.

● It provides him an option that will alleviate his present end result, and also provides a key to control for the future.

● It draws on specific facts which were there all along but organizes them in a form to be used better.

(5) *Using innovative processes to generate options.* While creativity in developing alternative solutions is hard to describe definitively, the general process of innovation isn't as obscure. Three major stages seem to characterize innovative action.

● The innovator first gets technically informed in the area in which he hopes to create something new.

● The feasibility of the new idea is tested to see if it fits the problem.

● A plan of installation is devised and put into operation.

Getting technically informed

Confronted with a problem which calls for some basic changes of an innovative nature, an apparently inescapable first step is to become very well briefed on all of the important technical aspects of the subject. Technical information may include scientific knowledge where this is germane, but it also includes all of the other specific information which would bear upon the subject. New and original ideas for options can be counted upon to come to the informed mind, rather than to the half-informed or uninformed one. Not that ideas don't come to the ignorant, but usually it is the unknown and uninformed whose ideas fail.

● To install a new computer in your office, or to install a new appliance in your home requires that you learn the *features* of the device if you hope to make a sound decision.

● If you plan to change a method you should be as close to totally informed about the method, its underlying theory, and its situational requirements as time permits before choosing to adopt it.

● To change the behavior of others you will stand a greater chance of success if you know them well, what caused them to behave in their present fashion, and what kinds of stimuli will lead them to amend their habits or actions.

chapter 7

CRITERIA —
A FILTER FOR OPTIONS

*Morality may perhaps consist solely in the
courage of making a choice.*
—LEON BLUM

In the common parlance "decision making" usually refers to the heroic single action of picking one alternative out of all those available. This chapter will show how criteria—tests of preferredness—aid you in making such choices. Let's illustrate with a simple case to show how criteria can help you make up your mind.

The case of the barked shins

A newly appointed supervisor in a small packaging room notes from his plant's safety report that his section's frequency of reportable accidents has risen to among the highest in the plant. He notes that almost all of the accidents have occurred in one small group of five women who package, weigh and seal items in cartons. He refers to his supervisory manual and figures the frequency for this group by itself. He discovers that if he could correct the accident frequency in that group, his rate would be well below the plant average. Applying the method described in this book he goes through the following process:

Facts: Present accident rate in whole department is one accident per week per 40 employees.

Objective: Reduce to no more than two per year per forty employees. This would be a reduction in rate from over 600 accidents per million man-hours down to somewhere about three to four per million man-hours, which is the plant average.

Analysis: He quickly applies a 20/80 analysis and recalls that almost all of the accidents have occured in the one small group, and that furthermore, most of the reportable accidents have occurred to one little old lady who spends plenty of time in the first-aid room. He also notes that the complaints have all centered around one kind of accident; Mrs. M. is constantly stumbling into things in the work place. This has resulted in these kinds of injuries:

> Skinned shins
> Stubbed toes
> Falls which barked her elbows, hands, and head.

Further investigation shows that Mrs. M shows a tendency to have such mishaps on Monday, although a few have been scattered throughout the week. A chat with the plant nurse, the group leader, and Mrs. M reveals that on "some days" she simply seems to be lacking coordination and bumps into things. One of the members of her work group confides that Mrs. M brags about her social life over the weekend. Another reports that she should be wearing glasses and several weeks ago was fitted with contact lenses. Still another reports that the work area is congested and hazardous. Several options seem to be available to reduce the accident rate:

1. Fire her
2. Have her eyes examined
3. Transfer her to another job
4. Buy her some shin guards
5. Reprimand her.

Any number of other suggestions for options might be developed, but for our purpose we might now turn to some criteria for choosing among them.

The process of developing criteria (test of preferredness) in this case—which is for illustrative purposes only—assumes that the choice will be made from among the five options listed. The criteria are those things which we would like to see as the ideal outcome of any action we take. For example:

1. *Contribution to objective:* We want the accident frequency *rate to drop.*
2. *Cost:* We would prefer the *least expensive* way, although we won't make the decision solely on costs. If the difference is a few dollars or even a few hundred we might pick any except one which is outlandishly high (sending her on a trip to the moon, or even around the world).
3. *Feasibility:* Will it work, or could you do it at all?
4. *Time:* Will the solution we choose be fast enough to meet the de-

mands of the situation? (In military or other emergencies we may spend money extravagantly to save time.)

5. *Undesirable side effects:* In solving this problem we want to avoid creating new situations which might be worse than the one we started out to improve.

These criteria often fit typical screening situations. If you have your options in hand and your criteria defined, now lay them out in a grid. This sets up the options so that you can make some judgments about each variable.

Here's how that might look for Mrs. M's problem (Figure 7-1).

	CRITERIA					
OPTIONAL CHOICES	CONTRIBUTION TO OBJECTIVES	COST	FEASIBILITY	TIME	UNWANTED SIDE EFFECTS	ACTION PRIORITY RATING
1. FIRE MRS M						
2. EYE EXAM						
3. TRANSFER HER						
4. SHIN GUARDS						
5. REPRIMAND						
DESIRED OUTCOME	HIGH	LOW	HIGH	SHORT	LOW	

SCREENING YOUR OPTION THROUGH YOUR CRITERIA

Figure 7-1

The actual ratings of how each option fits each criteria, it should be emphasized, is a *judgment* of the person making the rating. He is like the umpire in the game who makes on-the-spot decisions about minutes, action, or situations. In order to make judgments about Mrs. M you must know her, the department, the company, its policies, and the like.

You'll also note that no single option seems to meet all of the requirements for the desired outcome perfectly, and seldom if ever, will do so. This means that we must choose the one which appears to come closest. In more complex decisions we may want to quantify—for example, rate in percentages—the probable effects of each option in achieving each criteria.

The needless rush to quantification where it isn't necessary to make a judgment may complicate matters however, and in fact will arouse some resistance among people whose allergy to mathematics as complex as square roots is severe.

The test of whether or not to quantify your prediction of consequences is whether or not in so doing you improve the prediction.

After screening all of the options through each of the criteria in turn you might come out with something which shows that the choice which most closely approximates your ideal criteria would be an eye exam. This of course doesn't assure success, since we don't know what the outcome of the exam will be. The optometrist has a whole series of facts he must collect, match them against his objectives, develop some options and screen them as well. This sub-goal and the process of arriving at it is often found in decision making. Before we can decide on the value of the decision to test Mrs. M's eyes, we must await the outcome of the optometrist's work. (The decision experts call this sub-optimalization, or optimizing a piece of the problem.)

Most important problems will break down into component pieces or sub-problems. This calls for several areas of control for the top decision maker before the other people involved start working piecemeal on the problem.

1. They should all be aware of what the major objective of the larger problem is, and how they are contributing to that objective.

2. The subordinates handling the sub-problems must be trained in the rational processes being used by the top people, or the pieces won't add up to the whole. This condition, widespread at lower levels in the military establishment, works contrary to the marvelously rational methods at the Department of Defense level. The thousands of lower-level officers and managers haven't the foggiest idea of what the Secretary and his aides are doing, and simply conclude that "he is a genius."

The point of the case of Mrs. M isn't how to achieve employee safety, but criteria. In the actual case Mrs. M's eyes proved to be perfectly fine from a medical viewpoint. The actual action taken was to provide shin guards. Not the kind Yogi Berra wore for the Yankees, but plastic strips sewn on the inside of the legs of some attractive slacks provided by the company.

The forms which criteria can take

The foregoing model for screening options is only one of a number which might be devised. "Cost-effectiveness studies" would include the first two columns in this chart. Here are some kinds of criteria you might select to test preferredness among optional solutions.

1. *Gain-loss calculation.* This can be arrayed in several ways and we'll run through an illustration of how this could be done (using a man and his investment program). One important note here is that we shouldn't fall into the trap of assuming that we can ever maximize gain while we are minimizing cost, at least not simultaneously. Maximum gain is infinitely large and minimum loss is zero, or even negative cost.

Cost effectiveness and gains versus cost calculations should aim at maximizing the amount after the costs are subtracted from the gains.

2. Given either costs or gains which are fixed and unchangeable, the best criteria will be to move the other (costs down or gains upward) relatively. For example, if you have $1,000 to spend for a car, your criterion then becomes maximizing qualities obtained in the car on the existing market. Your criterion used as a screen then becomes almost wholly a description of the desired features.

A young man has $1,000 which he has saved for the purpose of buying a car. He finds that for that sum in the agencies in his town he can obtain:

a) A 1956 two-seater T Bird which has these features:
- stylish design and body work
- greatly admired by his friends
- in need of some work, which he can do
- probably high maintenance costs

b) A 1963 Chevrolet Impala which has these features:
- good body and engine
- engine may need tune up, which he can do
- low maintenance and operating costs
- considered conventional by his friends

Since the cost is the same for both, the choice must be made on the basis of gains which he hopes to achieve in buying a car (social standing, transportation, reliability, etc.).

3. *Absolute costs* as well as relative costs must be considered. The shopper who finds things cheaper by the dozen may not be making an optimum choice in buying a dozen, if the chances of economically using a dozen are rather slim. It is cheaper, per ounce, for instance, to buy aspirin by the barrel than in small tins of tablets. The chances of using a drum of aspirin for family use makes the saving unrealistic, since the absolute cost goes far beyond what would be expended for an item which is used infrequently. *Ratio tests* of cost effectiveness are often misleading and shouldn't be used loosely.

4. *Undesirable side effects* as criteria are preventive criteria which force the decision maker to look for and predict the consequences of undesirable

side effects. In some cases these spillover effects can more than undo all of the good effects from the original decision.

Undesirable side effects are often in the form of ruffled feelings which emerge unforeseen as a result of the original rational solution, and lead to losses.

In the case of Mrs. M, there are a number of undesirable side effects which could more than offset simply achieving a lower frequency rate. From the first option, "fire her," would come an immediate and heartening reduction in the accident rate. The undesirable side effects could include such things as union grievances, arbitration, possible upset of managerial decision, loss of morale in others, breakdown of confidence in safety programs, and perhaps a tougher line by the unions generally when bargaining time comes around.

It is quite obvious that figuring costs in a matching of cost and effectiveness is laden with pitfalls. A few others might be pointed out.

● You might optimize at a lower level and thereby create a loss at a higher level which isn't visible. The director of quality minimizes spoilage, but at a cost of meeting delivery schedules, thereby causing the customer to drop the company as a supplier altogether.

● You might overlook certain inputs which are needed that have a massive effect on costs but aren't figured into local calculations. Take the case of the university where costs were calculated to the penny for direct out-of-pocket outlay for research without any allowance for university overhead and administration required to support the research. The cost-effectiveness of the research was greatly overstated, leading to some important headaches later.

● You might reverse this and calculate into your costs certain "sunk costs," those costs which have already been paid out, charged off, and therefore not rightly includable in the costs of the option. When one firm found itself with an extra plant, almost wholly amortized at the end of the Korean war but in good condition, it calculated capital expense of the plant in comparing costs in one location with another where a similarly used plant had to be purchased. Since they were identical in age and condition it seemed to top management that each should be costed the same. A passive (and perhaps befuddled) controller agreed to include the sunk costs into the cost of making the new line.

A different but related kind of sunk costs would be the case where a receptionist in the lobby of a laboratory was also assigned the added duties of certain typing tasks. Based upon some methods studies, it was recommended that she be relieved of her typing duties since "the unit cost per letter for her typing letters is almost twice that of the typing done in the typing pool." This recommendation was solemnly followed, with the result that she spent the time between visitors reading novels.

Pressing into detail

In certain kinds of decisions the criteria of gain-loss can be applied in more depth than the foregoing criteria chart would allow. It is also noted that some decision may not be sharpened by quantification, but others may be considerably improved.

Construct a gain-loss table for each solution proposed

In selecting options one of the safeguards which should be placed around the solution and decision is that of predicting outcomes of various alternatives. This is more than being a seer, but rather is a means of weighing the alternatives to choose the one which will have the greatest gain or will minimize losses. It should also show relative effectiveness of each option by visually presenting the possible combinations of solutions and outcomes in a single place.

The gain-loss table is a most effective tool for showing such relative effectiveness of your options. This method is a chart showing possible outcomes for the major available choices of action. Although the specific details of the chart may vary we'll use it for a specific purpose, to screen out options in terms of gains and losses with respect to our objectives. In the following examples, some important considerations are omitted for simplification.

Take the case of the man who is mapping out a short-run investment strategy for a sum of money he has come into. After talking to a number of people, his banker, his broker, some friends, his wife, and studying his present financal condition, he decides that the two alternatives which stand almost equal in his mind are (a) putting the money into a savings bank; and (b) buying some common stocks. He notes that the return on common stocks averages 3.9 per cent, that the market is somewhat mercurial lately and that as many stocks have gone up in value as have gone down. This means that he must spend some time studying the market and must watch his investment portfolio with some care in order to avert losses if his stock should suddenly take a slide. On the other hand, if he is successful at this management of his portfolio he may be able to select rapidly growing stocks and increase the value of his holdings far beyond the 3.9 dividend income. Bank savings accounts are now paying 5 per cent. There is no growth of principal here beyond the interest income, but he doesn't have to spend any time managing the account. It simply sits there and draws interest. Setting aside the many factors which might have gone into his definition of his problems, let's assume that in his mind he has reduced his options to either one or the other of these two. He is then ready to construct a gain-loss table. It might look something like Figure 7-2.

Gain-loss Table for Personal Investment Between Bank and Stocks

option	possible gains	possible losses
savings account	1. 5% interest 2. save personal time etc.	opportunity cost of higher earnings from growth stocks
common stocks	1. possible growth up to 50% 2. 3.9% dividends	1. possible losses up to 50% 2. consume much personal time in supervision and management

Figure 7-2

Naturally, he'd want to list all of the available factors under each one, such as security of the capital under each, insurability of principal against loss in the bank, and any other gains or losses he might be able to devise. Having started out with an analytical framework such as this, he is more likely to seek out all of the possible gains and losses for each alternative than if he tried to do it intuitively or think them out in his head without such an aid.

As a final summary he might use the chart in two other ways.

1. He might figure out the likelihood of each outcome and apply some of the rules for calculating certainty spelled out in Chapter 2. For example he might take the level of return from both interest (banks) and from stocks (dividends). Suppose he figures that the possibility of obtaining 5 per cent interest from a bank is about 90 per cent probable. That is, he figures it most unlikely that interest rates will go down in the near future On the other hand, he is far less certain that dividends on the stocks he

option	expected return on principal	probability of achieving this return	expected value
interest income	5.	.90	4.5
dividend income	3.9	.50	1.95

Figure 7-3

purchases will remain at 3.9 per cent and assigns that rate a probability of 50 per cent. His calculations of the gain-loss value take on the nature of the largest expected value table shown in Chapter 3. His calculation on interest-dividend income expected values might look like Figure 7-3.

The last column, expected value, is the realistic estimate of relative interest worth to him, if his objective is to obtain earnings on principal without personal effort or management. If this is his only objective he can stop right here and the decision is clear. He will put his money into a savings account. Suppose, however, that he plays the market constantly, knows the ins and outs of the security business, has a good broker, and wants to increase his capital. At this level of objective he will work his risk-gain calculation for gains through growth of principal. He knows that half the stock on the list goes up and half goes down in any specific period. He also knows that the chance of his choosing 10 per cent annual growth stock every time is about 50 per cent. This means that by reasonable management of his speculations he might choose 10 per cent annual stocks half the time. His calculation of expected value from growth of principal might appear as in Figure 7-4.

option	expected growth	probability of this annual growth	expected value
savings	0.00	100.00	0.00
stocks	.10	.50	.05

Figure 7-4

By adding the two expected values together for each option he can come to a total expected value (Figure 7-5).

option	expected value
savings	5. plus zero = 5.
stocks	3.9 plus 5.0 = 8.9

Figure 7-5

It then appears that if the investor chooses to put his funds into stocks he will have an expected value of 8.9, contrasted with 5. from savings. The difference also represents some personal effort and time for management of the portfolio. His options are now clearer to him and he knows the price he must pay to gain his possible outcomes. The final determination will depend upon his objectives. The professional stock market operator would find that the second option would be more suitable. Others might find the first would be preferable.

The point here, of course, isn't how to play the market, or even to figure investment decisions. Other variables must be considered. For example, there's calculation of the effect of inflation. The point is that the gain-loss chart is a useful way of getting to true worth of various options to be weighed against your objectives.

The feasibility study

An important criterion once you have the options in hand is to determine how the device, or method of changed behavior, will fit the situation as it presently exists. Usually this requires that three considerations be studied to predict whether or not a solution will *fit*.

● Is it technically compatible? It's fruitless to decide that Indian reservations would be cleaner if the Indians were given vacuum cleaners, if you overlooked the fact that there is no electricity on the particular reservation you have in mind.

● Is it culturally compatible? Many ideas which are technically and rationally brilliant are perfectly useless because they can't get past cultural barriers. These may be the resistances which can be expected from the boss, your wife, the union, your peers, or the customers. If they won't *accept* the option then it must be considered non-feasible unless such acceptance can be gained. We'll spend some time later discussing means of accommodating logic and rationality to acceptance.

● Is it economically sound? Many options can be developed which would work well, but nobody can afford the costs of using the solution developed. The costs of an option and the comparison of those costs with alternative costs are an important knock-out in calculating feasibility of ideas.

A well-devised installation plan to predict effects

Another stage of applying criteria is to devise a thorough installation plan. This means that you start at the beginning and follow through a step-by-step projection of the application of the option. Obstacles are predicted and methods of overcoming them devised. Alternative courses in the event of a block, and allowances for contingencies are part of such a plan. The installation plan should anticipate potential problems, and take preventive action against causes of these problems. Thus the plan becomes not a fixed regimen, but may be divided into a basic path and branching routes in the event of roadblocks in the course of the original. It also entails some preventive planning to circumvent the occurrence of events which could cause failure. Spare tires, small tools, and a spare gas can in your car would be examples of such contingency provisions. The life raft in the overseas aircraft, the fire extinguisher in the school, and the provision of fire escapes for buildings are normal examples from our ordinary experience which illustrate planning for the unexpected as well as for the customary course of events.

What you prefer is important too

Not all of our options can be screened by using the laws of chance or a rational system, however. Our own preferences are an important ingredient in deciding which choice to make between available alternatives. Here are a few guides to making our preferences (our natural tastes) go to work on solving the dilemma of making up our minds.

1. *You can simply list all of the choices in order of preference.* Take the problem of the man who wants to make up his mind whether he should accept one of five assignments which are offered him. In sifting his preferences he decides that he'd rather have an assignment which will give him a new learning experience. He then ranks them 1-2-3-4-5 according to that standard, and chooses the first one which is offered which comes closest to teaching him most. If by chance his first choice and third choice fall by the wayside or the offer is withdrawn, he uses his preference ranking to sort the remainder. He is left with 2-4-5.

● This of course won't work if the choice is between things that are incomparable. "Would you prefer to walk to work or to carry your lunch?" The two choices are not related to one another and really can't be compared on the same basis.

● This method won't work if your likes and dislikes are vague as they relate to the choices. "Do you prefer an auk to an armadillo?" If a person doesn't know what either one is, and would have no earthly use for either, his preferences are not a very good guide to sorting them out.

2. *Your chances of getting a favorable outcome are decreased if you compound your chances.* In Paris there is a lottery in which the winner wins a lottery ticket on a larger lottery. If you take the easier (or cheaper) route you should be aware in advance that all you can gain is a chance at another—and more remote—outcome. Aspiring actors who want to act on the stage often take jobs on Broadway as soda jerks, with the hope that they'll be "discovered" by a talent scout who drops in for a soda. If they take the job because they need the pay, then they have made a necessary kind of decision. If they choose this route to being cast in a play in preference to haunting stage doors and casting offices because they find it's easier to get a job as a soda jerk than to get hired for a part, they are compounding their chances and decreasing the overall likelihood.

3. *Some decisions present alternatives so drastically different that they make the final choice of specific action easy.* Take the case of salesman who is offered three choices: (*a*) cover the Chicago territory; (*b*) cover the Milwaukee territory; (*c*) get fired. Since he needs the job badly, either

alternative a or b would be a matter of indifference to him, as long as it avoided the third alternative.

4. *Where there are absolutely no differences between a whole family of alternatives, then any choice will do.* Some choices are like the entries in a lottery. Since you can presume that each number in the lottery has the same chance as any other chance, none is preferred. Any casual method of making up your mind will do. You may pick the number from a passing car's license plate, your age, or choose any other basis and one is just as logical as any other. (All are illogical but OK.)

Faced with the same set of circumstances, however, any means by which you can obtain two (or more) choices is preferable to only obtaining one choice.

5. *Decisions which entail a greater chance of failing should usually offer opportunity for greater reward than those that have no such risk.*

The reason many men go into business for themselves is because they hope to get rich. There is always a chance that they will go broke and end up in debt for years to come. Yet, the choice to enter the business is preferable to doing nothing or working for another to such persons, because they see possibility of great gain. Given a choice of getting rich or going broke is easy—we all would choose the former. The decision to go into business at all requires first the expectation that we will probably get rich, or at least not go broke. The risks are accepted because of the possible gains.

One convenient way of making such a decision is to prepare a simple chart that outlines all of the possible outcomes for most of the available choices of action. Let's look at the foregoing situation if it were presented as in Figure 7-6.

| | *possible outcomes* | |
your actions	failure	success
keep your present job	won't get rich	won't go broke
start your own business	go broke	get rich

Figure 7-6

This simple method of arraying possible outcomes against the corresponding range of possible actions makes it visually possible to see the range of choices and their outcome in a way that permits your preference to be applied in its purest form. Purity of preference in this case means that you don't have a true preference blocked by lack of information, or clouded access to the range of alternatives weighed against gains and losses.

Now to put these tools to use . . .

These tools for approaching certainty in choosing between options of course won't find it for you. They merely provide some further avenues to wringing out of a situation all the factors which can help you make up your mind.

Suppose, however, that you're convinced that you've explored every option and chosen the best one, but one thing stands in your way: Other people won't accept it. What then?

chapter 8

USING GROUPS
IN DECISION MAKING

*The adventurer is within us, and he contests
for our favor with the social man we are
obliged to be . . .*
                                    —WILLIAM BOLITHO

In making up your mind you'll be confronted with two simultaneous problems. The first is coming up with a rational and logically sensible kind of answer. This is sometimes called the *right* answer by those people who have an excessive respect for logic, systems, mathematics and the rules of science. The second problem is to produce a decision or solution which other people will *accept*.

For example, if you deal with the problem of declining profit in your manufacturing operations, you might have two solutions. The first is the logical, rational one which your accountant tells you is correct, and your engineers swear by. The second one would be one which the unions wouldn't strike over, and which the sales department would accept. Perhaps you feel that you can hornswoggle the union, but the sales manager has some emotional reactions to certain actions which logic suggests should be taken. For example, all the logical analysis shows that you should close the old plant in Buxville. It is obsolete, in bad repair, and inefficient. The president, however, started the company in that plant and is emotionally tied to its existence.

The ideal decision is one which best combines the needs of both sets of requirements—logic and acceptance.

Experts in decision making are divided into two major camps. The first group is those who would stress the *quality* of the decision, its mathematical or logical basis, its rigor and efficiency. The other group, while not unconcerned about such matters, emphasizes that quality alone is not the sole criterion of a decision's usefulness. Rather, this latter group proposes, the decision must be acceptable to a group of outsiders who have the ability to make even the most logical solution fail. What is the importance of this acceptability of your decision?

● Children today are educated in a climate in which the unexplained order is considered to be offensive. While many children do not complete school (the drop-outs) and may not be greatly impressed by this necessity, the majority of the middle class children do complete school and have been indoctrinated to believe that their opinions are important.

● The pervasive effect of democracy in our society, its ever-enlarging scope, and the rise of human relations training in home, office, factory and institution have made acceptable ideas better than unacceptable ones.

● There is an increasing amount of research evidence that people who participate in decisions that affect them will execute the decision more effectively than when it was dictated. This is especially true among middle-class people, a growing group in our society.

The opposition to group decision making

On the other hand there are many opponents of group decision making. Generally such opposition can be classified into several major classes of people.

● Scientific types of opponents. These are persons with training and experience in applying the scientific method. From their own experience in laboratory research they have noted the rigid demands of rationality for systematic analysis of problems. It has often been their experience that when groups of persons get together, some informed and others relatively uninformed—perhaps downright ignorant—that equal sharing of contribution into the decision leads to chaos. The best decisions are made not by floundering through the ignorance of others, this group suggests, but through listening to the most informed mind, using the most logical processes.

● The mathematical types. In this group are applied mathematicians whose thesis is that gabfests can't possibly utilize the rigor and simplicity of mathematics in decision making. In specifying the problem a model of it constructed mathematically can eliminate superfluous and confusing variables. If the problem can be shaped in a way which will permit use of the computer, speed and accuracy can be added. For example, if the definition of the cause can be programmed in a method that discriminates clearly between the two polarities IS-IS NOT, it is natural for handling on a digital computer through the use of a language called Fortran.

● The individualism school. This is a group of writers and scholars who are opposed to group participation in decision making because it results in a decline of individualism in our society. It produces conformity, organization men, and persons who are victims of group-think. This decline of leadership by individuals and its replacement by leadership of groups is seen as a threat to the free society, and the possibility of being taken over by demagogues. In a few instances, such group thinking has been identified with the political and ideological left. (On the other hand, excessive individualism is seen by its opponents as a resurgence of the extreme right by some.)

Can rationality and acceptance be reconciled?

One reason the two schools of decision making have so seldom met on common ground is an unwillingness to try. The principal barriers to a synthesis of the two lies in the unwillingness of the protagonists to see the values—even in a limited way—of the other's position. The scientific, rational and mathematical school, for example, will snort scornfully that a group cannot follow the tightly disciplined course of the scientific method in identifying the problem, finding its causes, and establishing controls over the solution to be sure it works. The conference-centered group latches like a snapping turtle onto a single explanation for the attitudes of the scientific decision-making group, their explanation being that individual decision makers secretly want to be dictators over their subordinates, and this thirst

USING RATIONAL AND PARTICIPATIVE METHODS IN DECISION MAKING

1. stage in decision-making process	role of the leader	group participation in the decision-making process
define objectives.	initiate goal setting.	propose goals based on group experience.
	insist upon final definition.	make counter-proposals.
	approve and fix goals statement.	learn and understand the goals as they apply to their function.

Figure 8-1

for power blocks them from being participative in decision making. Hanging tightly onto their fixed positions, they throw out the possible application of the alternative method to their own.

It is proposed here that the process of decision making should include rationality and the scientific method, coupled with the skillful use of participative methods when they are appropriate. Figure 8-1 shows how such a combination of the two methods can be applied.

This is merely the first stage in the decision-making process, but an important one. In it the leader provides an essential function, but the group's share is important also. The leader states that objectives will be set, and initiates the goal-setting process. If he knows any limiting conditions which must be met he states them ("The board has established a 10 per cent profit as a minimum, and this is *not* a subject for debate on our part"). At this stage he permits the group to contribute from their personal and professional experience what they see as being the possible objectives. Because the technical knowledge of subordinates is increasing, it is not uncommon for the subordinates of a leader to know more about their own area of responsibility than their leader, it is only sensible for him to use that extensive knowledge in determining the *possibles* in terms of objectives.

If the group is apparently floundering, the leader has the task of pressing for a final definition. One option which the group is not allowed is to end the discussion without having set objectives. They may make counter-proposals to one another, and to the boss, but they are not permitted the luxury of wandering into the future without specific standards. The leader, or any member of the group, may point out that the proposed goals are too low or too high, and defend his position. Voting on the final result may not be feasible, but a consensus should be sought. This differs from a vote in seeking unity rather than division among the for-and-against proponents for a specific goal.

A consensus having been reached, even those whose proposals are not accepted will know that they have had a full hearing of their ideas, and the possibility that they might ultimately prove correct is always a possible consolation to them. As one leader expressed the consensus of a group setting goals:

"It now appears that most of us lean toward a direct mail campaign to move the product, mainly because we can measure the results more readily. A few of us are still reluctant about that route and would prefer a radio-TV campaign. In order to keep from getting stalled, we'll go along with the consensus, but we should note that the radio-TV plan was proposed, and we may still come back to it after we have tried the direct mail program as a starter. This decision can be reviewed after we've looked at some results after six months."

The final fixing of the goals rests with the leader, but he has a further responsibility to communicate such objectives clearly to each affected person, especially with respect to how it will affect that person's own areas of responsibility. This can be done in individual dialogues with the affected parties, or can be explained in a group with cross-comments by other members relating their colleagues' responsibilities to their own. In complex organizations such interchange has many values in the objective-setting process.

Before turning to the second step in the process of decision making, it should be noted that using the group's ideas doesn't relieve the leader of working vigorously and intelligently in applying the process. His purpose in including the group in the objective-setting process is to obtain clearer, more feasible objectives. He will also get more manageable predictions of expected achievements, because the group will understand more thoroughly those objectives which they have helped shape. Even where they may not accept wholly, understanding the aims thoroughly will have numerous advantages. Let us look at the respective roles in stage two, getting the facts.

STEP TWO — GETTING THE FACTS

stage	leader role	group member role
2. getting the facts	ask for a list with evidence	contribute facts and evidence
	make classification chart and ask for facts to complete it	contribute facts for each category listed
	make visual charts and ask for definition or relationships	state relationships and evidence to corroborate
	construct relationship grid to be completed	contribute data for relationship grid
	polarize facts ● before–after ● is–is not ● for–against	present facts and evidence for each pole
	ask for expert views	present expert views

Figure 8-2

In the second stage the leader is specifying the problem area in which a decision must be made. Using the tools described in Chapter five, he focuses the thinking of the group into channels where their local knowledge of the facts will be concentrated on identification of the problem. This may include only a few of the tools or in complex problems may entail almost all of them. The leader asks for a simple listing of the facts, and later may ask that these same facts, noted on a chart without critical comment, be classified, visualized, polarized or supplemented by expert views from such persons as lawyers, tax men, engineers, or functional heads. It might be noted that at least two of the tools deal with relationships, not merely hard facts of a physical nature.

The advantage of group meetings in such a format permits the pooled experience and information of the group to be funneled into rational lines. There is no lacking of rational method. It merely provides that the group won't flounder along in a chaotic fashion, at the same time it meets the stringent requirements of both logic and acceptance. The composition of the group meeting must be such that most of those attending have something to contribute to the rational process of finding the problem. If this is done the necessity for endless running about, appointing investigators, and phoning for fragmentary bits of information can be averted.

The major advantage is that inaccurate information, such as might be received from casual interrogations, can be checked against the knowledge of others, who may respond with rebuttals when they hear inaccuracies presented.

The lone executive who attempts to ferret out the facts through telephone calls to persons who might have information will lose much of the truth. The executive who abruptly calls his plant manager and asks, "Have you changed any materials down there in the past two weeks?" will be subject to a variety of responses depending upon the quick-response ability of the person questioned, his perception of the reason for the questioning, and his ability to produce full and honest responses.

In the group meeting each individual has a chance to size up the purpose of the meeting, to have his fears of personal injury alleviated, and to see the total purpose of the investigation. Finally, there is the simple power of one mind to influence another in eliciting information. The comment of one person serves as a "reminder" to the next person, and by association one idea thrown into the conference triggers another in the mind of another. In one conference for example:

A. "Down in my department I've noticed that people seem to be avoiding jobs where the maintenance is poor and the machines are running poorly."

B. "That's intresting. I guess we have the same thing happening in my department. I hadn't thought of it, but now that you mention it I can see that my people are doing the same thing."

Stage three—identifying the problem

In the third stage, having clarified objectives and defined the present situation, the leader can summarize the final problem definition (Figure 8-3).

stage	leader role	group member role
3. define the problem	summarize and define the problem ask for individual segment definition	agree and modify define their own part of the problem

Figure 8-3

The group can then agree or can modify and clarify the problem if it sees this definition as too limited or too broad. Next, the leader can press on into definitions of what the respective members of the group must accept as their segment of the problem.

Take the case where excessive machine breakdown was resulting in downtime 40 per cent over the year before. The group has identified two major forces at work as the cause of the problem. The first was that operators were not following specified procedures in putting material into the machine. The second was that machinists were not following the preventive maintenance plan. The two fed on one another. Because the operators were careless, the machinists became disheartened and merely repaired things when called upon to do so. The operators found that machines were down for long periods of time and saw little advantage in trying for perfection in their own work. Nobody could clearly state which came first; the problem was to alleviate the present condition. Members of the production supervision group specified two major responsibilities which they assumed as their problem and area of concern: training operators who were not aware of the proper method, and controlling their performance through checking and correcting while they were working. The maintenance people saw their problem as reviewing the system of preventive maintenance with the mechanics, and checking and correcting their compliance with it.

Are there any instances where group participation could be fruitless and individual use of rationality and logic would be superior in problem identification? Clearly, yes.

Where the problem is a systems problem it might better be solved by engineering and other rational methods.

Where the problem is one of supervision or of training it might better be solved by group involvement.

Some typical management problems which might be better handled by a systems analysis approach (individual) would be the following:

- defective shipments are being received due to packaging failures.
- manufacturing equipment failures due to malfunctions.
- organization of sales territories leads to lost sales.
- sales compensation systems fail to give sales incentive.
- missile failures due to component malfunction.
- the organization has conflicting policies.
- labor contracts with ambiguous provisions.

The single common characteristic of such problems is that they can be tracked back to a single cause, or a combination of a few causal forces. The cause can be found by logic, and the process of finding it is always highly satisfactory to the decision maker because he has a comprehensive method (the scientific method) and has developed skill in applying it to systems problems. Pure logic causes little or no discontent, since nobody has any particular vested interest in the present condition. On the contrary, they are ordinarily most grateful that the solution was worked out.

The case of the worn-out plates

A large mailing house was confronted with a crisis when the manager of the mailing department called to state that "all of the addressograph plates have been worn out and must be replaced." This would be serious because it entailed shutting down all mailing operations until the new plates were cut. The manager called a conference of most of the interested and informed parties. Here were the contributions of the conference members:

- The manager reported that the call had been received. He called upon the manager of the mailing room and asked him to explain.
- The manager of the mailing room held up a zinc plate. He stated that since the plates were old, worn down by two thousandths of an inch, they would not hold steady in the guide rails of the imprinter. This caused the machines to jam. The jams were getting progressively worse, and now it was impossible to finish a single job.
- The sales manager deplored the situation and asked how it could have occurred. He explained how serious this would be to sales if the machine were out of service for several days waiting for new plates to be imprinted.
- The purchasing man stated that he had obtained an estimate of four days for delivery of the newly imprinted plates.
- He states that their customers would have to wait, since that was the shortest possible time.

All of those present had contributed their expert views and the manager was left with nothing but frustration and lost business.

At this stage he decided to press further into the case. He walked down to the machine room, and leaned over the machine with the head of the machine department. A service man was there. The manager asked him, "Do you agree that the plates are worn?"

"Yes, I have checked with a micrometer and find them worn by about two thousandths of an inch on the edges."

Leaning over the machine, the manager, totally without mechanical or engineering training, asked, "Where do you put the plates into the machine?"

The machine room head pointed to the feed where stacks of plates were piled.

"Do they jam at that point?" The department head shook his head, indicating a negative.

"Where do the jams occur?"

The department head pointed to a point in the guide rail just ahead of where the imprinter rose to print the address onto the envelope.

The manager leaned over the machine and noted that the guide rails were held down by large springs, which pressed the plate against the bottom of the slide.

"Won't these springs adjust for a small difference in the thickness of the plates?"

"They should but they don't."

The manager took a handful of brand new plates and ran them through the machine. In a few minutes they jammed at exactly the same spot as the older ones.

"It can't be the plates if the new ones jam. What is special about this spot in the machine that causes them to jam up?"

The service man inspected the machine and reported it perfectly adjusted. The manager peered into the offending area.

"What is that black smear I see on the rails?" he asked.

"Ink and oil from the old plates," he was told.

Taking a paper tissue from his pocket the manager dabbed off the oily smear.

"Now run some plates through."

The plates ran perfectly for awhile, then finally jammed.

"Where is that oil coming from?" the manager asked.

"It comes off the plates. When they have been run heavily they build up oil and lamp black from the ink. Our ink consists of oil and lamp black."

At this stage the manager rubbed several of the plates across his finger. A smear of oil appeared on his fingers. The service man snapped his fingers.

"I think I have it," he said. "When you use that kind of ink the oil builds up on the plates and rubs off onto the slide. That way the springs won't hold the plate in position and they slide out. That could cause them to jam."

"What should we do?" asked the manager.

"First clean the machine, then wash the plates in solvent and the old ink will wash off."

The department head prepared a tank of solvent and dipped several trays of plates into it, washing off the built-up ink. The machine slide was wiped dry. The newly washed plates were run through without a jam. Provision was made to wash all of the plates immediately, and the delay was reduced from four days to four hours. The offending ink was changed.

What conclusion might we draw from such an example? Clearly the initial conference was worse than useless; it was a clear-cut, harmful vehicle for solving problems. Experts may dominate, and not be pressed. The logical questioning of the manager, the quest for specific facts was moved to the plant floor. There the experts were tested and required to defend their logic. You might say that the conference around the machine followed the requirements of a conference, but was clearly managed by one person. The question of autocratic behavior in the conference or the attitudes of subordinates had little to do with failure to solve the problem.

If any criticism on this solution and decision were to be made, it would perhaps be that the manager held on too closely to mastery of a method that should be widely taught in the organization. If the department head, the machine room supervisor and the service man were trained in similar methods of individual analysis the manager might not have been required to demonstrate his mastery of rational analysis.

Stage four—developing options or alternative solutions

Perhaps the greatest single advantage of the conference method comes after the problem has clearly been defined and the search for options begins. Most experts in rational decision making tend to gloss over this aspect of the decision-making process. Yet the generation of original and creative

stage	leader role	group member role
4. develop alternatives	ask for many alternatives accept all and write down	produce numerous alternatives suggest everything that comes to mind without evaluation

Figure 8-4

alternatives can often be assisted by the people who have worked most closely with the local situation (Figure 8-4).

With the problem clearly in hand, group decision making presents one of its more fertile areas for contribution to the improvement of decisions. *It can be used to develop a wide range of possible options.* The imagination of a group is wider in scope than the imagination of an individual and can be drawn upon for the development of numerous suggested options. The quality of the answers need not be of special concern at this stage of the process. In fact the attempt to suggest and evaluate at the same time may have a serious inhibiting effect upon the ongoing stream of ideas.

Dubbed "group think" and "mental popcorn" by its critics, and brainstorming by its advocates, this method of developing optional solutions, when properly managed, has a capacity to enliven jaded minds, which have fallen into ruts of conventional thinking and acting. Its origin was among copywriters for an advertising agency, and it was extended to problem conferences in all lines of business, in some instances where the pertinence of the method was of dubious value.

The use of brainstorming to identify problems, for example, can hardly supplant digging into facts and matching them against objectives through rational analysis. To attempt brainstorming under such circumstances is inevitably an attempt to supplant rapid-fire guesswork for thought and analysis. Inevitably it must be followed by intensive analysis of each proposal to determine whether or not the willing surge of problem statements will hold water under scrutiny.

The same scrutiny must be applied to the alternative solutions also. The difference between identifying problems and eliciting a wide range of possible solutions is that feasible solutions may be more readily recognized if they have followed and can be matched against a carefully devised statement of the objective and the problem. Such a means of developing alternative solutions can achieve these advantageous results:

- It can produce more suggested alternatives in volume.
- It can produce more refinements of a basic idea.
- It can uncover all of the unfeasible options as well as the feasible. Each will be evaluated later, and in the elimination of the unsatisfactory ideas, more reliability on the final adopted option can be placed.

Whether the group meeting development of alternatives entails the brainstorming method, or is simply a group meeting conducted on more conventional lines, the requirements of the leader remain about the same. "The leader's role is to state the objectives and the problems to be solved in attaining them, not to relay predetermined solutions or plans of action," suggests Norman R. F. Maier, Michigan psychologist.

Having specified what decisions are being asked for and what the other purposes of the meeting are, the leader then awaits the generation of alternative ideas from the members of the group. In the initial phase he may simply accept all of them, perhaps noting them on a chart part. This visual display of the cumulative effort of the group has suggestibility to others, and under leader prompting, a broader spectrum of suggested option will be produced.

When it becomes apparent that no further options are to be forthcoming, the group may then turn to discussions of advantages and disadvantages of each. They may be weighed against the statement of objectives, and summary of the problem.

chapter 9

MAKING ACTION PLANS

> *That book is good which puts me in a work-*
> *ing mood . . .*
> —EMERSON

Implementing the decision is more than simple activity or a single event. It consists of opening a series of moves designed to achieve the objectives arrived at in the first stage of the decision process. The decision shapes the plan, but it is modified by experience and learning curves as the plan is entered.

Action plans as operational maps

From the deliberations going into the decision, a major product is a plan of action which serves for the executive the identical function which the road map does for the automobile traveler. In addition, it includes other essential features which are not included in the tour map. This is because the action plan places more restrictions upon its user, yet fails to provide as much information about the total terrain in which the correct path is highlighted.

The necessary, if not sufficient, conditions for the execution of a program are threefold:

1. The principal executive responsible for the achievement of the program is clear in his own mind where he stands now, where he should be in terms of results expected, and at what time he should have achieved those results.

2. He should be familiar with the major limitations on means he may use in getting there, including such matters as time, budget, personnel avail-

able and other resources he may apply.

3. He has identified or is informed on the methods which will be used as measuring posts for progress along the way.

Numerous industrial engineering and other instruments used in management, such as production planning, could be applied at the point where decision makers need to convert decisions into action. In fact we find that in their most effective use, they will serve best when this bridging of analysis with action is called for. Among the proved instruments for making such a bridge are these:

1. Pilot plants or prototypes which test the idea in simulated and smaller-than-life fashion. The product of such instruments are modifications in the rest of the plan.

2. Progress plans. These are the schedules, timetables, PERT diagrams, Gantt charts, production control boards and other visualizations of the course to be negotiated.

Pilot plants as first-stage action

Before committing all of one's resources to a single course of action, a microcosm of the whole is a useful testing ground for the decision. In this testing, the test involves more than a validation of the preceding analysis, although it certainly may prove to be exactly that. Rather, if the analysis has been meticulously done, the pilot plant or preliminary test of the action serves to predict practical and empirical pitfalls which lie ahead. The logic of theory and the logic of practice are not identical, however strongly the theorist would pretend they are. In the pilot plant stage we move from the logic of theory to that kind of logic which deals with signs, signals and information which express our urges to project our scheming, planning and analysis. This practical reasoning has been governed by theoretical insight. The theoretical is considered more stable, assumed, and fundamental. The logic of practical application must be tentative, conditional. To use the words of one manufacturing manager, "When we launch the new model everything becomes iffy."

Before launching a new product we may wish to test the market for acceptance. This is not simply taking a small part of the market and making a go-no-go decision from the results of the sample. The action tries out the various options which fall within the spectrum of the final decision. It may be tests at various price levels, tests in various marketing channels, tests of various advertising methods, or tests of various package designs.

The pilot plant may also be used to test the effects in such areas as human relations, in which all of the effects may be theoretically unpredictable.

A printing plant in the East installed a gauge which employed radioactive isotopes for scanning printed material to control ink thickness. The technical aspects of the project were working according to plan, but workers began to protest. The possibility of radiation poisoning alarmed them. The management explained that government safety standards were being more than met. They pointed to the lead shielding around the very small isotope which was being used. Finally, the issue was resolved when one of the workers requested that the company install a shower where those leaving the shift could have the opportunity to take a hot, soapy shower before leaving for home. Despite the technical lack of necessity for such an action, the management agreed to the installation of a shower in the locker room area, and those desiring to use it were permitted to do so. The problem resolved itself with this addition. When the technique was extended further throughout the plant, the shower's availability was pointed out to all workers. Many of them continued to use it.

In making the first moves in turning decisions into action, standards for the remainder of the action and continued operation may be developed. One such test was the application of programmed instruction to clerical training at the J. L. Hudson department store. Programmed books (a variation of teaching machines) were written by the training staff and were tested initially upon a small group of persons entering the sales position. Modifications in the program followed. It was next tested upon a sizable group of new sales persons hired for the Christmas rush. Sales procedures, cash register methods and other systems were taught to about half of the new persons hired. The remainder were trained by conventional training methods of coaching and lecture. The relative effectivness of the two was measured. The findings showed programmed instruction to be more effective, less costly and time-saving. The test also provided ways of improving the program itself to widen its advantages.

A variation of this design is to pick a single department where the program is to be tried out. This can have the values of pilot plant testing and verification. It also can be used to prove the values of the new plan. By biased selection of the department to be used for the test, its success in the pilot run can be assured. As one plant manager put it:

> Whenever we have a new idea of technique we want to install we always take it to Joe Smith's department. Joe is a fellow who has an experimental mind, and enjoys new and novel methods. He takes a lot of pride in being asked to try out new ideas, and busts a gut to make them work. If he sees anything that needs to be done to make it work he does it, then tells us how to change the program to improve it.

Using such testing-selling methods of pilot plant action often leads others to request that they be permitted to try the new method as well. One variety of this is to withhold new ideas from those departments which have indicated early opposition until it has been installed and is working successfully in most or all of the other departments. This creation of an isolated position often has the effect of bringing the lagging department into the fold by its own request if not demand that it be permitted to rejoin the entire group.

The management of information in experimental action groups may be more complex than some of the sample actions or practical schemes previously outlined. Often the data must be managed mathematically to prove significant difference attributable to the new method of process. The classic model for such experiments can be sketched quickly (Figure 9-1).

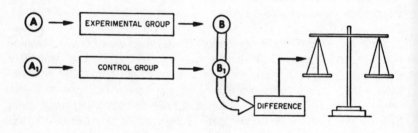

Figure 9-1

First we select two groups upon which measurements are to be made. The first is the experimental group, which will operate under the proposed new method or system. The second is a group called the control group, which will continue to operate under existing methods. At point (A) the measurements of output will be taken for both groups. The experiment is then conducted for the experimental group, while the control group continues under the older (non-experimental) condition. At the end of the period (B) the final or cumulative results for each group is measured by the same instrument. These two results are then compared and their difference is analyzed. The most important question about the difference is whether or not it is *significant*. This means that we wish to note whether or not any differences which exist are statistically greater to an extent that could not have occurred simply by chance. If differences exist, however large or small, they have important meaning only if they are caused (and most specifically caused) by the change introduced.

This assumes that differences in results between two groups such as these must either be attributed to *chance* or to *cause*.

The assistance of a statistician is often required to devise the specific tests of significance. The most common of such tests is the chi square test. More discussion of this tool of decision making is included in a subsequent chapter among the *tools* of decision makers. Modern statistics suggests that classic tests of significance can be made more meaningful if subjective probabilities are also incorporated into the calculations. In business decisions this introduces the hunches and opinions of the subject into the quantitative measurement of specific results.

With pilot plan out of the way, the execution of decisions may proceed according to progress plans.

Progress plans to guide action

The essential ingredients of progress plans are threefold: (1) What is supposed to happen, (2) When it is supposed to happen, (3) A commitment between a responsible person and another whose opinion is important to the responsible person. This important person is ordinarily the boss. Several commonly used devices from manufacturing, for the most part, have potential for widespread use in planning progress in other lines of activity, including clerical and white collar work, engineering programs, insurance sales, or institutional management.

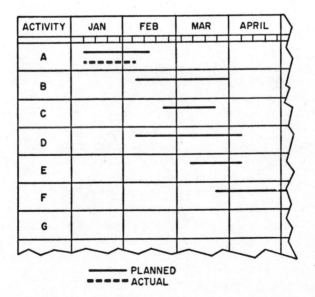

PLANNED
ACTUAL

Figure 9-2

The Gantt Chart

One of the earliest, simplest and most pervasive of such tools is that developed by Henry L. Gantt, an engineer of World War I, to expedite defense shipbuilding. In numerous variations today it is widely used in all forms of progress planning and in control (Figure 9-2).

The major ingredients are three: (1) across the top row are dates and units of time against which progress is to be measured. (2) Vertical down the left side are the units of scheduled results in terms of tangible numbers. (3) Provision for a parallel posting of actual amount achieved by dates.

PERT as a progress plan

A step beyond the Gantt chart which includes some newer applications of probability is the PERT diagram. PERT are the initials for "Program Evaluation and Review Technique" initiated by Defense Department pressure in the 1960s. This technique shows a more complex pattern of alternatives (Figure 9-3).

Visually the Gantt chart is really a predecessor of the PERT. The Gantt chart showed tasks as bars on a chart. PERT represents tasks by interconnecting arrows. This has the added advantage of showing how each stage is dependent upon earlier stages. By referring to the PERT diagram you

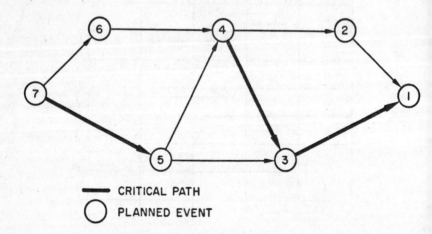

CRITICAL PATH
PLANNED EVENT

Figure 9-3

may note that there are some key ideas in PERT which are most useful in making an action plan.

1. Two key words in PERT are *activities* and *events*. An activity is represented by an arrow, and indicates that some kind of work or task is being performed. An event is a kind of milestone, and usually is so labeled because it is where two or more activities come to meet. One difference between Gantt charts and PERT is that in PERT activities can be shown as being parallel (being done simultaneously) or sequential (if starting one depends upon finishing another).

2. Using these two diagrammatic tools (arrows and circles) we can do something which wasn't possible with the Gantt chart—we can construct a *network*. This is a visual display of a program using arrows and circles that show all of the relationships, whether they are sequential or parallel. Let's try a sample to see if you are still aboard:

Mr. and Mrs. Smith are headed for the downtown areas for a shopping tour. Mr. Smith suggests, "I'll go to the hardware store and the garage, and you go to the grocery and the drug store, and I'll meet you here at noon."

Sketch that using a simple PERT diagram.

Is your sketch sequential or parallel?

Now suppose Mr. Smith had said: "We'll have to go to the bank to cash my check; then we can each go do our shopping. I'll go to . . ."

What does this do to the PERT diagram?

Occasionally there is a dummy activity (one which requires no time or effort) which is required to represent the network. This can be shown by a dotted line.

3. Once the network has been constructed, the next step in PERTing your action plan is to estimate the time that it would take to perform each activity. This is done by writing the estimated time along the arrow. Suppose for example it takes Mrs. Smith two hours to do all of the things she does inside the grocery store. This would be shown as in Figure 9-4.

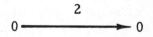

Figure 9-4

Since the network may include some alternative paths, the estimates should be made for all events. Mrs. Smith may detour to another market for meat

before going to the drug store. With a network completed with time estimates, you are ready to locate the *critical path*, which is the chain of
activities which would take the optimal period of time. If any one of the
critical activities were delayed, the whole project would be delayed.

4. Your network also permits you to estimate the *earliest time* in which
an event can be completed and these are marked into the event symbol
(the circle). What is the earliest which Mr. Smith may expect to meet
his wife if the activities she is planning will take two hours and one hour
respectively? If his own estimate for his two events is one hour and one
hour? Which is the critical path?

The *latest time* is also noted in the PERT diagram and is shown in the
event circle underneath the earliest time. The latest time is figured by working backward

earliest time
latest time

from the final or terminal event. Thus the bottom figure shows the latest
time at which each event can be completed without delaying the whole
project.

Now refer to your simple PERT diagram for Mr. and Mrs. Smith. What
is the latest time for Mr. Smith to enter the garage activity? Suppose it will
take him one hour in the hardware store, and one hour in the garage?

5. *Slack time* is the difference between the earliest time at which the
activity could be completed and the latest allowable completion time. Refer
again to your completed PERT diagram for the Smith family. What is the
slack time, and for whom? Does this agree with your own personal experience as a husband? What use could Mr. Smith make of this information?

6. Like Mr. Smith, however, as a husband you realistically know that
time estimates by women shoppers are notably unreliable. Far more realistic
would be to estimate the probabilities for each activity to take place (such
as one hour) but without much difficulty we can draw on our subjective
knowledge of his wife (after all they've been married twenty years) and he
concludes these things about her time estimates.

a) She never entered a grocery and emerged in less than an hour.

b) Two hours would be about average.

c) She could run into neighbors, bargains, or crowds and take as long
as three. If she is longer than that he will go in and drag her out.

These *three time estimates* (optimistic, realistic, and pessimistic) lend
themselves to statistical probability estimates, using some of the Bayesian
methods shown earlier in our table of expected values, and outlined in
slightly more detail in the last part of this book. Now, working from your
PERT diagram of the family shopping, complete the following chart for
various completion times. (You'll have to make a subjective estimate on

your PERT diagram, then calculate final probabilities for each expected time of completion.)

Completion time for shopping trip	Probability of meeting this deadline
1 hour	
2 hours	
2.5 hours	
2.75 hours	
3 hours	

This probability calculation gives us a basis for promises and the extent to which we can give assurances of completion. What we've produced is a series of projections about the outputs of the whole operation stated in these terms:

Expected date: The date on which the activity has a 50-50 chance of being completed.
Latest date: The last date on which an activity can be completed and still not delay the completion of the entire project (still using a 50-50 probability).
Schedule date: The deadline date for an activity.
Slack: The difference between the earliest date and the latest date. Thus, zero slack means critical path. If you have some slack you may be able to trade off some resources.
Probability: The chances of meeting the deadline date based on subjective knowledge of the situation.

All of this can often be handled on a computer; in fact, where the projects are complex, such as a missile or a shipbuilding project, the computer becomes necessary. Yet, for many other projects the idea itself is valuable for purposes of leveling labor force, spreading out pressures on equipment and plant, or managing cash, receivables or inventory. It comprises a valuable instrument for controlling action while it is going on.

chapter 10

TAKING ACTION

Behavior is what an organism is doing—
—B. F. SKINNER

HOW MANAGERS MAKE THINGS HAPPEN

When all of the planning is done, the analysis is complete, the decisions are made, the tests are performed and the plan is perfected, it remains for the manager to make things happen. This is more than watching what goes on, but includes compelling actions which change the behavior of people, modify the direction and correct it, and press through to the successful completion of the plan. What are some of the behavioral skills of managers who make things happen as contrasted with those who watch things happen, at best reacting to them? Heinz Hartmann has studied the behavior of a variety of managers and notes as a distinction group those whom he identifies as the "entrepreneurial type." This is the type, whether president or foreman, who accepts the personal responsibility for the achievement of his goals, and adapts his behavior to the situation and the goal to influence others. The manager has a unique position in getting action which doesn't fit the operator, or individual professional.

(1) *He has followers.* This means that his leadership will be measured by the performance of these followers rather than his own personality, his background, or even a pattern of behavior. This implies that he had done a suitable job in selecting them, training them to perform, and using the systems of salary, bonus, promotion and coaching to stimulate productive behavior rather than allowing them to remain uninformed, ineffective, or apathetic.

(2) *He manages by objectives.* He sets high standards for his people, defines results which will utilize their best abilities and enlarge them. He

is more concerned with letting people achieve their objective than he is in controlling their specific behavior. His concern extends to defining results, training those who cannot behave in a way which will get results, and defining any limits in means of getting results. He measures performance in terms of results which were agreed upon prior to the period in which the measurement occurs.

(3) *He works through organization.* His contribution is not necessarily in heroic and charismatic behavior. He builds organizations and makes them perform through effective group action. High on his priority list of managerial duties is maintenance of a team which displays unity of effort and high group achievement. At the same time he has individual measures for responsible persons. His decisions are not individual masterpieces in logic which he reveals magically to those not armed with his rational arsenal. Rather they are combinations of great skills inherent in the group, dynamically pressed into fruition by his personal action upon the group. His efforts aim at a rising level of group initiative and responsibility, turning the individual members and sub-groups into a decision-making machine.

(4) *He is an agent of change.* The manager who makes things happen sees himself as a rebel against the present status of the organization, and a foe of the status quo. His eye scans every operation, every product, every process with a critical eye. He asks how it can be done better, cheaper, faster, easier, safer, or with higher quality. His goal is growth and improvement of everything under his direction.

(5) *He has a range of behaviors at his command.* The manager who makes things happen has a repertory of discriminatory behaviors. He may be as patient as needed if waiting will achieve his goals. He may be solicitous of others, or he may be as tough as a Marine drill instructor if such an approach is called for. He shows enthusiasm when it is needed to stimulate enthusiasm in others. He likewise can show caution and temperance when he hopes to transmit such behavior to others who are perhaps improperly exuberant. This discretion and adaptive behavior arm the manager to confront a wide spectrum of situations in guiding the organization in motion. All of these behaviors demand a tough-mindedness which he must develop through experience. This isn't simply tough talking, but rather the willingness to stick with a particular mode of behavior to the point where some evidence shows that a change is needed. It takes as tough-minded a man to persist in a waiting game, or to show tolerance and patience, as it does to bark orders and chew out subordinates.

WHICH STYLE OF LEADERSHIP GETS ACTION?

A matter of great concern to social scientists these days which has spilled over into the plant and office has been that of selecting a leadership style. The wrong leadership style, we are told, can importantly affect the output and productivity of the organization. Which style of leadership is most appropriate for productivity.

Clearly the question is a vital one. The methods of arriving at answers to this question have usually been those of the research psychologist, the sociologist, or the anthropologist. Often, however, such styles of leadership were cast in an Aristotelian model in which blacks and whites are distinctly discernable. Theory X versus Theory Y posed two separate philosophies of management. Under Theory X, the average person is seen by his boss as being basically lazy, disliking work and avoiding it when he can. In addition to this the boss sees his workers as requiring direction, coercion, intimidation or control in order to make them productive. The presumption of such managers is that workers are less intelligent and creative than their masters, and the world can rightly be divided into the order-givers and the order-takers.

Theory Y, on the other hand, is a belief on the part of management that average persons find work as natural and pleasant as rest or play. They enjoy being productive and creative, and when they are given suitable goals and a reason for getting on toward them, they will exercise self-control. Clearly one style of management is distinct from another, yet, the assumption that either style of management exists in fact as a universal all-purpose approach to getting action is absurd and extremely damaging to constructive management theory. As a mode for decision making it sets management and decision practice back several decades. It leads managers to believe that the two styles are the limits of decision-making and action-getting methods, and leads them away from the hard tasks of identifying the complex behavior required of a manager to get action from others. Yet entire companies have proudly identified themselves as "we are a theory Y company." In one instance, a supervisor wrote the university, "My company has arbitrarily dictated that all supervisors will manage by theory Y. Isn't this inconsistent?"

Autocratic versus democratic management

Still another widely held result of behavioral research has been a concern with the styles of management in which three available positions on a continuum ranged from autocratic at the left edge of a line to laissez-faire at the extreme right of the scale. Democratic management is posed as being at about the middle between the tough kind at the left to the extremely permissive (or let-alone) brand at the right extreme.

The prescriptive advice which is given by a majority of the behavioral scientists has little foundation, even in their own research, and there is contrary evidence to show that leadership styles as chosen by the leader unilaterally are not the only determinant. What does affect productivity?

Professor Likert has put it this way:

> Supervision is always a relative process. To be effective and to communicate as intended a leader must always adapt his behavior to take into account the expectations, values, and interpersonal skills of those with whom he is interacting.

Based upon numerous researches by the staff of the University of Michigan's Institute for Social Research, this conclusion might be explained in real-life terms this way:

1. *Consistency* and predictability of managerial behavior are key ingredients in making a managerial style work. The boss who is an affable, friendly, permissive leader for a while, then becomes a domineering tyrant, may find it difficult to revert to his earlier friendly, supportive style. Everyone will wait for the next event which will trigger his rage, his martinet applications of rules, or his arbitrary choice of actions. Far better that he remain the tyrant, for at least his people will be able to predict his actions and accommodate themselves to them—provided they have no salable skills which permits them to leave.

2. *Expectations* becomes a key variable in determining the success of a leadership style. If people have been led to believe that a boss will act in a certain pattern of behavior, they are likely to be upset, disturbed, or suspicious when that pattern changes radically. These expectations aren't wholly determined by the personalities of the followers, but are also secondary, acquired, learned and psychogenic in nature. Life in the foundry is unlike life in the library. The foundry foreman is perhaps a more rough-hewn sort, acts tough and is tough. He uses the language and manners of the foundry. Clearly the manners of the librarian would be unsuitable, ludicrous and comic in such a setting, and the workers there would respond with incredulity if he tried. Likewise, the employee in the catalogue department, reference room, and order department of libraries could hardly be expected to work as usual if confronted with a foundry foreman's tactics by their heretofore refined leader. They may accommodate themselves to perfectionism, waspishness and backbiting or excessive attention to status and manners if they work there too long.

While these two illustrations are dramatically apart in their content, they make Likert's points. The leader who hopes to change the leadership style must expect that he will encounter shock, disappointment, decline in performance, and perhaps open hostility and resistance when he changes the leadership pattern from what the group has learned to expect. This doesn't mean he must never try, but that he should foresee this effect when he does. Most supervisors should be trained and practice discretionary behavior which guides them on when to be firm (or tough) and when to be permissive and soft.

3. *The kinds of objectives* often determine the style of management

which is germane. Where there are regular and minimum requirements of a job, firmness may be required to prevent failure. The paymaster who fails to meet the weekly payroll, the tax manager who omits an important tax report, or the worker who grinds without goggles should be led to expect firm and arbitrary action on the part of the boss.

Problem solving and innovative behavior call for a much more permissive style, since the behavior sought is one which is often doubtful, of uncertain outcome, and is largely under the control of the worker himself.

4. *Three variables* generally will cover most of the requirements for choosing a leadership style to get the most effective action from a group.

   a) *The leader himself* is one important ingredient. His behavior should be autocratic only when he has complete power, no restraints on its use, is capable of behaving tough, has some unique knowledge that others don't have, and is firmly entrenched in his position. Otherwise he might find that his autocracy can only lead to chaos. When should the leader try permissiveness? When he has little or no power, there is no time pressure, his tenure is based upon the pleasure of his group, he has no sanction to exert, nor has he special knowledge that the group lacks. He may also be incapable of dominating anybody—maybe he has never tried it, and his first attempt will probably fail.

   b) *The followers* comprise the second determinant of a leadership style. The leader can be autocratic with followers who have always been leader dependent, are temporary employees, have never had their opinion asked, where there is a great labor surplus, where the followers are autocratic people themselves, or where the followers are low on independence drives. On the other hand, the leader must adopt a laissez-faire or democratic style when the followers have more power than he does, dislike orders, can rebel successfully if they so choose, are volunteers, are loosely organized, or are in tight supply.

   c) *The situation* is a third determinant of leadership style. Autocratic leadership will work when the situation is one in which tight discipline is historically present, strong controls are ordinary, time pressures are constant, low profits margins or tight costs are prevalent, physical dangers are widespread, low skill requirements of workers are common and frequent changes must be made quickly. Permissive or democratic management is more suitable if the situation is without a clear purpose, no controls have existed in the past, time pressures are non-existent, the changes which occur are few or very gradual, the environment is placid or safe, the work calls for conceptual or highly creative behavior.

The conclusion? The most suitable action for leaders who want to achieve results is to spend time studying context, or frame of reference for the action. This frame of reference should become the basis for the choice of a leadership style, with the realization that the likelihood of a universal all-purpose leadership style fitting all situations, or even a single situation at all times, is astronomically improbable. The age, experience, stage of growth, organizational structure and relations, organization climate and organization culture all comprise the context in which action must take place.

A range of available behavior and skill in application—sometimes defined as mature behavior—is the plain but very difficult suitable pattern of leadership called for.

chapter 11

CONTROLLING EFFECTS
OF DECISIONS

*Tis the part of a wise man to keep himself
today for tomorrow, and not venture all his
eggs in one basket.*

—CERVANTES

The essential closing of our decision-making system is the feedback of
actual output to a measuring point where the output is compared with the
input. This basic cycle of control is exemplified by the myriad instruments
which are used to control temperature, the course of ships, the steam
pressure in a generating plant.

Feedback—the cybernetic system

If we study the entire system of decision making we note that our
business decisions, especially those which lend themselves to logical
analysis, are all designed for optimal solution. Like a proposed play in a
football game, if it were perfectly executed, and every little circle on the
blackboard were indeed to block out every little square on the other team,
then the resulting score would bring back the glorious days of Willy Heston
at Michigan when the fabulous teams of the early 1900's scored 2,000
points to their opponents 2. (They lost to the University of Chicago 2-0
in the last game).

In real life we know that perfection in planning does not assure perfection in execution. The proposed solution is confronted with unforeseen
obstacles, obstinate people whose interests and desires are contrary to the

106

optimal solution, or simply the perversity of inanimate objects.

This requires that our decision-making processes include a control stage. Furthermore, this control stage must be devised before the implementation of the plan begins, for planning of a systems nature is near impossible in the heat of battle. Once in action, it is the logic of practice which takes charge, and we'll defer this subject for subsequent chapters. What do we expect of this final stage of the decision-making process?

1. It should make accurate measurements of what *just happened* or what is *happening now*.

2. It must provide for a judgment as to the similarity of the existing condition with the desired condition.

3. It should permit or arrange for corrective action to restore the actual performance to the desired level which is on course to the objective.

These requirements indicate a cybernetic loop, which not only measures but steers as the decision and its subsequent action move onward.

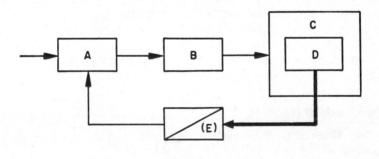

Figure 11-1

Illustrated in Figure 11-1 are the respective stages of a simple closed-loop system of control. The commonest example from our experience is the operation of the thermostat system for controlling the operation of our furnace. At (A) is the switch which turns off or on, permitting oil, gas, or electricity to flow into the heat producing unit at (B). The furnace has two functions, it may produce heat, or it may rest idle waiting further orders from the switch. When it is directed by the switch to work, it converts the input energy into heat and shoots it into the distribution system of ducts, pipes, or coils. This emits heat into the environment (C) of the house. The level of temperature is measured by (D), a thermostat in the immediate area in which the thermostat is located. Presumably this thermostat is located in such a way that it can report faithfully what the temperature typically might be in the entire house. This recording of actual temperatures simultaneously is sent to a comparator (E) which checks the actual temperature reported against a predetermined desired temperature. It makes instantaneous decisions with regard to conformity of the actual to the desired. If the temperature falls below the acceptable pre-set range, it turns the switch on and more heat will be produced by the furnace. If the comparator shows that the temperature has risen about the pre-set temperature, orders will be sent to the switch to turn the furnace off. The environment presumably remains within the upper and lower limits of pre-set temperatures.

The point here, of course, isn't how to control your house temperature, but to illustrate the basic ingredients of a cybernetic system. It is this system which provides the means for control over performance of operating units. Not that every control problem can be handled by electronic, electrical, thermal or hydrostatic devices. The point is that the system will apply to social, economic and business problems with roughly the same facility with which it can be applied to such engineering problems as temperature control, flow control, liquid level, pressure and the like.

Some distinctions are in order however when we begin to apply the cybernetic control system to making decisions work effectively.

Two kinds of feedback

Two kinds of feedback may be observed in the application of the principle.

1. *Automatic control.* This is instantaneous or almost instantaneous feedback of the comparator to the switch. The process is thus described as self-controlling and the time period for the completion of the closed loop is extremely short. Such loops are more likely to be characteristic of physical and engineering kinds of feedback systems than in social processes. Controlling the inputs in a petroleum process, a machine feed, or other technical processes makes great sense and improves efficiency.

2. *Periodic feedback.* Certain social and business processes may not lend themselves to such continuous control. It may not be economic, it might engender resistance from people controlled so tightly, or it may be simply impossible. Under such circumstances periodic review and feedback for correction is a perfectly sound application of the principle of cybernetic control. It is also somewhat different in application.

INSTANTANEOUS FEEDBACK

Two major types of instantaneous feedback device are available in establishing controls over decision. The first of these are the measuring devices of the engineer and scientists. The second device is the human being.

Physical devices. Ordinarily those parts of the decision which may be implemented and controlled by devices must be selected by engineers. The major ingredients in this process include the selection of the variable to be measured. The output must be converted into a physical quality to be measured such as pounds of pressure, foot-pounds, kilowatt-hours, feet per second of flow, or degrees of temperature. This will call for devices which may be based on mechanical, electrical, thermal, hydroscopic, or nuclear principles. The units measured must fit within some predetermined limits, and the measures must be responsive, but not overly so. The temperature control which was pre-set to maintain a perfect room temperature of 70 degrees without a single degree variation would result in the

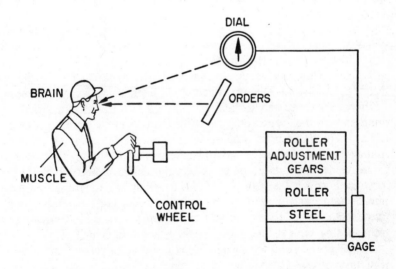

Figure 11-2

furnace switch going off and on constantly until either the switch or the furnace broke down. The principal advantage of physical devices over human sensory measurement lies in the reliability of the machine to report accurately, to remember infallibly, a..d to work without fatigue. This also has distinct cost advantages over employing humans to work at "watching and adjusting," since the idle and observation time is extremely high as a ratio to total time being paid.

The human as a thermostat. Until recent breakthroughs in instrumentation, many operations now done by devices and instruments were done by human beings. The popularized idea of automation may extend beyond this major contribution. The essential ingredient of automation, however, lies in this substitution of decisions of an immediate nature by devices for decisions of an instantaneous nature by human beings.

The thickness of rolled steel was formerly controlled by a rolling machine operator. Upon starting his job, the operator stood before a large adjusting wheel which controlled the thickness of the finished rolled plate. Slightly above his eye level was a giant dial which indicated the thickness of the finished product going through the mill. The relationship of the man, machine, control indicator and the product are depicted in Figure 11-2.

As the steel went through the rollers it was measured by a set of gauges which sensed the thickness of the finished steel to a thousandth of an inch. This thickness was transmitted to a dial which was visible to the operator. He received this information with his eyes, along with information posted on the production order which gave such standards as, "Must be no more than .0115 or less than .0105 thickness." This meant that he attempted to adjust the control wheel downward whenever the thickness as shown on the dial ran upward of .0115 inches. He would likewise adjust the control wheel upward whenever the thickness of steel indicated on the dial ran below .0105 inches. This was done by an internal mechanism of the man himself. His eyes received the data from the dial, transmitted them to the brain, where they were compared with the pre-set standard. A difference determined in his brain would set off a message to the muscles which turned the control wheel to make an adjustment in the appropriate direction.

In one instance, users of the wheel noted that almost all of the steel produced ran on the higher side of the permissible range. They watched the operator, and noted that he was indeed maintaining the thickness at close to the upper limit stipulated in the order. Asked for his reasons for so adjusting the machine the operator stated confidentially:

"I get paid by the ton on piece work, and the thicker I run the steel, the more money I make."

Couple this interjection of human interest in matters which were not calculated in devising the system with similar unforeseen inputs, and the control was somewhat less than perfect. Operators get tired, the brain may be fatigued from events the prior evening, the muscles may become fatigued, and the ability of the brain to maintain continuous unbroken attention to such a repetitive task means that error is more likely than if an inhuman device could be assigned the same task. The cybernetic system eliminated the operator and replaced him with a gauge which measured thickness against pre-set orders, and when variation appeared, directed a roller adjustment motor to shift the rollers to bring the process back into line.

Many processes, however, will not allow for such mechanical or physical measurement and feedback, and the process in which humans serve as instruments and motors must be utilized. The supervisor who patrols the floor and checks his department is serving in a more complex way as a controller in part. Manual operations such as driving a car employ the same motor skills as were used by the steel mill rolling operator.

● As a general rule, when the human is using only his cybernetic function he can be easily replaced by a non-human device.

● Where the data being received are complex, varied, and perhaps operate against uncertain standards, the human may not be replaced.

The latter includes most of the controls which must be exercised over work. Service occupations have not been especially subject to non-human control, since the variety of behaviors required to produce services has so few standards, has little uniformity, and demands the production of an infinite number of cybernetic decisions, not one of which is identical with the one before, and only the human can produce such a continuous spectrum of behaviors.

This use of the human as a thermostat requires much extension of his senses, however, and the development of conceptual tools and logical instruments which can facilitate the work of the brain. The control over decision making is less one of personal control over what is going on than applied information theory in which the decision maker obtains information and controls through information. He may, for example, note how well others are controlling their own behavior through information. This may demand that he have access to information, that he establish norms so that exceptions will come automatically to his attention. The machine operator may be self-controlled, fitting his behavior to the standards which his brain has assimilated.

It may be generally concluded that managerial work which aims at excessive personal control through putting the manager in the role of the thermostat which sees all and controls all must be done at the expense of informational control.

PERIODIC FEEDBACK

It is far more likely that the manager will function at a feedback level where he receives information in organized form. This organization requires that information be accumulated and classified before it is transmitted to him. This clustering effect requires that the process have operated for some period of time (longer than instantaneously) during which data are building up.

Decision-making controls through information control often include some preventive measurements which will be collected on a sampling basis at periodic intervals to detect possible variance before it has become so serious that major surgery is required to make the plan right. Such controls are forecasts of the possible pitfalls and are developed before starting on a major program or plan. They consider optional outcomes which could block the entire program from being carried out, and cover the insurable risks.

A few of the instruments which may be designed in advance to control the effects through periodic review of a decision or pattern of decisions are these:

1. *Use of logical premises.* This is the simple use of the scientific methods of rational analysis, and empirical facts. Certain companies are very dependent upon the weather for their sales volume predictions coming true. The gas company, for example, sells much more gas during a cold winter than a warm one. Breweries find that beer sells vastly better in a hot summer than a cool one. Ice cream companies, air-conditioning manufacturers, and soft drink bottlers all make certain estimates in advance conditional upon an average temperature that has proved indicative of corresponding sales income. This can be historically projected in several

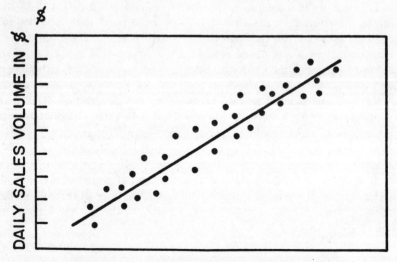

Figure 11-3

ways, including the generation of a statistical chart showing correlations between heat and sales volume (Figure 11-3).

The accompanying chart, which is included as illustrative rather than factual, is compiled by plotting for some time a series of points which indicate sales and corresponding temperature for a product which is known to be subject to variation for this cause. The line is based on a statistical fitting to the dots. It might be a curve.

The value of such premises in preparing in advance periodic review points is that historical record of temperature by dates for years past may provide a logical basis for making plans for materials, personnel, cash flow, equipment maintenance, and other key variables, thereby preventing their being unavailable at crucial times.

2. *Mathematical and quantitative methods.* Management has increasingly incorporated into the decision-making process the skills of mathematicians, usually where the decision to be made can be reached best through the treatment as a problem solving behavior. Such methods are less often used where personal hunch or preference of the decision maker is the only possible guide, as in choosing objectives. The purpose of mathematical decisions is closely allied with the subject of this chapter, since many of the quantitative-method decisions incorporate decisions of outcome in their methods. Ordinarily there are three classes of decisions which can be treated quantitatively:

1. Decision under certainty, or where at least the process will lend itself to probability-type treatment in the face of uncertainty.

2. Decisions where there is an opponent to be outwitted. Sometimes the opponent is a state of nature (such as weather) or the opponent is a rational person.

3. Decisions made by an individual or a group.

The use of a model to obtain control

One of the key processes which mathematicians use in decision making is the construction of a model of the problem. The first stage in model making is to abstract from the problem those things which are significant. This is based on the assumption that some attributes of the problem must be ignored if a decision is to be made. A model is a symbolic or numerical counterpart of the empirical problem, which duplicates the essential behavior of the process. A simple model might be constructed from the following paragraph:

> As I look at all of the costs which go into making my product I note that some of them are carried by the accountant as fixed expense whether or not we are producing a few units, many units, or no units. Then as production costs go up, each added unit of output adds those costs which are added to produce each unit. These costs are variable

cost, varying with the number of units. These two costs together comprise the total costs of doing business.

This might be made into a model which looks like this

$$T = f + v$$

where T represents total cost
f represents fixed costs
v represents variable costs.

For simple repetitive problems which can be carried in the mind, there's no point in making a model. When complexity enters, the model provides discipline and order. It gives the manager some variables to watch, helps him to relate those variables and helps him derive conclusions from premises. This means that his periodic reports will be taken from different parts of the process with a specific purpose of flushing out the model with real data. This discipline of the model provides one of the best guides to developing periodic feedback to control the decision which has been put into operation.

If the model has been used in the choice of options, it also has a consistency in use for the control of results.

Management by objectives

The essential feature of all periodic feedback is that the actual results are measured against statements of expectations prepared prior to entering the action stage. Where such matters as responsibility of subordinate managers to deliver certain results are involved, the statement of results expected and the measurement of results achieved becomes a way of managing. The essentials of the process are the statements of goals prepared in advance and to which commitments are made. The performance of the subordinate against these statements of objective is an on-going process. The manager and his superior sit down at the beginning of each period and conduct a dialogue on three areas of responsibility

● regular or routine responsibilities
● problems to be solved
● innovations to be programmed or attempted.

As we've outlined in Chapter 4, this classification of objectives has a hierarchical nature that places a greater value upon innovative change than upon maintenance of the status quo.

The reporting system of results against such objectives in the management of managers is basically a two-part process.

1. The individual manager operates under self-control and provides his own instantaneous feedback of results against goals.

2. The superior provides information of a cumulative or periodic

nature to the subordinate to confirm or correct this observation of his own performance.

This means that the superior must take regular measurements or arrange for their collection through a variety of channels to obtain accurate periodic reviews of results attained, and also arrange for a systematic feedback to the subordinate of the periodic summaries.

Performance review

The deferment of performance review to fit a periodic schedule can have a harmful effect in the controlling and improving of the operation.

● When specific actions of an offending or undesirable nature occur, they should be treated by instantaneous feedback, and not accumulated for some future period. The teaching effects are totally lost when they are deferred until some arbitrary periodic review is indicated.

● Only those actions which are under the control of an individual should be included in periodic reviews to him personally, if such feedback is interpreted as reports of his failure or success. For example, the local plant manager should not be held accountable for rises in local tax rates, or administrative costs of the home office.

Conventional reporting instruments

The periodic reviews discussed in this chapter will include not only statements of results against objectives, but statements of accounting performance against revenue and expense budgets, statements of sales performance against targets of volume, gross margin, contribution to profit and sales expense. Manufacturing performance may be measured against costs, quality, safety, housekeeping spoilage, yield, downtime of machines and a host of other standards. The variety of such reports is limitless in industry at large and is extensive for even the smallest firm.

SUMMARY

Control in the decision-making process is meaningless by itself. It has significance only if there were goals and standards to begin with. If the final objective has been defined and intermediate stages laid out, control can be added. It consists of noting actual achievement against hoped for and the taking of corrective action within as short or long a period of time after the information about results are known as is feasible. Some controls are so important that they should be instantaneous, while others, for economic or practical logistics, can't be taken immediately and should be taken periodically. The control process itself doesn't control the action, however. It is the action which is taken by the person receiving the feedback which turns the organization about in its tracks and starts the action back into proper channels once more.

This "action" will concern us in the next section. There are certain aspects of decision making on the run which have been largely ignored by decision theorists. Yet, when all of the thinking and theorizing has been done, somebody must move, and think while he is moving. What are some of the major ingredients in such behavior?

Part II

Decision Making On the Run

The Logic of Practice

Some decisions are finished and perfected when the analysis is complete and the general course of action outlined. Other decisions have merely been initiated when the analytical work has been finished. What remains is the vital portion of the decision making required to achieve the objective.

chapter 12

THE LOGIC
OF PRACTICE

Man is not a fact . . .
                        —J. W. KRUTCH

In business, in war and in personal affairs a certain part of decision making remains an imponderable. It is the decision that worked which appeared to have small chance for success. Its counterpart is the decision which failed in the face of every indicator which seemed to predict that it would succeed. Measuring what caused the failure or the success requires more than simply reviewing the plans.

> *The plan which succeeded where success was not predictable often was carried through because of the subjective vigor and ingenuity with which it was implemented. The plan which failed often fell short because of the lack of such vigor, ingenuity, and logic of practice.*

It is this inexplicable difference, occurring in and limited to the field of practice and action in implementing decisions, which will concern us in this section.

Theorists, even decision theorists, are characterized by their method. They attempt to fit the rich content of actual concrete experience into the framework of rigid theory. In attempting to simplify and generalize, the danger of warping actuality is ever present. The tastes and proclivities of theorizers are toward abstraction. The commonly held presumption that intellectual work at this level is superior to that which deals with reality, description and phenomena is widespread in the western world.

The danger here is that we may accept too readily plausible explanations and easy generalizations which fail to do justice to the rich detail of reality which they intend to subsume.

In fact, it is far more difficult for the intelligent person to cope with human nature in the specific than in general. It is far more difficult to describe one manager than it is to write a whole philosophy of management. It is harder to describe one of his actions in his work than to describe the manager. The more limited the material, the harder it is to describe. The test of applying the powers of description is an infinitely more complex and difficult task than preparing generalizations, accumulating statistics, extracting essence for a model, or even applying method such as the scientific method. The more one depends upon generalization, the easier the task. The assumption that generalization is difficult and the concrete is simple is an assumption which is open to serious question.

What confuses the subject of management and decision making is that people do not always notice that they are operating with a concept, and that the concept "action" is perhaps the most difficult of all. The existence of the manager and his behavior in decision making and action to implement decision are not conceptual but real. Most decision theorists do not live in the buildings they build, but rather dwell in a small tent some distance away.

The superiority of the practical over the theoretical is more likely to be found in ancient philosophy than in modern science. Plato, Aristotle and Augustine emphasized the supremacy of the practical over the theoretical. We should engage in speculation to save our soul or our hides, not for the truth itself.

Action is subjective—theory is objective

The purpose of theory is to describe objectively the process or procedure by which a result is arrived at, a goal reached. Reports of scientific research follow a rigid objective format:

> 300 cc's of isopropyl alcohol were combined with 300 cc's of water.

It is most unlikely that the scientist would describe his action in terms of what actually occurred.

> I was working late in the lab one night, and had decided to try a mixture of ethyl alcohol and water for the next step. I looked around for the ethyl alcohol and found that somebody had borrowed it and hadn't returned it. I tried to get into the supply room for another bottle, but it was locked and the guard was across the street for coffee. While I was waiting I made a cup of coffee and was fuming. Then my eye lit on the bottle of Isopropyl. It was all there was and suddenly I had an idea: "Why not try that? I thought about it for

a minute and decided that even though it wasn't what I planned originally I would try it instead. After all I could always try the ethyl alcohol tomorrow. The first results looked so good I forgot all about the original idea, and I called my wife to tell her I was making progress and wouldn't be home for a couple of hours.

Such a report would of course reflect reality, but wouldn't be of special interest to the theorist, who is interested only in the replicable portions of the experiment. It is most unlikely that future students would be asked to establish an exact duplicate of the environment in which the experiment was conducted. No college, for example, would ask the student to work alone in a lab late at night, have the guard leave for coffee, steal the original alcohol, and make the student go through the actual process by which the original discovery was made.

More likely, the scientist, if he mentions the incident at all, will make a brief mention of the influence of "serendipity," which is a theoretically acceptable word to cover such accidental events that make something work in a way that wasn't expected.

The subjective life of the decision maker in implementing his decision is comprised of his own existence, and the brute facts of his existence can make or break the quality of the decision. The variety and richness of this existence are too complex to be known or explained theoretically. This is not wholly true for groups or populations, but is perfectly obvious for individuals. Explaining individual existence in terms of the group will inevitably miss the differences that comprise the logic of practice.

Action means movement

The essence of action is movement. The soldier who would grasp the essence of combat must learn that "walk and shoot" are the essential actions for the foot soldier. For the pilot it is "move the instruments," including those required to fly the plane, release the bomb toggles, actuate the triggers of his guns, and the myriad other movements entailed. For the manager it consists of speaking, gesturing, writing, walking, sitting, standing, or listening. Clearly these are controlled action from a central brain. But the ten systems of the body are in movement (not all at once, of course) and the mechanical functioning of the human machine is importantly involved in the implementation of decisions. The decision to execute a complex program of mass activity such as communicating employee benefits, conducting a cost-reduction program, reaching a new market, takes reality in the actions of people which in turn may activate things. Effectiveness in management must always be measured in terms of effectiveness of the action taken. The decision-making process as it moves majestically through the stages, terminates in movement of the striped muscles, the skin flaps of the lip, the vocal chords, the arm-hand motion used in writing. It is to control this movement that systems are designed.

The individual who takes action executes the decision which is objective and which further assumes that the individual will treat it objectively. The theory of decision making, especially that which is mathematical and quantitative in nature, may fall into the pitfall of assuming that the choice to move on its implementation is one achieved by theoretical reflection alone. Certainly we are pressed strongly to "be objective about ourselves" despite the impossibility of ever achieving more than a fraction of such a dictum. The conversion of objective decisions and theoretical objectives into subjective movements, and the choices to make those required movements into personal decisions to move are essential parts of the decision's effectiveness.

An executive who travels by jet planes may make his trip to the west coast or London nothing more than an overnight stop.

Recently an executive for an automobile company left Detroit at 7:45 A.M. on a jet for Los Angeles, arriving there at 9:05. He completed four appointments that day with several staff members on the West Coast. A two-hour conference took place in the morning. A technical plan and recommendation was proposed to him, and he reviewed the materials with its advocate. After thirty minutes of questioning, he approved the idea. He left for lunch with several of the larger dealers on the West Coast. He discussed with them some of the more serious problems of marketing which they reported in that region. He made notes of these to report back to his staff in Detroit. That afternoon he interviewed a prospective employee for one hour, and ended the day with a session in which he talked to a management executive from a steel company which supplied parts for the firm. He outlined the company's grievances with the supplier's performance, suggested some specific changes in operating practices to the supplier, and assured him of support if the corrections were made immediately. He boarded the 5:55 P.M. flight for Detroit and, after drinks and a leisurely dinner, read a report, wrote some notes and took a nap. He was met by a company car and was home in bed by 1 A.M.

A fairly full day, and not one to be completed every day to be sure. Yet it is not an impossible one, and recognizable in the experience of many executives. An older person, for example, or one without time urgency would have stayed over and traveled the next day, perhaps spread the whole day's activities over another day. Yet, in the past such a trip would have occupied a full week of travel and work time.

What actually occurred here that is of interest in the logic of practice?

1. There is the collapse of time. From the viewpoint of his home office, this executive's secretary could simply respond to calls, "Mr. Smith isn't in today, but will be in the office tomorrow morning. May I have him call you?" What she might accurately have stated was the factual report: "Mr.

Smith is now engaged in a process of flying 650 miles an hour for 5,000 miles, riding 50 miles in cars over freeways, talking to executives from a radius of 150 miles of Los Angeles, and will take action on some aspect of three extremely important decisions."

2. Mr. Smith actually collapsed this time for decision through movement. The decisions entailed making progress on a technical program in which he reviewed the work of others in fact-gathering and presenting proposed solutions. He gathered facts on dealer relations and marketing problems as the dealers saw them. He gathered further facts as a segmental part of a total decision on hiring (or not hiring) an applicant for an executive position. He concluded his ground time on the West Coast by implementing a decision with relations to a supplier. He issued the conditions under which the supplier would be retained, making an ultimatum as a conditional decision. His reports and record-keeping were recorded on his flight back, to be more formally noted in his office the next day.

3. No single complete decision was carried out, but progress was made in the execution of all of those which Mr. Smith touched. No doubt he was able to report a "satisfactory trip." Were an interviewer to have asked Mr. Smith if he had followed the theoretical stages of decision making, it is entirely possible that he might receive a blank stare. The logic of practice requires that such a numerous array of large and small decisions be retained personally by the individual. It means that in any particular instant in time he may not be conscious of being engrossed in the "fact stage" or the "developing alternatives" stage.

The management of this work pressure, numerous projects in different stages of completion, and the time which it must be telescoped into bear little resemblance to the theory of decision making. The governance of

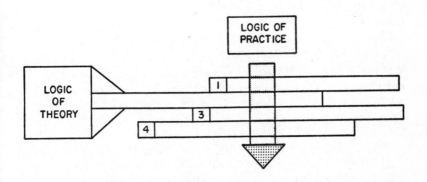

Figure 12-1

such time and action is managed more by the logic of practice than by the logic of theory.

The difference in perception of the logic of practice from the logic of theory is illustrated in Figure 12-1. The logic of theory arranges the stages of decision as an orderly, rational process, moving from the setting of objectives to the determination of the final course of action to be taken. It has symmetry, logic and a beginning and an end. The logic of practice is made up by the time and interest of the executive, his pressures, and the day-to-day judgments on numerous decisions which he goes through in a single day. He makes a fragmentary judgment on a single part of a larger problem, then awaits further developments. He seldom has time to stick wholly with one major problem to carry it through more than two or three stages of action. If the problem has "high priority," he may spend more time on that matter. Usually he must await other's actions, and accordingly turns his attention to the currently required stage of another of the numerous problems with which he is dealing. The admixture of actions he takes comprises the logic of practice. He is more like a juggler than a weight lifter.

Such a logic calls for skill in opening a drawer for awhile, then closing it and opening another. He deals with the next important phase of one problem, and when that phase is complete he turns to another problem at exactly that phase of it which calls for his attention at that moment.

The logic of practice, then, is less one of being systematic in pursuing a problem through its various stages than of working on numerous problems at once, deciding which small aspect of which general problem he will turn to next (or respond to), and what specific action to take on each at the moment he is working on it. It requires that he be able to drop something and pick it up later at exactly that point at which it returns to him.

The well-known story of the captain in the Pentagon is illustrative. Each day he left the building in chipper spirits and fresh from a day's work. One evening a haggard colonel asked him how he did it. "Simple," the young captain reported. "Whenever anything comes to my desk I simply write 'refer to Colonel Smith' and drop it into my basket. I never see them again, and I assume that there must be enough Colonel Smiths in the Pentagon to cover the problem somehow."

The haggard colonel nodded. "I know," he stated. "My name is Colonel Smith."

Judgment and practice

Conspicuously missing in the theory of decision making is any suitable explanation of what *judgment* consists. If any assumption is made here, perhaps it is the assumption that judgment doesn't exist, but is to be supplanted by models or theories of decision making. The reason for such a gap is that judgment is part of the logic of practice, is unmanageable in theoretical terms, and is subjective with the individual decision maker.

Judgment is that untheoretical and apparently intuitive (at least often described as such) reaction to questions which are presented without much warning and to which almost immediate responses are demanded. The quality of this reaction to an inescapable demand for decision forms the quality of judgment which we attribute to the manager.

Judgment is of higher quality when the instantaneous responses to dilemmas of an immediate nature are correct and fast. It is a sporadic burst of intelligence spaced among long stretches of routine.

Judgment apparently grows through experience. The persons who have been through an experience more than once are more likely to have facility in making the decision right than the person who is presented with an appalling situation for the first time.

The retention of general guides to handling small situations is the development of judgments. Such experience may be translatable to new situations through the building up of a considerable body of knowledge in the logic of practice. Some examples may be of assistance here:

> Most senior executives realize the importance of face-to-face confrontation when they find themselves in serious disagreement with someone whose continued good relations are important to them. If an important customer is reported to be disgruntled, it is part of the logic of practice for the senior sales executive involved to make an immediate contact with the highest level executive in the customer firm as soon as possible. This face-to-face contact is always considered superior to writing a letter.

> Subordinate executives who understand that the boss is inflamed over some behavior of theirs, on the other hand, often get out of their office and let a decent amount of time pass in which the old man will have a chance to cool off.

If we were to ask either of these men why they would hold firmly to such tactics, without necessarily being able to explain in any conceptual, theoretical or logical terms why they know it to be true. In some instances they might be able to cite a specific case in which they had behaved in a different fashion and had seen disastrous results ensue. One executive explained his proclivity for talking before writing letters this way:

"When I was a kid I had a paper route. One day I was going on vacation and I was briefing the kid who was going to deliver my papers while I was gone. I wrote out some notes on each customer to help the replacement along. The old man was a grouch. I wrote this on the customer's order ticket in black pencil: "GROUCH." Somehow the customer got his hands on that ticket, and when I got back from the vacation I was called into the circulation manager's office and got the dressing down of my life.

The substance of what he told me was 'Never put it in writing kid, especially when it's true. Stick to telling other people.' "

At the same time this person was noted as one of those who never said anything in an agreement which he wouldn't later confirm in writing. Confronted with what might seem to be a logical contradiction, he reflected for a moment, then stated:

"I guess what I find best is to talk first, then when you strike an agreement or a bargain, confirm it in writing. The reason to confirm it in writing is that you might both recall the details differently, and both would be unhappy. I guess we all know how to rationalize things we've said in the past—usually in our own favor—and a note confirming the discussion avoids that kind of error.

Such presumably scientific, non-theoretical and often intuitive judgment comprises the majority of the logic of practice. Since it is comprised of a myriad detail bits of knowledge growing out of subjective experience, it lends itself but poorly to the logic of science. Often it is based on situation and is personal with the individual executive and his immediate peers, bosses, and subordinates, and wouldn't do at all if it were generalized to every managerial situation.

As we press into the logic of practice we uncover such an array of small judgments and intuitions growing out of subjective experience which are adaptations of theory that it begins to dawn on us that here is where the bulk of the decision-making process lies. Judgment then is logic of practice which doesn't lend itself to science, but which is reduced when firm scientific principles are developed. The areas of judgment have been reduced by rationality and will undoubtedly be more reduced as future management research is accumulated. The possibility that such judgment will ever be eliminated and that the manager will be nothing more than a systems engineer operating mechanical procedures is a chimera adhered to only by those who have isolated themselves in theory from the real world where the logic of practice prevails.

Management through mathematics

The monster electronic computer is relentlessly widening its dominance over industrial and military decision making. Mathematicians with neither business nor military experience are riding these machines to positions of power and influence. The idea of such machines regulating those who are not computer-oriented to positions of minimal importance is highly hazardous in administration.

While it would be naive not to concede that some of the criticism of the Defense Department was politically motivated, there is no doubt that some of this opposition stemmed from former Secretary Robert S. McNamara's heavy reliance on the electronic computer to solve complex problems. The secretary, according to some critics, became the *pater familias* of a mathematics cult.

As recently as 1940 one could still find books which treated mathematics as an obscure and frankly hopeless subject which needed special treatment to be made palatable. Edward Kasner and James R. Newman wrote a popularizer of higher mathematics that year in which they justified their work by stating that "the popularization of science is a duty to be performed." "The mathematician," they added, "is still regarded as a hermit who knows little of the life outside his cell."

However much truth this may have had in 1940, it is most certainly not true of higher mathematics today, nor of mathematicians, as is seen in the full-page ads in the help wanted pages, campus recruiting trips to hire those who are trained in it and the immense power now vested in those who understand its deeper mysteries. Sufficiently great is the new power of the quantifiers that their earlier protestations of innocence and impracticality take on an ironic air. Mathematically trained people today exert immense influence in business, in science and in government, especially in the Department of Defense.

To the extent that they substitute mathematical methods for some of our traditional values, they comprise a source of alarm to some observers.

Where scientists might previously have spent countless days or months performing routine manual calculations, they now have at their fingertips great masses of finished data upon which to apply human ingenuity. Without these giant number-manipulators, the advance into rocketry and the space age would have been impossible. To stock its ravenous memory drum has demanded countless breakthroughs in electronics and solid state physics.

In return for this application of the physical and biological sciences, the computers have brought forth ever more prolific families of thinking machines.

The impact of this tribe upon mathematics has been revolutionary. In the field of finite mathematics, the need for higher analysis has become a most urgent necessity in order to arrange data into "programs" which speak the coded grammar of machine language and cope with the logic of computer math.

Thorstein Veblen once suggested that the world would be better ruled by a "soviet of engineers," eradicating the business and financial domination of production. While few now see this goal as possible, it is not impossible, some say, to see a world ruled by a "soviet of mathematicians."

Leaders now select their successors by statistically valid tests which predict success for some and reject others. Computed ratings have become the basis for redirecting advertising, for firing TV stars, and for corporate policy changes. Consumer surveys are avidly read by decision makers who attempt to foresee (and, some say, control) prosperity levels.

"Operations research," the popular label for computer-oriented decision making, originated with the British armed services during World War II. After the war, operations research found widespread civilian use in the United States, as applied to such problems as warehouse location, transport networks, and production and inventory control. In recent years Secretary McNamara returned operations research to military use in establishing defense policy and for decision making in strategic defense, all of which places mathematicians a long way from Whitehead's "refuge from the goading urge of contingent happenings."

So pertinent has automated mathematics become that some critics now consider its "divine madness" in a new light. Operations research enjoyed immense success in its progress through industry, so much so that it sometimes outdid itself. Young Turks without business experience began to find computer decision making the way to bypass the long stairway to the executive suite. Because they promised to substitute certainty for uncertainty in business decisions and replace intuition with rationality, they were sought out by top management.

Intuitive decisions went upstream against the scientific advice of young quantifiers, and all too often came off second best. Old hands, ill equipped to argue with computers and quantified logic, could only retreat, baffled and rebellious. In the face of many such defeats, a growing corps of anti-mathematicians emerged. "These young operations researchers just won't listen to experience," one company president put it, vowing to have none of it.

A few operations research teams were brash enough and green enough to tackle problems that went beyond their new-found art and fell on their faces. One agricultural chemical company lost $8 million by trying to predict the future market in a particular commodity. When this happened, the anti-mathematicians were quick to reassert control.

The battle of operations researchers versus the anti-mathematicians has moved onto a broader stage in recent years. Senators, generals, admirals and industrial defense contractors aligned themselves among the anti-mathematicians, as operations research in Department of Defense strategy threatened to take military decision making away from the generals and vest it in the Secretary of Defense and his youthful staff of operations analysts—often referred to as the "whiz kids."

The struggle for control over military strategy decisions went back beyond Secretary McNamara. It had its roots in an order by President Eisenhower made late in his Administration which vested greater power in the Secretary of Defense, especially in financial matters and the promotion of senior officers. The unification of the services and the construction of the Pentagon aimed to put the three services under one roof. It did so physically, but they continued to fight each other until Eisenhower's order gave the two new powers to the Defense Secretary.

The full impact of this was not felt until McNamara came in from Ford to serve President Kennedy. McNamara quickly established clear civilian direction at the peak of the military establishment. In part, this direction drew upon the powers established by President Eisenhower. It also carried a distinctive McNamara style of pure rationality, which came under criticism as being excessively so. Since the attack on National Guard ineptness, which enraged many state governors, successive hammer blows of logic and financial power have rejected Skybolt, spurned the RS-70 airplane and committed the U. S. to nuclear power. This rationality turned on the Navy, threatening the existence of the big ships in favor of Polaris-bearing submarines.

Emboldened by open skepticism on the part of friendly legislators such as Senator John Stennis (D.-Miss), many military men have become frankly critical of the "new type of civilian expert." Seasoned military men feel they are being shunted aside by the young scientists who shape decisions through operations analysis and the computer.

The new nuclear war plan described to Congress by Secretary McNamara evoked frank doubts from Senator Stennis on the Skybolt and big bomber decisions. Senior officers leaked the opinion to columnists that we would become a second-rate power in ten years, with "bow-tie boys" or "whiz kids" calling the plays without consulting our military leaders.

Most of the corps of younger undersecretaries in McNamara's strategy group were under 40 and without military experience. Actually the computer played a not-so-important role in their methods, said Department of Defense Comptroller Charles J. Hitch, the principal whiz kid, but to the anti-mathematicians "the computer was their symbol." *The New York Times* military analyst Hanson W. Baldwin presented the position of the officers in an article, when he stated that the new centralization based on "slide rule statistics" and "computer analyses" comprised "almost as great a threat to a secure and free nation as the attempted military coup envisaged in the novel, *Seven Days in May*."

As *The New York Times* columnist James Reston put it, "McNamara has been run over by the gravy train." Yet McNamara's *modus operandi* was of long standing and had carried him to the top at Ford Motor Co. Even there, as one Ford executive anonymously expressed it, "We can now see that he created a monster in the comptroller's department" in his rush to the top.

Gravy trains and battling admirals and generals aside, there is a deeper discontent which grows out of the new treatment of people as numbers in calculating the effects of nuclear war. Drawing on the precise calculations of his operations researchers, McNamara told the House Armed Services Committee that both Russia and the United States would suffer 100 million deaths in an atomic war, with another 100 million falling in Europe and elsewhere. This "megadeath" sort of arithmetic, which Defense Department adviser Herman Kahn called "thinking about the unthinkable," seems to some critics to be an ultimate in quantifying human relations.

As the quietly civilized *Manchester Guardian* wryly put it, perhaps we should prefer that such people devote their brain power to "thinking about avoiding the avoidable." Many people attribute the chilly results of reducing our population to such an abstraction simply to the reign of mathematicians.

The suspicion which developed into a national feud over policy has been building up rapidly in plants and offices around the country. Among the working population at all levels there is still a strong preference for the idea that each man is unique, and this idea resists the leadership of quantification which engulfs him. The centralizers who would operate firms by the numbers can cite the efficiency which indeed results. Yet where this clearly suppresses individuality and uniqueness, we tread a path that leads us to goals which are quite unsatisfactory in terms of being employed, to say nothing of life goals on this planet in general.

St. Augustine still strikes a responsive chord with his observation that there are "hidden deeps" in men which we may never explain, not with survey research, psychological tests or operations research. The popularity of books such as *The Brain Watchers*, by Martin Gross, or W. H. Whyte's *Organization Man*, is an expression of the unease which Everyman feels when he becomes identified by a trait which he has in common only with everything else which can be so identified—his number.

The use of numbers to accomplish a task more easily is not quarreled with. In a scientific world it is sound and necessary. A fond father may state that he has six children, which is useful to know at bath time or when loading the car, yet he never loses sight of each one's individual strengths and weaknesses, likes and dislikes. The danger point in leadership is where it is no longer possible to convert back from numbers to unique individuals.

Even if there were not the improprieties in logic often associated with operations research and quantitative management, such as the production of tautologies which deal with only half the truth, there is a basic rightness in maintaining the uniqueness of individuals for its own sake. We can be confident that this viewpoint will prevail over the new society of mathematicians.

chapter 13

THE MANAGEMENT OF TIME

The mass of men lead lives of quiet desperation . . .
—THOREAU

Scientific laws are intentionally fixed and timeless. Even if they subsequently prove to be fallacious and are modified, it is expected that they will remain as proposed explanations until disproved. The logic of practice is dynamic and temporal. Most of the language of the logic of practice is expressed by verbs which are tensed. We deal with answers to questions of "What should I do, do differently or stop doing?" A further distinction is that the attention paid to "do" isn't really a succession of discrete "nows" but entails the management of time in which the projected future dominates the present.

If we can obtain information on the unfinished projects which a manager carries in his mind today we know more about his logic of practice than through any other measure we might devise.

The project itself introduces the logical element of decision making. The subjective logic of practice introduces the incompleteness of the project and the element of time. In the logic of science time may be managed by PERT, by tree diagrams, by flow charts, and by engineering estimates. For the manager or executive of the project, the time is internalized into pressures and priorities which are subjective, personal and even visceral.

Scientific concepts of time, including past, present and future, in a regular measurable flow are essential to the physicist, or the astronomer. The nature of subjective time for the manager is more manageable, and has a different nature in his logic of practice.

The executive and time

It has been said earlier than when the executive gives of his time he gives of himself. The appointment pad of a typical executive is often crowded with meetings, appointments, inspections, and telephone calls. Subordinates often complain "you can never get to see the guy," and one of the most valuable assets to the subordinates is time spent with the boss, especially the successful one.

The total time which the executive has to spend at the practice of his profession is limited. It is limited by his mortal character, and his working life is ordinarily limited by the requirement for education until he is 21 at the lower end, and the compulsory retirement for most firms at age 65 at the other. This period is further eaten into by the requirement that he work his way upward through a hierarchy, and it is not common for him to achieve general management rank until he is well over forty. This leaves him about two decades in which to make his mark on the organization and the industry, and often much less.

Opportunity to dispel this time in projects or activity which are non-productive tends to increase as he rises in the organization, because other people who do not see their own areas of concern as trivial seek to involve him in their projects.

There is a common knowledge among executives of the price which must be paid to achieve the projects which are unfinished, or even unstarted, for himself. The time to achieve comprises the price he pays. He might abandon all of the projects and go fishing. Often he has the financial means to do so by the time he has reached the top or come close to it. He might simply complete the projects which are developed now or which are forced upon him. Even more demanding are the projects which might be initiated if he makes a choice to start them, and which will never be started if he chooses not to start them. This ascending hierarchy of goals and projects which he chooses to pursue also is a hierarchy of the demands upon his time—and himself—which are inherent in his position.

This range of attention to time and the giving of himself extends from such mundane questions as "Should I answer my own telephone or make my own travel arrangements?" to more grandiose questions as "Should my company attempt to merge the five major firms in the industry into a single firm with me as principal promoter and perhaps chief executive, or should we coast along for another five years holding the status quo?" The mundane matters can occupy fully as much time as the more grandiose ones, can be managed with greater assurance and certainty while they are going on, and rely heavily on assured judgments in which he has garnered extensive experience in the past

One of the determinants of the allocation of an executive's time is his subjective choice of what the highest priority projects will be.

The avoidance of error

One family of projects are those which are designed to avert error. The manager who carries as his project tester the single dossier "mistakes need not happen" will manage his time far differently than the manager who has different projects. The prevention of mistakes in others has numerous psychological virtues to commend it to many managers. First, it is a full-time occupation, since there are many who move at variance with the letter of the law in policy, procedure, and regulation.

Several requirements are very helpful in filling one's time with such projects:

1. It becomes necessary to obtain a grasp on communication channels at a juncture where approvals are needed before the initiator can move further. This requires that eventually everyone must acknowledge the power of the guardian against error. His project lies in thwarting and checking information, then issuing judgments.

2. It is also fairly important that the standards and guidelines not be specifically spelled out and widely disseminated. If this were to be done, the lesser persons might *learn* what the standards were and begin to apply them under self-control. This would then eliminate the need for the error-avoidance activity of the superior and would force him into a confrontation with other more difficult judgments of a forward-looking and creative nature.

The illusion that time thus filled with choices and decisions is effective executive time is a form of narcotic which beguiles the manager. The use of managerial time for control and avoiding mistakes in others stresses conformity to the system, objectifies the people in it, stifles creative use of time, and puts a heavy damper on creativity and innovation. This conformity isn't merely one that's imposed from above on the subordinates; it is a self-imposed conformity on the part of the manager.

The following lists two kinds of time for managers. The first is an actual activity list, the second a list of specific accomplishments during one day.

Manager A (ACTIVITY)	Manager A (RESULTS)
Read incoming mail	
Answered mail—dictation	Learned of problem
Checked and signed purchase order requests	Issued four decisions
Met with three subordinates who were proposing a new method	Clarified confusion of three subordinates

Checked production report for prior day

Eliminated excess production cost on night shift

Prepared notes and sent queries on variances

Soothed angry customer

Answered afternoon mail

Prevented recurrence of error

Conference on customer complaint

A fairly full day? Possibly, yet in the management of time we might find that many of these activities would be classified as the avoidance of error. The solution to such a concentration in mistake-prevention? It entails placing the people who are being checked under self-control. The reason for such delegation isn't simply the desire of subordinates to be free of domination, but the efficiency for the manager himself. The finite nature of time itself means that before this time is available to use for creative decision making, other types of activity must be shed.

Even among the error-avoidance activities there are categories of time expenditure which make it a variable of great flexibility. The sorts of questions which are brought to the manager for control may be vital or trivial. The structure of the organization which prohibits the smaller issues from getting to the top while permitting the large ones to arrive there promptly modifies very significantly the time utilization of the manager.

Creative and authentic use of time

Two alternative uses of time exist for the executive. The creative use of time is considered here to mean that which is applied to manipulating information (memories) into new and unique combinations. Authentic use of time for a manager is spending personal energies becoming what he really is. This search for authenticity and creativity drives hundreds of thousands of employees annually out of their comfortable positions in large firms into new small businesses of their own. This year some 750,000 new businesses will be established. The sad fact is that almost as many will fail, but the persistently high level of new business formation despite the preponderant evidence that most will fail within ten years is a tangible testimony to the search for personal expression of creation of the new, and for authenticity.

Authenticity is most difficult to find in executing the system of another, or in controlling others in subordinate positions who must be checked and corrected to prevent error.

The greatest limitation of tight personal control through error avoidance activity is that it makes prisoners of both the guard and the prisoner, destroying the authenticity of each. Analysts, reviewers and critics often have an unease about their function because of its lack of authenticity. There are a few if any opportunities of self-expression in destroying the possibilities inherent in others' ideas and proposals. The possibility destroyer gains little sense of personal fulfillment of his subjective self when he totals up the end of the week's achievements in such terms as "This week I ruined thirty proposals."

A modicum of creativity is possible in the work of the critic, reviewer and corrector of error, however. The development of new and unique forms of control and preventive action, however stultifying its purposes for those controlled, is a manipulation of past experiences into new and unique combinations, and meets in its own way the requirements of creative behavior. Some of the most fiendishly clever inventions of our time are found in the programs of controllers, systems men, industrial engineers and forms designers.

The logic of practice, however, must rank among its higher values those which are decisions that something should happen which isn't presently happening. The use of time which is spent in choosing new and original goals, shaping these projects into tangible form, overcoming the obstacles which stand in the way of their becoming real comprises a creative activity which permits more authenticity for the manager than any other kind of activity.

Far too few persons in managerial positions ever grasp the vision which is before them always of building an organization as a form of creative activity. The originator of an idea who converts it into a permanent, going, productive organism, staffed by individuals of great talent, all seeking to find their own authentic existence, and each expressing his own creative talents is performing an act of the highest order of creativity. The organizers of the world, perhaps typified by the "great organizers" of Ernest Dale, perform work of the highest creative order. Alfred P. Sloan, Ernest Breech, George Love, Theodore Vail, several of the Du Ponts, and others who built great organizations or restored sick ones to health must be judged among the most creative persons of our time. In smaller scope such opportunities lie before every manager.

Natural distractions and diversions from such insights exist in many kinds of organization. This is often true in engineering and research administration. Here, the overriding concepts of "creativity" and self-expression are limited to the work of the basic researcher or development engineer. The presence of work which provides authenticity to so many people, and the opportunity for creativity in the physical sciences obscure the endless opportunity for better organizations in such environments. The administrator is considered a form of lesser person, and his work less significant than that of the people he administers. A similar viewpoint is common in universities as well. The teaching and research faculty finds its work authentic and creative, and views the function of the administrator with disdain if not open hostility. Unfortunately the administrator in such establishment accepts such a view and behaves in a fashion which chews up administrative time in activity which proves true the jaundiced viewpoint of the professional. Uncertain or unaware of the authentic role of administration, he fritters away time in establishing new systems of disapproving purchases, of vetoing budgets, and of managing personnel administration with the outlook of the provost marshal. Pervaded with such an outlook, the work soon attracts people who are essentially clerks—defensive, passive and uninspired people. Deans who should be generating grand schemes for new levels of education spend their days in endless rounds of administrative clucking at the actions of the hostile and rebellious professionals.

Research or educational administrators who should be encouraging creative projects spend their days engaged in form and procedures, checking locks on the doors, inspecting the housekeeping, and auditing the books. The result is that such organizations are normally the worst managed to be found.

Of systems and time-saving

The basic block diagram so beloved of the system man offers a key to the effective use of time. If we note in Figure 13-1 that most systems consist of inputs, activities and outputs, we find the thief of time in activity.

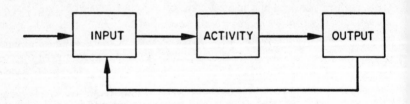

Figure 13-1

The genius of system as a time saver is that it starts with a definition of the outputs sought prior to releasing the inputs or resources required. It also enforces a harsh and hostile discipline upon the activity applied. It demands that they come forth at the time most effectively engineered to produce the most output, and they eliminate those activities which might contribute least to output. Such a systematic approach to life certainly is the core of human and managerial efficiency. *Effectiveness must be defined as contribution to outputs and objectives.*

1. The rationing of inputs means a careful husbanding of labor, material and supplies, and capital. As Charles Hitch so amply demonstrates in his *Economics of Defense*, resources are limited and possibilities for their use are unlimited.

2. The possibilities of using up the sparse supply of time available to man are limitless in the category which we call *activity*. We may simply fritter away our time in matters which consume resources and produce nothing. We may in fact work very hard and find the sun has set having engaged the entire day in activities half of which canceled and negated the other half.

3. The key to efficiency lies in *defining goals* and sticking to them rigorously, eliminating those activities which do not contribute to objectives and outputs or consume too much of the scarce inputs in doing so.

Among the means by which we economize time is that of elimination of activities, delegating both activity and result to others, which economizes our time if not theirs, and studying methods to eliminate superfluous activities which are self-canceling.

Yet, man is not a machine, and the words of Thoreau have some relevance for the time-pressed modern professional and manager.

> Most men in this comparatively free country, through mere ignorance or mistake, are so occupied with the factitious cares and superfluously coarse labors of life that its finer fruits cannot be plucked by them.

There are, Thoreau's words suggest, matters in which efficiency and behaving like a smoothly oiled machine are irrelevant. Enjoyment of personal pleasures are often found in purposeless activity. The search for God, the reflection upon esthetic things, the whiling away of idle hours, the pursuit of an elusive idea in a poem, the tracking down of a hypothesis solely for the pleasure of the hunt, and the desire to learn simply for the sake of learning are outside the cybernetic system we've sketched in Figure 13–1. The inward-looking man, the man who leads the examined life, does so when he consciously steps outside the systems approach. He is concerned with such matters as relating his own thoughts with his own feelings, and the problems of operating on both levels at once. Systems demand that you set aside one kind of values in order to achieve objectives. Most of the tyrannies and inhumanities of man to other men have grown out of system. The progress of civilization has often been made by people who would have nothing to do with system, but were concerned with their own character. Such activity has nothing to do with either time or efficiency. Where systems can lead to leisure and idleness through finding resources to permit them, they may also become so all-obsessing that they incapacitate the human being, who sells himself to systematic living for asking the meaning of life.

In the logic of practice there must be more than personal efficiency. It means that systems and logic can serve only as a means of earning surplus time which can be deposited, and against which substantial withdrawals may be made. The endless application of system to a life can become pathological, and when it warps the man it becomes his master, not his servant.

chapter 14

THE ABSURD
AND THE AUTHENTIC

A man's thought must be the building in which he lives.
—SOREN KIERKEGAARD

In operating firms, even the most successful, there are significant numbers of people for whom the absurd is a daily companion. This absurd, belonging nowhere in the logic of theory—unless in existentialism—grows out of lost authenticity and of lack of meaning in work. The employee who is bored, apathetic, or suffers from a dread of his work is often a victim of the absurd which abounds in business.

> I am simply bored stiff by my job; I find it a burdensome chore to get into my car and head for my office. I look forward to the day of repetitive action and wish I could go somewhere else, do anything else.

This quotation is not from an assembly line operator, but actually was told to the author by a divisional chief engineer. Engrossed in systems not of his own choosing, doing work devoid of creativity, robbed of much discretionary behavior by company systems and procedures, he found no creative challenge, and was engulfed by the absurd.

Illustrations of the absurd

In one large insurance company a supervisor attended evening school and studied methods of improvements and industrial engineering applied to the office. Returning to his job he began to apply the principles. He found much of the work was repetitive and unnecessary. Applying his newly acquired knowledge, he was able to combine, change sequences, simplify and improve operations in a way that made it possible to produce the same amount of work with thirty-nine people as had been produced with forty-four. Within a short period of time normal turnover had eliminated five people from his staff, and he simply omitted requisitioning new employees to replace them. Shortly after this the personnel department came through the department and applied its system of job evaluation to the supervisor's position. Shortly afterward he received a notice that his pay was being reduced. The reason? "Our studies have shown that you have less than forty employees, and this reduces your final point score in our system below that for supervisors with more than forty employees. Accordingly your salary is reduced by $11 per week." Not being especially stupid nor unaware of his own interest, he immediately requisitioned the five employes, and put them at busy-work, and his pay was prompty restored to its prior level.

In a manufacturing plant a department supervisor was called into the office of the cost accountant and some new cost standards for his department were explained. "Your department will be measured by its compliance with an output level of 1,300 units per hour" he was told. As he reflected upon this he went into his own operations and discovered that with thirty machines under his direction the range of possible production levels ran from a low of 300 a day to 5,000 an hour. He quickly worked out some computations which showed him how the optimal level of 1,300 could be achieved. It often entailed operating machine making useless product in order to "beat" the figure established for him. This occasionally meant that he accumulated embarrassingly large surpluses of these unwanted items, and he was required to dump them into a scrap car as surreptitiously as possible. The loss to the firm was enormous, but he beat his figures regularly. The absurdity of such a system was apparent in the logic of practice, although in the logic of system and theory it was perfectly sound.

An office supervisor was concerned over a high turnover among his secretarial help. An investigation showed that they were leaving for higher pay. He immediately filed a request for pay increases for those remaining. The request was denied. "It is not our policy to review salaries for experienced personnel more often than once a year." Several others left for higher pay. Yet when he sought replacements for those leaving, he found that the employment office of the personnel department was sending replacements who started at higher pay than those who had been there a long time. Upon his query he was told, "We are authorized to pay competitive rates to fill vacancies." Faced with this absurdity, he immediately discharged all of his secretaries and ordered them to reapply for the now-vacant positions. All were hired at the higher level.

A large petroleum company found that it had completed several large engineering projects. After some delay, a directive came from above that the engineers who had been working on these projects were to be released from the company. At the same time the company was conducting an extensive recruiting project on college campuses to hire new young engineers for other work. The recruiters reported their feelings of absurdity in their work.

> *The absurd emerges when the logic of system developed for two problems is each perfectly executed—and the two actions cancel one another.*

The possibilities for involvement in the face of the absurd are diminished considerably. Systems which perpetuate the absurd in business evoke a particular attitude in those affected. They see management systems (and decision systems) as a sleight-of-hand trick to evaporate reality and people who see it into an unreal theory. Absurdity for employees and subordinates emerges when the systems builders pretend to comprehend everything but are able to make intelligible only their own abstractions. Such absurdity is the graveyard of spontaneity and creativity. The erroneous presumption is that concepts are things or actually operating processes. It is the man who pretends to know everything who is the originator of the absurd.

Authentic decisions in practice

One of the most common remarks heard during interviews with employees and subordinate managers in large corporations has the following substance:

> Does anybody up there (in higher management) know what I am trying to do? Do they know what I want to do, and am capable of doing? Do they even know what in h--- I am actually doing?

College recruits enter their first position and leave in large numbers after a year or two. One report states that they turn over at a rate of 75 per cent in three years. What do they report as their reason for searching elsewhere?

> They found no challenge in their work.
> They saw no opportunities to use the skills they brought to the job. The company was reported to have no specific plans which come through either explicitly or inchoately to them.
>
> Being fairly far down in the organization, they find no opportunity for commitment to tough and challenging assignments by which they can become authentic. They are surrounded at the lowest levels by cynical persons whose eye for the ever-present absurd is grist for a kind of sardonic humor which makes life tolerable in the immediate sense. But in measuring themselves by the projects they have unfinished before them, these young men see no projects not riddled with absurdities which rob them of authenticity.

The logic of practice calls for decisions in practice which add authenticity and eliminate the absurd from the lives of those whose subjective actions make the decision a reality. In innumerable trade and professional association meetings of specialist groups such as traffic managers, purchasing manager, personnel men, engineers, and accountants the most warmly received speakers are those who can bring reassurance—temporarily at best —by telling the assembled group, "Your job has a larger meaning than perhaps you have seen in it in the past, and here is that meaning." A sure-fire formula for success in making speeches to such groups is to combine a good speaking voice with a sincere message that explains to those assembled how their work contributes to a larger whole, why its significance is great, and what contribution it makes to society, the economy or even to their own firm. This hunger for authentic meaning to work, and the uneasy evidence of the absurdity which surrounds them comprise the greatest single problem in shaping a logic of practice.

Top management members often are shielded from this absurdity, since they have a clear picture of the theory and logic of decisions to lean upon, and seldom see the absurd. When they have personal contact with lesser ranks, it is most unlikely that they will uncover the absurd which is rampant in their organization at the practicing level. For one thing, the very occasion of personal contact with the top-level decision makers itself is an authentic experience for the subordinate, and is widely sought after. If the foreman in the Jersey City factory meets the chairman of the board, it is most unlikely that he would bother such an apparently important and authentic person with the absurd detail that the master mechanic is a phony who has combined incompetence and persuasiveness in a masterpiece of absurdity. In the presence of the great man, whose life is obviously authentic, the lesser figure will concentrate on studying the top man with the hope that he too might grasp the essence of this authentic person and have some of it rub off on himself.

> "I think the chief is a pretty great fellow, but those fakeroos he has around him are a disgrace. It's amazing how he can be so smart and be taken in by those guys," is the way one worker reported to an interviewer.

The search for authenticity in practice has taken many forms. Suggestion systems which produce new ideas and methods are sometimes a vehicle for uncovering and uprooting the absurd. Employee attitude and morale surveys using pencil and paper questionnaires are a sometimes useful form of doing the same thing. Yet, the requirements go beyond such stop-gap measures.

Authenticity demands joint commitments

One cause of failure for such stop-gap devices as suggestion plans and survey lies in the lack of commitment to common projects between superior and subordinate. When suggestion systems fail, reports by the National Association of Suggestion Systems show, it is often because the higher levels of management fail to stand behind the purposes of the suggestion plan. Suggestions are submitted but not processed, or processed slowly. The suggestor's superior criticizes the suggestor for proposing the change. Rejections are not clearly explained. Such behavior by the superior of the suggestor is more than a mechanical failure to follow a suggestion plan. It is symptomatic of a lack of commitment of two parties to a common objective. The absurdity for the suggestor lies in his being asked in the first place, then being ignored.

Similarly, attitude surveys have the same fault when they fail (not all of them do fail). The questionnaire asks the opinions of subordinates in questions eliciting his attitudes toward certain conditions of work. He responds, and having been asked, finds his responses ignored. The absurdity lies not in the questionnaire, but in the lack of commitment of the superior to be responsive to answers to questions which he himself initiated.

This commitment means that the project and purposes of the organization, having been established by higher management, have been communicated to the lower levels and there is agreement between the levels as to the objectives of the total business. There is also understanding about what responsibilities the subordinate has for assisting in the deliverance of the final goals.

Surveys by the author and by other researchers have shown that lack of commitment is far more common than might be supposed by persons relying upon logic or common assumptions.

Given a manager and three subordinate managers, a series of interviews was conducted, using the pattern of questions as follows:

(1) Two questions for the superior manager:
   What are your subordinate's (Mr. X's) major areas of responsibility? In each of those areas, how will you measure his performance in terms of results expected at the end of this year for purposes of figuring pay raises, bonuses, promotability, coaching and delegation?

(2) A similar set of two questions for Mr. X, the subordinate:
   What are your major areas of responsibility, as your boss would define them?
   In each of these areas, how do you think your boss intends to measure your performance in terms of results expected at the end of the year for purposes of pay, promotion, coaching, and the like?

In hundreds and hundreds of pairs of matched interviews using this dual format a startling condition was uncovered.

*The average manager and subordinate manager are not in agree-
ment on 25 per cent of the responsibilities, and not in agreement in
30 per cent of the definitions of how the subordinate will be measured
at the end of the year.*

With such a widespread condition the possibilities for the absurd are
great, certainly as great as the lack of understanding. It is safe to generalize
that when the manager and subordinate manager are not in agreement on
what the subordinate's job consists of specifically, the door is opened for
the absurd. It may further be generalized that without a dialogue and a
confirming memo dealing specifically with these matters, commitment cannot exist.

To put it more personally, unless you and your boss are now jointly committed to a set of specific projects for the coming six months or year, you
have less than necessary commitment and a significant portion of your
relationship is in the realm of the absurd.

The correction of this area of the absurd is not an addition to your job
nor his. Such correction aids both of you. Commitment means that both
superior and subordinate understand two vital aspects of the subordinate's
job:

1. What are the responsibility areas in which the subordinate should be
working now in order to help achieve the common objectives of the entire
unit?

2. In each of these areas, how will results be measured in specific terms,
and what is the time commitment by which this measurement will be taken?

Authenticity is impossible without these fundamental definitions for every
employee in every kind of organization.

Authenticity demands the logic of practice

Two systems, each perfect in themselves when conducted side by side,
may lead to conflict and the absurd. It is patently impossible and uneconomic to attempt to foresee all of the possible manifestations for the absurd.
It is possible, however, to arrange the day-to-day environment to permit
its quick eradication.

The absurd cannot be subjectively countenanced by persons who take
themselves and their lives seriously. It can only be tolerated by people who
detach themselves subjectively from what they are doing. Under such circumstances they will remain objectively at their tasks for reasons such as
money or security. Indifference, error and perpetuation of further absurdity
can be the only results of such loss of authenticity on a widespread basis.

What then of those decisions where the logic of theory and system have
generated conflicting actions producing the absurd? In the logic of the system there must be flexibility to permit the practical manager and the logic

of practice to modify the system, however logical and efficient it seems from its internal viewpoint. When salary administration and methods systems conflict and produce the absurd, a whole new problem is created which can only be solved through discretion of operating persons in charge of the action phases of the decisions.

A similar discretion must be permitted and encouraged when the functioning of a perfectly fine system conflicts with other facets of reality. Such conflicts are productive of the absurd, and restoration of reality and the logic of practice should never be delayed in order to preserve absurdity.

In far too many large corporations the absurd becomes an instrument of control and bars the lesser ranks and middle managers from being what they are. Rather than behaving in a manner which is fluid, dynamic and creative, the man governed by the absurd tries to become something fixed and systematic, which he is not. His head nods affirmatively at piously stated nonsense. Employees have a firm and serious sense of duty which permits them to accept the absurd as if it were authentic, the inconsistent as if it were consistent. They are the humorless ones who seriously and heavily justify the policies to which they adhere, even when such policies are self-canceling, confusing and patently absurd.

Even more serious is the increasing corps of defenders and creators of the absurd. Intelligent men, usually mathematicians, engineers and scientists by training, they become architects of the absurd by their very obsession with the logic of theory, and a corresponding scorn for the logic of practice. Unwitting, they perpetuate a bad faith to logic. In a few instances they are men without experience who hide behind their own norms and reasons. In others they are self-aggrandizers who use their systems and logic of theory as instruments of aggressive self-assertion. The logic of practice in the face of such behavior lies in the direction of organizing decision making to avert the absurd and permit the authentic in practice.

chapter 15

DECISIONS AND PEOPLE

Liberty consists of the ability to choose . . .
—SIMONE WEIL

Most of the tyrannies, totalitarian states, and barbarities which have been characteristic of our century have grown out of some overriding logic or system. The master systems-maker of our times has been Marx. Principles and system lay directly behind the concentration camps of Hitler. "When a man lacks character he requires a system," says Camus.

The logic of practice in human relations must be opposed to that kind of system which would treat humans as objects. The logic of system requires that humans be treated as a resource. Behavioral science manages data about humans with the same detachment as it does data about pigeons, rats, and primates of non-human levels. Only in practice can these harsh requirements be made human.

The dehumanization of man is not a result of the logic of practice, but of theory. On the contrary, the logic of practice demands that each person be observed and contacted as a distinct individual. In the array of actions which comprise the work day of the manager, he shares the work days of dozens of others. The logic of practice is one of giving and receiving information, and observing the behavior of others and being seen by them. For the most part, in our everyday lives, we understand others by observing what they do, the functions they perform. To each his behavior is a personal thing.

A prominent cleric was making an announcement before a large congregation in the course of his Sunday morning service. One of the features of the service that day was the presence of an eminent organist who was scheduled to play an extremely difficult Bach piece. In the fashion which is cultivated by many elegant members of the cloth, the minister solemnly announced: "The organ will now play." At this signal, the eminent but temperamental organist, clad in voluminous robes, bounded from the bench of the great organ and flounced to the front row of the church, where he sat defiantly. "Is that so? I think I'll listen to it" he announced.

This objectifying of the functioning of a human who is keenly subjective is the major function of the logic of theory. The logic of practice means fitting lifeless decisions to living people.

Man is not a fact

Nowhere is the difference between the logic of system and theory from the logic of practice more apparent than in human relations. The human is quite properly treated as a resource in the logic of theory and system. He is a number whose common characteristic with others is that he often shares the same number. Number is an intensional characteristic which destroys uniqueness for the sake of manageability. This number is an abstraction, without which our modern world of science would be impossible. As long as the extensional characteristics of the individual Adam can be reclaimed at will from his intensional character as a number, little is lost and much is gained.

The doting father who takes a large family on a trip will use numbers to be sure the car is properly loaded with all of his offspring after each stop. If the number is insufficient, he will stop the car and search the grounds and the rest room until the proper number are on hand. Such efficiency is most logical. It would be unthinkable, however, if his concern for his loved ones stopped at this definition of their characteristics. Yet, this reduction of man to an intensional definition, irrecoverable from thence forward, is an increasing part of the logic of system and logic.

The director of the military draft may find it to his advantage to call up 20,000 anonymous numbers to be sent to the distant war. The general may commit faceless regiments of thousands on his acetate war charts. The operation researcher may locate his warehouses by use of a model. The leveling of production may wipe out plants, shifts, or departments objectively. The world of efficiency and our own demand for a rising standard of living not only permits it, but demands that it be done in order to feed the hungry thousands and maintain our economy on an even keel.

This is not to suggest, however, that once this logical process has been completed that a new logic should be debarred from taking over. The logic of practice is reality-centered. It faces the people who accept responsibility, who must subjectively behave in ways which are personal to them and their manifold differences from every other person in the world. Such a logic of practice can exist only when the logic of decision theory ends at the point of action and the experts in the logic of practice are free to move. It also means that modification of the system may be essential in the hands of the operator when it dehumanizes the individual.

When man is treated as a fact, and the logic of theory prevails where the logic of practice should do so, the exceptional is always leveled down toward the average. New and original insights which diverge from the plan are dismissed.

The systems maker remains confident and self-assured that no such insights in practice can affect the ultimate outcome, and insistence upon the absurd becomes petulant and dictatorial.

In 1965 the Secretary of Labor of the United States read the figures on unemployment in the United States and concluded that there were great surpluses of low-skilled workers among the unemployed. When fruit growers in California and pickle growers in Michigan insisted that Labor Department restrictions on importation of migrant workers were leading to great shortages in supply of such labor, the secretary patiently insisted that "there is no shortage." Great piles of fruit and pickles in real life lay unpicked and unsorted. The hard facts of the fruit proved small persuasion to the secretary, whose system showed him that such a condition couldn't theoretically exist.

The logic of practice for human relations is a real world. It is phenomenologically real to the practitioner, who must make his decision on the evidence he sees and receives from people he talks to. The logic of system at this point must be set aside. The influence of the logicians of system must be curbed and overruled when it demands that the practitioner engage in the humanly absurd. The alternative is a depersonalization of human relations which has proved devastating in our times. The ontological mistake of confusing a human person with the thing, object or artifact is the most potent threat of system and logic in our time. Logic and system are neutral. The system of production in the death camps at Buchenwald was not unlike the system of production in the food distribution center in the Midwest during a flood. It is not the method which was at fault in Marienbad or Dachau. It was the purpose and the extension of the logic of ideology, and of system to practice where individual officers and employees of the camps could objectify the miserable thousands who staggered from the box cars daily. The concentration camps of Siberia had an unassailable logic of system to them, but their logic of practice was bestial and inhuman.

Depersonalization of human relations practice is a constant threat. Its forms may vary, its intensity may waver. Man in the modern age is a functionary of timetables, of procedures, and the time clock. Even his leisure is tightly scheduled, and he plays and sits as spectator in a tightly systemized fashion. In an age of modern technology, our very existence depends upon this great web of meshing systems which surround us. This is no plea for a return to an agrarian society, nor a proposal that we should become hermits. The logic of system, however, should be tightly circumscribed and divided from the logic of practice. This logic of practice should defend itself from the other logic, and urge every man to look upon himself subjectively, to accept personal responsibility for his own action, and even to engage in rebellion where it is necessary to preserve his individuality.

Systems can treat individual humans as part of an aggregate to be conditioned by propaganda, standards and mass rule. In this respect they are in conflict with a higher logic of practice. In logic the mass become unspiritual and inhuman. Human existence is seen as analogous to a beautiful, well-oiled machine.

Communication in practice

American businessmen who do business in modern industrial Italy find one aspect of business relations there hardest to understand. When two Italian businessmen are engaged in the practice of commercial negotiation, the noise level often appears to be unthinkable. The reason? Both talk at the same time; hands wave frantically, emotional outbursts simultaneously erupt like fireworks. Suddenly out of this apparently incoherent battery of words emerges agreement. The two parties shout "agreed" and adjourn business to the nearest cafe for wine to celebrate a mutually profitable agreement. What is less apparent than the confusion is the unbelievable feature of the event that somehow the two men were talking and listening simultaneously, a feat which modern communication theory has yet to recognize as possible.

I directed a casual inquiry recently to the president of the leading speech and communication teachers' association in America about research done on this dual listen-talk form of communication. He indicated that no such research has ever been done to his knowledge. Yet, in many parts of the world the practice is common. In bazaars, markets, and in certain women's social organizations in this country this practice is but one example from a host of real instances from life. It indicates that common practice of communication has not been amply explained in modern communication theory.

In business the major emphasis in the study and teaching of communications has been that of communications systems, the logic of communication and information theory. This has added considerable insight into the organization of communications networks, and especially in the physical communications which are converted in physical hardware. Modern telephony would be impossible without theoretical breakthroughs made in information theory. At the same time, it is a patent error to assume that human communication can be compressed into the same logic of system which works so admirably for physical communication.

The concept of feedback is one which has grown out of information theory and is an invaluable addition to communications practice. It is not, however, anywhere near a total explanation of the subjective, chaotic and personalized communications which characterize managerial and business communications in that area of decision making where the logic of practice retains its influence.

Undoubtedly it has been possible to isolate the elements of communication in many respects. The manager in practice talks, writes, listens, watches, confers, and reads behavior of others through cues which are simultaneously received, interpreted, and converted into responses in a complex fashion that has little order or system. The attempt to strap such complex behavior into theoretical framework can only explain the individual components theoretically, but does not grasp the whole in reality. Such a grasp of the entire process or welter of communications for a single individual or group of individuals as it essentially is would require such a multiplicity of measurements and variables that it would be uneconomic and unmanageable. The attempts at such theorizing come out resembling reality in the same way that musical compositions contrived on a computer resemble a Beethoven symphony.

Does one then simply throw up his hands at the impossible and treat all communication as a mess which should be abandoned? Obviously not. The kinds of communications which lend themselves to system should be systemized and theorized upon. Little harm is done and much good can result. The good comes in differentiating those parts of communication which can be treated systematically from those which cannot. Those which cannot may then be considered part of the logic of practice, and accorded the treatment which permits that logic to function in its most effective media.

And what, we might legitamately inquire, is the treatment that can make sense of the logic of practice in the area of human relations? The logic here lies in making individuals free, and responsible for their choices made under that freedom.

Self-control as a logic of practice

When the systems have been developed to the ultimate, and theoretical logic is at the boundary of its possibilities, subjective logic takes over. This boundary is a theoretical one, we might note, and largely unrecognized in management theory. Subjective logic, considered inferior since it uses few of the conceptual tools of the physicist or mathematician, nonetheless exists and stubbornly resists attempts by the logical positivists to "assume" it out of existence.

The major breakthroughs at a conceptual level in space flight were made when a theoretical proof was generated that sub-sonic flight was governed by an elliptic curve, whereas supersonic flight is governed by a hyperbolic curve. A similar kind of transitional theory is needed for the transition from the systems theory for decision making to the logic of practice, where decisions are implemented through energetic barrages of subjective choices.

A great deal of attention has been paid to the effects of self-control by behavioral scientists in recent years, but almost all of this research has been characterized by these common characteristics:

- It has aimed at general theories of behavior, or sub-theories in general areas.

- It has relied upon two instruments of data-gathering for its empirical flesh for its designed experiments; the questionnaire and the interview.

- Uniformity and order have been imposed upon all of the human relations studied, all of the personalities and human behavior under investigation.

- It has leaned heavily upon mathematical, especially classical, statistics for verification of findings.

As with other systems theories, insights can be achieved by such technique, but reality cannot be grasped entire.

Self-control in practice is likely to be situational, that is, the relationship of the man to his environment is important in determining the amount of self-control permissible. Such are the major findings of modern behavioral research. The worker on the assembly line has less self-control than the scientist doing basic research. Theoretically the self-controlled man is more productive in his work than the controlled man, and even more clear is the evidence that the self-controlled man likes his condition better than the controlled man, whose actions and choices are less of his own choosing. However valid such conclusions may be theoretically, they may be of little value in specific applications where the logic of practice takes over.

- Dr. Jones works for a large pharmaceutical lab, where he conducts research. He sets his own pace, has ample budget for assistants and equipment, and feels little of the pressure to produce that characterizes workers on the assembly line. Near the end of the year he goes before the research committee—composed mainly of scientists and administrators—and submits proposals for research programs. One year he goes before this committee and proposes a continuation of his research into antibiotics. The committee listens carefully, then explains that it cannot invest further funds into an area where the output of new products commercially usable has apparently dried up, and suggests that he generate a new proposal—perhaps in the area of virology, which is "hotter." Dr. Jones sees this as loss of self-control, as dictation by non-scientists and commercial influences. He adopts the behavior of a man who is not under self-control and engages in thoughts of leaving or of open rebellion.

- Mrs. Sage is a widow with two children, whom she supports. She has attempted to live on a meager pension and has barely made ends meet. She finds the world of the poor to be one where officials of all sorts exert unbearable pressures on her. Bill collectors hound her, and she feels keenly her loneliness and defenselessness in the face of power from the world around her. Her diet, her clothes, the limitations upon her children to take part in activity in school and with other playmates depresses and defeats her. One day she decides she will answer an ad for female laborers in a television factory. She is accepted and works on an assembly line. She wires carriages from diagrams, and is paid $90 a week. Her foreman is an amiable and helpful young man, and working conditions are pleasant. The rules are strictly enforced but nobody is unfair or abusive. She finds the other ladies are congenial, and she enters into some social life on the outside among them. Her pension, plus her pay, permits her to buy many things she never had before: her children enlarge their social life and take music lessons. She buys small things for the house, and some long-desired appliances. At work there are prescribed starting and stopping time, she has no discretion over what she will wire or how, and she must "keep up." Her personal viewpoint is that she is vastly better off because now she has self-control.

These two examples would be perfectly explainable from a subjective theory of practice, but conflict with many of the findings of modern behavioral theory, which generalize that the attitudes of the two persons would be diametrically opposite. This isn't to suggest that assembly line workers may not feel loss of self-control, or that scientists may not have a high degree of it *en masse,* or in a generalized (theoretical) framework. It merely suggests that when human relations practice takes over, a new kind of choice exists.

In practice, what is the logic of self-control?

Victor Vroom makes a useful distinction in a behavioral research study on the subject of participation. He demonstrates that participation by a person in the decisions which affect him can be subjective or objective. The person who thinks he has participation may behave as if he has, even when he hasn't by some objective standard. On the other hand, a person may have wide opportunity for participation by objective measurement, but when he thinks he is being short-changed in this regard, he may behave as if he were afforded little.

1. *Self-control in practice refers to a spectrum of available choices.* From the standing point of any individual his practical self-control—sometimes called participation by the theorist—is determined for him by the available choices he sees. If the choices are there, but he fails to see them because of defects in his vision, then they are not effective choices. The miner whose job is eliminated in West Virginia by the closing of the mine may not in fact have any choice but to remain as a redundant worker in the same town because his vision doesn't extend to moving to Detroit or Chicago. This defect in ability to see the actual spectrum is often painfully subjective. Objective facts which prove the existence of the spectrum not-

withstanding, his self-control is limited.

2. *The spectrum of available choices can be enlarged.* The world, being dynamic in many respects, does not present a fixed and unchanging spectrum of choices to people in practice. While it may be fixed for an instant, it will be larger (or smaller) later on, and conscious effort to enlarge it can produce greater ranges of choice—which is to say greater self-control. The greatest enemy of self-control is that which effectively limits choices available.

The Negro youth in the South may be born with native capacities which would have made him a Ralph Bunche or George Washington Carver. His home environment, his social peers, and the physical conditions of his existence may carry him to an age where further growth of the spectrum is most unlikely. The accidents of birth, growth, education, and parentage affect available choices.

This isn't to suggest a fatalism for everyone in predicting growth and widening abilities. A Carver may rise from a slave's cabin or scion of fine family descend to playboy or lush.

3. *The ability to see the choices can be enlarged.* The theory of relativity was born in the mind of Albert Einstein, not in the mind of Irving Einstein, a conductor on the 42nd Street bus. The choice to sing in the Metropolitan opera is available to only talented and trained voices; the chance to select which job offer to accept may confront only the man who has trained himself in skills which are salable on the job market.

The greatest media for enlarging self-control for employees in practice lies in exposure to opportunity to gain experience in a range of positions where different skills may be learned. Useful in this respect are training courses conducted for employees, tuition refund plans for evening education, and work experience under a superior who takes his teaching responsibility seriously.

4. *Self-control entails responsibility for choices made.* The choices made under self-control, as has been noted, aren't totally free of environmental forces which shape them. The responsibility for the choices, however, is subjective. Many current systems of management take away this assumption of responsibility. In doing so they rob the individual of his individuality.

This bald statement should be quickly distinguished from the conclusions of the ultra-conservative and member of the radical right who applies such a statement to suggest that child labor laws rob the child of his individuality and freedom of choice. Such arguments have been used against collective bargaining, social security, and most other social legislation. There is nothing in the assumption of individual responsibility which should militate against public policy nor company policy that widens freedom. The widening of self-control occurs through public education, or health and safety laws (the cripple has limited choices open to him). Exploitation consists of limiting another's freedom to choose from a broad range of alternatives.

Recent examples of the executive who conspires to violate the law are perhaps a germane case in point. The law limits the power of the firm to engage in conspiracy, in order that buyers of their products have a wider choice of suppliers. Packaging regulations, food and drug laws, and regulations on advertising limit choices of some to enlarge them for many.

5. *The boundaries of choice grow out of the human condition.* In the logic of practice as contrasted with the logic of theory, five major limiting conditions are subjectively present, even when the practical decision maker attempts to sweep them under the rug. The situationality of existence, death, guilt, luck, and conflict are the perimeters of the logic of practice which constrain it, move it, and shape its patterns. No amount of system and logic sweeps them away. Confronted with these limits, the logic of practice beats its staccato messages for the individual, sometimes working against the system, often for it.

Self-control for oneself is a product of others' concern for self-control as a principle. Unless I have concern for preserving self-control for others, I may expect that the amount of self-control which is available for me will be circumscribed as well. The executive creates self-control for others over whom he has economic power. This is more than a simplistic system of delegation and human relations techniques prescribed in technique-laden training courses. It is in written and actual policy by which the company is run. It is in the daily choices the executive himself makes which are imitated by his followers. It is the rewards and punishments which he administers. It is the promotions he makes, the raises he awards, the bonuses he administers, his assignments of work. Coupled with this is the teaching he engages in with those whom he contacts. When these actions widen the spectrum of available choices for the people in the organization, improve their ability to see the entire spectrum, and make them responsible for their choices, he makes men free. When he limits the spectrum by any means, he reduces them to objects to serve his pleasure, and enslaves them.

chapter 16

SNAP JUDGMENT

We have made many decisions to become what we are.
—PAUL TILLICH

A major barrier between management theorists and practitioners is that of "practicality." The decision theorist, for example, developed extensive equipment to improve managerial decisions. Operations research, group decision making, and the like are widely used Yet all of them require *time* —sometimes an inordinate amount. The virtues of not rushing off half cocked are stressed explicitly. All of this is perfectly fine for certain kinds of decisions. For those decisions which are a long time in coming to fruition, for those which have long-run consequences, and for those where the costs of error are unthinkably great, such slow-paced decision making is imperative.

Yet, there is another kind of decision making which for many operating managers and supervisors is far more prevalent and necessary—the snap judgment. For the plant superintendent faced with a wildcat strike, the sales manager confronted by an enraged customer, or the labor relations manager in tight negotiations, the practical exigencies of the situation call for rapid-fire judgments. Furthermore, such judgments must be right more often than they are wrong. To decide nothing is to make the wrong choice. To call for more *time* is to be *impractical*.

This isn't to deny the importance of reflective judgment where it is called for. Yet, many decision makers fail to note the necessity in certain situations of the *hip-shot opinion*.

The anatomy of the considered decision

The literature of modern managment is replete with the anatomy of the well founded, scientific decision. Modern systems theory, operations research, and the behavioral sciences all have made significant contributions to this area which Professor Simon calls the "new science of management decision." The application of rational methods of management to choosing among alternatives, the choice of criteria, and the use of technical methods and statistical instruments for decision making comprise an impressive body of research. Briefly summarized, such systems ordinarily include several stages:

1. defining an objective to be achieved;
2. clarifying the factual situation which exists;
3. discovering possible causes for the gap between the two;
4. developing options, or alternative ways of alleviating the difference;
5. screening these options through criteria such as cost or profitability, or contribution to objectives until the "optimal" or best is discovered;
6. executing that option, with appropriate adjustments and controls, and evaluation to see its effect.

Although this pattern varies with the respective theorists (the foregoing is probably much closer to Simon than any other) it generally adheres to most such decision-making methods. All of these decision methods however imply a certain amount of conscious reflection on the part of the decision maker. This requires time for execution. Many decisions, even important ones, simply don't permit such a time span, but must be made immediately. How are such quick decisions made, and how can they be improved?

The anatomy of hip-shot decisions

Snap judgments can be conveniently classified into four major categories:
1. the steel-trap memory;
2. the speedy recall;
3. the faster-than-anybody recall;
4. the universal procedure to circumvent fast response.
Let's look at each of these in a little more detail.

The steel-trap memory and total recall

In the early days of TV one of the more popular shows for the millions was the audience participation show. Huge prizes were awarded to contestants who could pull out of their memory drum answers to such questions as: "How many hills are there in Rome?" or "Name the first five books of the Bible." Beginning as an interesting spectacle of watching mortals display their phenomenal memory for apparently obscure information, it blossomed into a game of mental gymnastics with fantastic prizes running into thousands of dollars for an hour of such mental virtuosity. Contestants were displayed in isolation booths, screwing their facial muscles into contorted agonies of thought as they produced gems of photographically recalled information to amaze the millions. The possibility that mere humans could perform such feats of mental magic was entertainment of the highest Neilsen order.

In a single thundering crash the entire fabric of this game was destroyed and with it the faith of millions of viewers in the possibilities of computer-like minds when the contestants were exposed as frauds who had been previously briefed on the topic and perhaps been given a chance to bone up on the subject.

The prestige which seems to attend upon the executive who can dredge up massive amounts of trivial information is high. The container company president who remembers that a beer can is two and eleven sixteenth inches in diameter impresses some people greatly. One of the reasons many would ascribe greatness to Robert S. MacNamara as defense secretary was his ability to recall vast amounts of factual information without notes. People long to believe in infallible minds at the top of the organization. An exceptional memory becomes equated to great brain power, which in part accounts for such adoration. Is memory really that invaluable?

Undoubtedly a retentive memory and ability to recall completely will be associated in others' minds with alertness or quickness. Yet, it's not really decisiveness, but a special kind of mental ability.

The psychologist Ebbinghaus many years ago demonstrated that memory is more related to learning ability and concentration than general intelligence. While memorization skill can be improved through training, it is not a "memory muscle" which can be developed by mental calisthenics. Given average mental capacities, a strong intention to learn, rewards and punishments, and other rules of learning, improvements can be made to ordinary memories to make them work better. We remember best things we have tried hardest to remember.

Selectively committing things to memory which can be useful later thus clearly gives one a distinct advantage in the competitive struggle in business. For the politician this may be memory for names and faces. For the general executive it may be financial figures. For the manufacturing executive it may be specifications of product or process. Such memories are most useful in the competitive struggle of a career simply because people generalize into them a wider reputation for all-inclusive intelligence and worth. The horse player who remembers that he was married "The day Twenty-Grand won the Wood Memorial" is drawing more on racing memories than romantic ones. His "steel-trap mind" works only for horse races.

The speedy recall variety of snap judgement

A refinement of the steel-trap mind with total recall is that mind which can produce answers to specific questions without hesitation. The key here is the instantaneous nature of the memory. A similar—and legitimate—game to the previous one was one played by comedian Herb Shriner and scholar Mason Gross, now president of Rutgers University. In this game, originated as a classroom exercise in philosophy classes at Columbia University by Dr. Gross, the contestants were required to race against a clock to produce correct verbal responses to impromptu questions. Contestants were ushered before the millions in their living rooms for a brief bit of badinage with Mr. Shriner. Clearly Mr. Shriner was no threat to anyone's memory. His rural wit and down-to-earth manner made everyone feel good. He was an Indiana farm boy of the Will Rogers school, his folksy style making him a sympathetic figure. The contestant was then ready to play the quick thinking game. Dr. Gross, urbane and scholarly, explained the rules. Each contestant would be given a question to which multiple responses could be made ("Your category is state capitals which have the same name as famous men"). Immediately the clock started and the contestant was required to spin out of his memory drum as many responses in this category as he might recall. If he responded with an incorrect answer, he might then expect one of two alternatives. If Dr. Gross recognized it as incorrect he would sound a loud buzzer. If the doctor sounded the buzzer and the answer proved to be correct and the doctor wrong, the contestant was generously rewarded. If he continued to answer correctly during the entire period, he received a prize based on the number of correct responses.

The test then became both a test of the individual in his memory and reproduction of facts under time pressure, but also became a battle of quick thinking against a human opponent. Only on a few occasions were contestants able to outwit the doctor, although many did win some substantial prizes simply by being correct.

Out-thinking everybody else

Still another variety of the game which has many characteristics of business quick decisions is that of out-thinking a group. Where the think-fast contestants on the Shriner show merely had to recall many correct answers and his mistakes would be judged by one man, the game of "College Bowl" pits one team of college students against another team of college students. The "toss up" question is read by the moderator, and the contestants may then push a button sounding a buzzer if they have a correct answer. Often the buzzer rings before the question has been completed. The information is generally in the area of the liberal arts, history, science, politics, art, music, and current events.

No time for the slow, patient, phlegmatic pace at which scientific research must be done. The clock, the scoreboard, and the quick hand at the buzzer by an opponent demand quick decisions of an almost impulsive recall nature.

A variation of this type in business is the man who performs rapid calculations in his mind. While others are still looking for a scrap of paper to find the cube root of 17024 he calmly states that the answer is "twenty-four," before they can take the cap off their fountain pen. He is quickly labeled as a genius. Carried to the extreme he becomes the idiot savant who can recall a string of boxcar numbers after one viewing; or can multiply two six digit numbers in one second. Because nobody else around can do such rapid calculation, he is accorded a special status. Thus, if he can't hold a job or tie his own necktie he is readily excused. For the rapid recall man there is no time for mulling over the niceties. No time to recheck a solution for correctness. No time to worry about the possible alternatives. Impulse becomes action as it erupts into the consciousness of the contestant. His hand must be quick to the buzzer. A well-stocked memory and an ability to recall an item from its depths to the surface immediately are the major requirements of the game.

Decision making on the run in business often takes on many aspects of such quick-thinking contests. In many ways it is antithetical to the kind of thought which is rooted in the application of a system such as the scientific method.

Procedures as substitutes for quick thinking

Because there is a certain innate nature to the quick response skill— perhaps an accident of inheritance or of early training—there is some hesitancy on the part of the person who hopes to come out ahead in quick-thinking situations to rely purely upon native talent along those lines. Far safer is the possibility of gaining mental leverage over others through applying techniques which will give a competitive edge to its possessor. The development of subjective and highly personalized pattern for handling such quick-think situations is part of the logic of practice. Having such a system allows its user to enter the hip-shot area and win without really having to be a hip-shooter.

Among the many such techniques which have been used to cope with pressure-laden situations has been the technique of non-directive interviewing. Psychiatrist Carl Rogers developed this instrument for client-centered therapy for use with the mentally disturbed, a stress-laden business at best. It was taken over by industrial personnel and training men to deal with employees in a temporarily emotional condition such as being angry, agitated, or aggressive. Its rules are:

● *Listen actively,* using reflective statements which respond to disturbed behavior by repeating in a simple acceptance the statements of the wrought up persons. ("I see, you feel that you have been wrongly passed over for promotion. Tell me more.") Such statements of simple understanding and acceptance lead the other person to unload his entire grievance, and incidentally to make it unnecessary for the object of his wrath to attempt to parry each point as it arises. It also eliminates the need for quick responses by the listener.

● *Listen for insights* by the complainer. In the midst of the flow of angry charges and accusations, the listener awaits evidence of insight. ("I guess my problem is that I haven't attended the training classes the company offered, but.") When such insight appears the listener reflects this back to the angry one, and seeks to get him to understand his own problem. Once the problem is understood, the two are then ready to proceed to solutions and action which the client or angry employee devises for himself. Thus what might seem to call for quick response is converted into more rational patterns.

Many variations of this Rogerian technique, useful in coping with situations where attempts at quick thinking would prove unfortunate, are observable. The manager who deliberately pauses in the face of verbal discussion and erects a sticky silence which hovers briefly before he responds is using *technique* in lieu of quick thinking. The executive with the slow, steady stare; eye fixations which resemble twin barrels of a forty-five pistol; the unblinking gaze while making a temple of one's fingers; all are useful techniques for controlling fast-paced interchange. Many a mediocre young man of regular features has moved nicely into higher rank—sometimes over his head—by keeping his trap shut at the proper time, when opening his mouth and thus demonstrating his shallowness of mentality could have killed him off.

Such techniques are those of non-commitment. If unrecognized by one's adversaries, they may take the place of quick thinking. If seen early however, they are traps. In the hands of a skillful cross-examiner such silences are exploited and turned into evidence of incompetence.

The major limitation of technique for avoiding quick thinking is that it must be applied in situations which are essentially the same as that for which it was generated, or in which it originally was tested.

CAN QUICK THINKING BE DEVELOPED?

Three major means of managing quick thinking may be of use here. This assumes of course that such demands for snap judgments exists. It must be developed where it is called for, not only at the lowest levels of organization, but at the highest.

The logic of practice often calls for the generation, invention, and testing of emergency procedures as part of the original control system in the stages of logical decision making. To attempt to predict every possible emergency is futile however, and practice demands that new, temporary and expedient procedures be devised on the spot by leaders and key personnel while the action is under way.

The three major situational keys to quick thinking can be classified as follows:

1. Those circumstances which are rooted in the interests of the people affected;
2. those situations in which experience has already shown the one best way of doing something fast;
3. finally there are situations in which procedures must be devised, and training in them required;

Let's look at each one in detail.

● *Seeing the main chance*

Most quick thinking of an innate nature usually has to do with somebody taking care of his own interests. The adroitness of people in letting themselves be outgrabbed for the check in an expensive restaurant is one illustration. When confronted with rapid-fire decision situations, the surest bet is that the average person will—consciously or unconsciously—do his best to take care of his own interests.

In practice, the impromptu development of new ways of doing work is commonplace. Even routinized jobs such as that of machine operator are characterized by such on-the-spot decisions. Time-study men, having devised tightly planned methods of work, are often baffled by the ability of operators on piece work to devise instantly new and original forms of doing the work in a way that permits them to bloat their earning beyond what any studious industrial engineer would have meticulously calculated as possible. In operations requiring hand coordination and motor skills, the varieties which can be devised by the individual are amazingly large, even within the prescribed framwork of methods of engineering practices. Deliberative efficiency experts are often outguessed by quick-thinking workers.

● This is possible since most of the work done in the world is subject to extensive development of on-the-spot procedures which are substitutes for following the system rationally chosen. Decisions must permit adaptive action by the individual worker, who will quickly see where his own interests lie.

In the logic of practice, decisions take on a coloration of psychology, especially learning theory. The manager as a learning organism learns as much from itself and its own experience as it does from underlying theory of the decision which it applies.

● *The importance of experience*

Two aspects of experience in quick thinking appear to be vital. The first is to have some memories or information stored up for use. The second is the ability to manipulate these quickly into new and unique combinations to solve specific problems for which time is short. The younger person often has more genuine alertness and is less distracted by his past frustrations and defeats. He often cultivates popularity among his young associates by being identified as a quick thinker, able to produce quick retorts and witty repartee without apparent reflection.

During the war in the Pacific, the writer was officer of the guard on the Solomon Island of Munda. Touring the base one night he came upon a sentry post unmanned. It was at the entry to a special service company which provided entertainment to the service men stationed there. Hearing a jazz band blaring away back in the jungle, he stalked angrily down upon the scene and found the sentry, complete with helmet and arm band, playing the saxophone in the middle of the band. "Why did you leave your post?" the officer demanded sternly.

"I'm investigating a disturbance," was the instant reply.

This combination of obvious surroundings (noisy music) with the legal requirements of his duties as sentry (investigate disturbances in the area of his post) was a sudden, unpremeditated bit of creativity that saved him from serious trouble; and the officer beat a hasty retreat.

This brashness of the young often permits boldness, but coupled with inexperience, lack of information, and irresponsibility, it often leads to unacceptable error. At the other extreme is the experience which has taught only caution, circumspection and hesitancy.

It is a common experience to inquire of a proficient practitioner how he was able to recognize and solve an emergency problem with such speed and accuracy, only to have him report, "Well, I had an experience somewhat like it one time, and I didn't do so well on that problem. I figured out what I would do if it happened again. When this thing happened just now 1 reacted as if it were that other problem and it worked."

● An engineer was placed in charge of an assembly operation in a mass production industry. His pattern of problem-solving was one he had learned in orderly engineering development. Thus when the chief inspector informed him that the line was turning out bad work, his experienced response was to call a meeting of all the informed parties to discuss the situation. Fortunately a less systematic member of his staff with more operating experience raced down the line, found the offending operation and corrected it. The subordinate's reaction was based on his own experience: "go take a look, then fix it," which was more suitable for his special environment.

● A foreman in a manufacturing plant often is confronted with such demands for immediate action. (1) A pump starts to leak, spewing a toxic acid onto the floor. (2) The shoring in a repair job shows cracks and is sagging and making ominous creaks. (3) His workers are turning off their machines and it looks like a wildcat strike unless he takes some action. All three such situations demand answers at once. The man who has been in similar situations before will think faster, perhaps save the day.

● *Immediate action procedures*

Where emergencies have happened in the past, procedures can be devised and employees and manager trained to apply the established procedure to the emergency. Such procedural planning can circumvent the necessity for quick thinking of an original nature.

● Infantry machine gun crews are taught emergency action in the event their gun fails to fire. They practice this action in training camp until it becomes an almost automatic response to the failure. Thus, under combat conditions where pressure and the need for quick thinking might produce panic, it produces instead remedial action of an instantaneous and conditioned nature.

● Children in schools are familiar with the fire drill, in which they move in orderly fashion out of the building at a certain ringing of the bell. A common experience in the event of real fire in a school is for the children to state afterward "I wasn't worried; in fact I thought it was just a fire drill."

● The most useful application of such principles occurs in business when possible emergencies are studied and procedures devised in case the unhoped-for event should occur. Once the site of possible emergencies is located, and the procedures arranged, then practice in remedial action can be taught.

● One of the more interesting methods of preparing for the undesired event is that of "role playing" the situation under safe circumstances. Automobile companies train foreman to handle grievances and disciplinary situations through acting out the roles of foreman and grievant or worker in training class. Salesmen in insurance firms are trained to cope with objections and unforeseen resistance by role-playing both customer and salesman. Bank tellers are taught to deal with emergencies from holdups to irate customers, by practice and role play. Having been through the situation in a play-acting form, the employee, manager, or salesman doesn't "lose his cool" when it actually occurs.

● The use of management games and simulation exercises aids the decision-making process and encourages skillful quick thinking by exposing the person to simulated real life situations. By acquiring familiarity and ease with the problems in simulated circumstances, he can think quickly and make sound snap judgments in real-life situations he may be encountering for the first time. Repetition makes snap judgment perfectly feasible. Inexperienced managers may falter.

Theory and practice

● Medical interns often find that the work of making diagnoses of patients takes an inordinate amount of time during their first weeks of internship. By the time their internship is over and they have approached their residency period, they find that the time required has become considerably shortened without eliminating any of the necessary steps. Their judgments and reaction appear to come more easily, based on the procedures they have taught themselves in other cases. The *practice* of medicine has achieved a reputable and definable stage of development. The *practice* of management has yet to be recognized as being different from theory. No medical doctor would deny the distinction between medical science and medical practice. The words "clinic" and "laboratory" have different connotations. This distinction is often denied in decision making, in which practical men often scoff at the value of theory, even as they use it, and the theorist brushes aside the distinct nature of practice as having a nature of its own.

Is quick thinking skill transferable?

Practical experience in quick thinking leads to future successes and can be developed subjectively in managers and employees at the point of implementation of decisions through teaching. The substance of what must be learned includes four things.

1. Developing quick thinking requires people who are steeped in the technical details of their environment. Every detail, however peripheral, may some day become important and simply storing away of all kinds of information can be of subsequent value when fast decisions are needed. The young man who is new in a position therefore should be as nosy as he can (tactfully) about every aspect of the operations around him.

2. He should inquire of experts why they do the things they do, and look for relationships between apparently unlike things.

3. Practicing snap decisions, even if they are not immediately implemented, can develop skill without damage to the results. Making hip-shot judgments, just for practice, then watching actual results to see what happened can improve the quality of later snap judgments made under such time pressure that there is no chance for a second guess. There is no virtue and there are many disadvantages to snap judgments when time exists to do a more sober and rational evaluation. Yet the development of such skills may grow out of practice, and they will serve the organization well if they are available when required.

4. The greatest use of snap judgments lies in making such judgments quickly, and counting upon percentages to make more of them right than wrong. This decision making by barrage is distinctly different from the rational stage of decision, but in countless circumstances is essential for the original objective to be approximated.

The need for two speeds

Complete decision-making skill then requires discriminatory selection of the kind of logic which applies in the task at hand. If the time exists to deliberate, it is obvious that deliberation is invaluable. Where no time exists and the decisions must be made in volume, then quick-thinking skills are called for and should be on hand. This is the limitation of theory. It takes time to develop and apply; sometimes more time than is available.

Alfred North Whitehead has decried the "foolish notion that it is possible for anyone devoid of personal experience of business to provide useful suggestions for its detailed conduct." The ivory-tower decision theorist who makes assumptions about time available for execution of decision omits an important ingredient of decision making: he overlooks timing. Systematic decisions are the product of intelligence, plus timing. Yet when business routine is fixed, intelligence must retreat and be supplanted by a series of conditioned reflexes. This is the basis for Whitehead's opinion: the timing may be wrong.

Division of labor demands a system to be aligned with. Routines must be established, but practice calls for short flashes of intelligence precisely timed. To stifle such creative intelligence from functioning means that our systems and rational decisions may be as rigid as cast iron, to the ruination of the firm they propose to improve. Outside judgments lose their worth mainly because they cannot include a sense of timing along with logic.

Without doubt, people tend toward one extreme or the other; they tend to act without sufficient deliberation, or at the extreme they can "never make up their minds." It's also apparent that each type is a source of major irritation to the other. Perhaps the time has come to add to the teaching of decision making the art of discrimination. Two speeds are needed. Some decisions you make slowly and deliberately; others you fire from the hip and count on volume and practice to improve the situation. A study of the literature of decision making suggests that too little is known of decision making on the run.

chapter 17

THE PERFORMING ART

All the world's a stage.
—SHAKESPEARE

Decision making on the run is split sharply from decision-making theory in its systematic logical form in another respect. Decisions on the run are made by performing managers and employees behaving as actors in a play, and their behavior is like a stage performance at the tail end of an inexorable process of logic. Having devised a consistent and plausible plan for the solution to a problem, the decision analyst may blithely assume that the executon and action which ensues is anti-climactic, subservient, and of less intellectual worth than the logical process itself. Yet, this decision making on the run, being governed by a different logic, may undo the logic of theory and in so doing, may untie the tightly strung train of decision which logic has prescribed. The means which make this logic of practice dominant in the efficient execution of a decision may be explained in terms of the logic of the performing arts. Management behavior in action is properly explained as an example of the art of drama.

The lively art of managing

In practice management has many characteristics of dramatic art. It's not uncommon for compelling managers to evoke the comment, "What an actor!" Often we refer to the dramatic nature of business. In training managers we often place them in roles which we ask them to enact. These roles simulate the real-life situations which may confront them in the plant, and in effect we rehearse them for the real play before the real audience when the acting is for keeps. The critical reviews of performance often adopt

166

much of the character of stage reviews. The performance review is a regular part of the personnel procedure for most well-organized firms.

One reason decisions of vast conceptual complexity and mathematical precision simply don't work is because the playing out of the scenes simply doesn't jell. Since the decision theorist in no instance has considered the implementation of his options for action in terms of dramatic roles to be written, his logic falls prey to the practical effects of dramatic motives when the logic of practice takes charge.

The manager considered as an actor

Given a hoped-for outcome, a goal to be achieved, a problem whose solution requires action, the final release of the action is to an actor. The staff analyst retires to the wings or the pit, where he may whisper cues, raise and lower some curtains, but the immediate, continuous and ultimate decisions at this stage are in the hands of the actor himself. Even his scene is not one which has been totally considered by the plot. His actions are a series of little choices. Shall he move to the center, or stand steady? Should he raise his voice or lower it? Should he slavishly recite his lines, or ad lib? How should he use his props? These are the multitudinous small decisions which can make the play, can execute the playwright's vision, or can remake it into an entirely new expression of the actor's own vision. Never really free of his script, he nonetheless has room to add his own character to the role he is assigned, enlarge it, botch it up, or raise it to heights of grandeur.

The scene for the implementation of decision may affect the way the part of manager is enacted by the actor cast in it. Life in a corporate headquarters, with its quiet opulence, its thick rugs, its Danish furniture, sleek women in bit parts, brings forth acts which would not be evoked in a foundry with dirt and smoke, uncouth players, and the roaring of machinery. In the latter setting the actor who plays the part of the manager may roar and bellow like a mad man, wear a costume and use language which would never do in the more subdued headquarters scene. The rifle company commander under mortar fire may find that the decisions devised in cool rationality a hundred miles to the rear by officers in starched chinos and polished brass are absurd for a company riddled by casualties, bathed in its own blood, and stupefied by fatigue and fear. A few imperative or inescapable limits of mission and objective may stick with the scene, but the decisions and acts and thoughts are wildly and grotesquely at variance with the plan. The improvisation of actors may determine the success or failure of the decision made in the rear, but for reasons never imagined by the decision makers. For the same imperatives the decision may fail.

The manager as an actor will be consistent with his scene. The scene designed by cool logic is ambiguous. It is the actor who makes it explicit by his choices and his acts.

The manager may be empathetic with his people if the scene permits empathy. Frantic scenes may generate frantic acts by the manager. Like Hamlet who is warned that "the very place puts toys of desperation without more motive into every brain," the physical and psychological climate of the scene bears inexorably on the decisions which are made at the point of execution. The logic of practice in decision making requires consideration of stage, scene and supporting cast. Much of this environment for the manager as an actor is of utter indifference to the systematic logician who sees decisions as execution of logical exercises. The architect who designed the work environment recognizes this in his plans.

Formal and theoretical decision making assumes unwittingly the reduction of acting to mere motion, predetermined by the logical plan. It assumes that the manager does not act; rather, that he is automatically moved. The manager as actor knows better. He knows that effective action is affected by the scene, and it is he who sets the scene to prepare for the desired action. He knows the truth of the military maxim that "terrain determines tactics." The stages of decision-making outlined earlier make a little pretense of picturing terrain, but proceed as if it were not important. This is a fallacy of some dimension in logic alone.

As an actor, the manager is not an empty organism, a puppet, or a black box. His own purposes and those of other actors are variables which color the logic of practice. The role of managing, its entrances and exits, its costumes and props may have the effect of galvanizing the beholder, and transforming the wearer. The manager who sees his role as being an instrument of a productive machine may comply with the plan more perfectly than the actor who sees his role as one of being human in a human climate. Theory cannot cope with scenes and actors who will bend the decision for low or high reasons. The logic of theoretical decision making is incapable of coping with either sloth or dedication to duty; with greed or altruism; with corruption or saintliness. Yet any of these in a scene as it is enacted may be introduced by the actors themselves.

The great electrical conspiracy of the early sixties provides a case in point. The pressures for results growing out of management by objectives in the leading conspirers led the system to a crashing failure. In the price-fixing conspiracies in steel in 1965, the rationale for the actors' behavior was explained in just such scenic environmental terms.

The social relations of decision making on the run in administrative scenes is still another incalculable in determining choices. The manager as an actor responds to the acts of others. The resistances of others, their upstaging, their fidelity to their roles and his awareness of his appearance to them are practical guides to the immediate choices he makes in action.

Management and the comic art

Every leader of organizations under stress knows the value of humor, wit and comedy to the maintenance of stability and sanity for the actors. Not every management decision is executed in a play which resembles a pageant, although the logic of decision making most often assumes this to be the prevailing manner of execution. The roles of the leader himself seldom include that of the buffoon, but in his staging the importance of this role is recognized. A carnival element in the staging of the action has numerous advantages for the manager.

Comedy being a legitimate form of the performing art, it has an important part to play in the choices made and logic of practice.

● It permits human folly to exist in real life and not overwhelm the actors and reduce them to despair.

● It is essential to the scene where the absurd exists, for the incongruity of reality with theory is one of the most fertile sources of humor in business.

● The more pressure and conflicting actions which are generated by the plans themselves, the greater the opportunity for wit to assert itself. In businesses such as television or advertising, where the planning is chaotic and the absurd abounds, humor flourishes.

The TV producer who was trying to sell sponsors on packaged TV shows attempted to convince the manufacturers of Volkswagen automobiles to sponsor the series "Twelve O'clock High." This series, having as its subject the life of bomber crews in World War II, had numerous scenes depicting heavy bombing raids on Germany. During the initial showing of the pilot films one of the actors reported on his radio with satisfaction that a hefty tonnage of bombs had been dumped on Stuttgart.

"They just bombed our factory," a guttural voice boomed from the sponsor's row. Needless to say, Volkswagen did not sponsor the series.

● The cartoon "Out Our Way" has made a classic comic figure of the Bull of the Woods, and the ordinary figures to be found in a large machine shop. The wry observations of ordinary machinists comprise a splendid illustration of the role comedy can play in dealing with the absurd created by formal organization and logical systems confronting the realities of life in the plant.

Sociologist Orrin Clapp has defined three major roles which have become embedded in our language as social types. These types, villains, heroes and fools, comprise a suitable beginning for the discussion of the consideration of the dramatic as part of the logic of practice. Ridicule and humor can make apparent to us the folly, humbug and incompetence of the social structure, Clapp declares. The practice of the Gridiron Club dinner which pictures important men as fools is considered healthy therapy for the pomposity of policy, logic and high rank. Clapp distinguishes five major categories of American fools.

1. The *incompetents,* who by their rashness, simplicity, clumsiness, are weaklings who illustrate ludicrous role failures.

2. *"Discounting" types* include those who claim more status than they deserve and include old fools, bush leaguers, punks, the small-minded, and nuisances.

3. *Non-conforming fools* play another role, and include freaks, characters, oddballs, cut-ups, and beatniks.

4. Still another role to be found in the cast of humorous characters are the *overconforming types.* Among these are the yes-men, fanatics, faddists, or eggheads.

5. A final kind of object of humor is the *comic butt or jester.* He may be a buffoon, joker, or the good Joe.

A form of safety valve, much of the humor found in practical areas of the business is turned against those who generate the decisions and policies resulting in the absurd. The effect of humor which treats the best-made decisions as the product of stuffed shirts, eggheads, fuzzy-minded nuts, whiz kids, young turks, or big shots isn't without significance in the practical art of decisions on the run.

The manager as a games player

In decision theory there is included a theory of games. In decision practice there is the performing art of the manager as a games player. In executing such logic of action he may apply some of the theories of games and simulation, or he may simply apply a subjective kind of logic, sufficiently complex that it fits either of the major premises of games theory.

Rather than being rational he may function at several levels of feeling and thinking at the same time. He may have a rational moment, interspersed with moments of apathy in which he is indifferent to whether the game goes on or not. Along with this he may feel an emotional spasm which restores a level of desire for a specific outcome. This is quickly supplanted by another mood in which he couldn't care less about the outcome, except that he decides to go along with the crowd, and it is operating at some indeterminate level of mass hysteria. Experts in the mathematical kinds of games theory admit the impossibility of encompassing all of the varieties of game behavior in their systems. "Game theory does not, and probably no mathematical theory could, encompass all the diverse problems that are included in conflict of interest." The mathematical decision theory of games presumes that people pursue their own interests, whatever they may be, and that each individual has a preference pattern among the available options. Statistically this may be sound, but in the logic of practice it's not the statistically average person, but the subjective individual who must be treated. He may indeed adhere to the same pattern as a majority, or he may differ from every other. The choices managers make, the little decisions which are made in executing the big ones, are subjective, local, individual, and cannot be treated as aggregates.

Gamesmanship. One of the more insightful descriptions of the practical art of game playing is found in the satiric literature of Stephen Potter or Shepherd Mead. Potter's books, *Gamesmanship, Lifemanship* and *Oneupmanship,* and Shepherd Mead's *How to Succeed in Business Without Really Trying* reach wide audiences and strike responsive chords because they evoke reality. Clearly not part of a statistical lump, the gamesman they describe is a subjective, ingenious, and devastatingly human figure. He works his ploys, his chicanery, his veiled moves, and his subtle insinuations with zest and Machiavellian ingenuity. In one sense he resembles the logician and mathematical decision maker. He has a clear-cut objective, he knows his preferences and adheres to them, and to the extent that these authors have described them, is subect to prediction and control. Real life examples can be found in abundance which fit this category of gamesmanship, which might not be predictable under the logic of theory.

● The group of subordinates who worked under a detested autocrat prepared a glowing résumé for the boss without his knowledge and circulated it among numerous management search agencies until finally he was offered a better job and left.

● The executive who used a secret buzzer system to his secretary in the outer office to signal for her to enter and remind him of a prior urgent appointment to hasten the departure of the undesired visitor was a games player.

The Potter brand of game differs from some other kinds of games which managers play which affect and control the choices they make in the instantaneous pattern of practice. Spontaneous social activity is interlarded with purposive and controlled managerial behavior in his day-to-day life at work. It is in this interpersonal social activity that he may show perceptible changes in voice, vocabulary, physical stance, and facial expression. The executive may behave in one way when making a presentation to a board of directors, another when coaching a junior executive, and a third way when kidding a good-looking secretary. This difference in behavior may also be accompanied by changes in state of mind and mental attitude. The logic of decision theory which assumes a constant pattern may prove inadequate for such varied experiences of managers.

Scientific psychology in its beginnings emphasized simple things, looking at consistent aspects of behavior. Each function was studied separately and one at a time. More recently psychology has turned its attention to varied experience. The motives of men drift, rather than remain constant. Playful behavior of animals, children and executives varies. The boss may be grumpy at nine and playful at ten. He suddenly develops a keen interest in the punctuation of his letters, or the quality of grass on the plant lawn, then drops it abruptly. This varied experience is a phenomenon which makes the logic of practice different from the logic of theory.

Psychiatrist Eric Berne has described the varieties of experience in terms of games which are played by adults. The adult, Berne points out, has three major ego states among which he is constantly moving. These ego states include:

● His parental ego state; everyone carries his parents around inside of him.

● His adult ego state; everyone has an adult inside him.

● His child ego state; everyone carries a little boy or girl around inside him.

The games which people play are based on the transactions which occur between individuals, each with these three structural states. This means that the relationships of people are not simple one-to-one relationships, but may in fact comprise a game in which each party in the transaction slides quickly into that ego state which makes the relationship more satisfactory or useful to him. A simple business conversation may start out as a transaction between two managers in their adult ego state:

> Mr. A: Harry, have you seen my dictating machine?
> Mr. B: Yes, Bill, mine was broken and I borrowed it. I hope you don't mind. I'll return it immediately.

In another instance the original transaction may start with an adult state being met by a parental state, which reduces the original persons to a child state.

> Mr. A: Harry, have you seen my dictating machine? (adult)
> Mr. B: Why the devil don't you take care of your equipment? (parent)
> Mr. A: Quit picking on me; it's not my fault. (child)

This complexity of dialogue takes the forms of games which adults play. The game is played on a social level and a psychological level. Certain kinds of transactions are complementary and the relationship works well. Others are crossed transactions and lead to social difficulty.

In the logic of practice such explanations of the choices people make are far more significant than the assumptions of the rationality of decision making. Berne suggests that much of our transaction time is taken up in pastimes. The titles he uses for such transactions represent the kinds of topics which are the subject matter. Parents play the games of PTA, Kitchen, Wardrobe, General Motors, and My Son Joe. Businessmen would be more likely to play the transactional games of Balance Sheet, Dow Jones, As I See It, and Ain't It Awful. The varieties extend from Walter Reuther to Wall Street Journal.

The game is one which should produce the best yield for the player in his social intercourse. Often it is the vehicle for preserving mental health, Berne observes.

We might easily illustrate how these games would be applied to the business world of action. Some games which have been noted might include:

Try and get away with it—The quality manager
Kick me—the middle manager
Now I've got you—autocratic office manager
See what you made me do—the alcoholic

The psychology of transactions permits an extremely varied pattern of choices for the individuals, roles to be assumed, ego states to be adopted. The choices, many unconscious, are subjective, and unless this logic of action is considered in the shaping of logical and rational decisions, the risks in the decision may be radically understated.

Much of the rational decision-making theory of our time assumes a tight, artificial and frankly unrealistic assumption of adult-adult relations in the organization which must execute the engineered decision. The greatest frontier in decision making thus remains in clarifying such over-simplifications and incorporating the realities of practice into the necessary logic of practice.

chapter 18

THE LIMITS OF DECISION MAKING

*One sees a certain prince today fortunate
and tomorrow ruined, without seeing that he
has changed in his character or otherwise.*
—MACHIAVELLI

Back in the early days of radio, a pair of comedians each evening put forth entertainment for the millions at their crystal sets. One such skit went as follows:

"Theories! Everybody's got a theory. I say that all those theories are bunk, and anybody who invents a theory is a fool."

"I see. Is that your theory?"

"Yes, it is." (Laughter)

One thesis of this book is that a general theory of decision making is impossible. You might say that's my theory. More accurately, we need an existential theory of management to clarify the issues in dispute in the jungle warfare of management theory and especially to decision making. This means that we look first at systems, then look at their great limitations.

Koontz clarified the jungle-like nature of management theory, first in the *Journal of the Academy of Management,* then in *Harvard Business Review. Business Week* magazine noted it for the executive reader. Waino Suojauen, Lyndall Urwick, and many others have leaped into the fray. William Frederick suggests that in ten years we will see from this jungle emerge a general theory akin to Keynes' *General Theory of Employment Interest and Money* in the field of economics.

Such recent safaris into the jungle of management theory show little

174

promises of finding the *essential* manager. The manager is an organizer, say some. No, no, he is a systems engineer, say others. Really, he's a decision maker, states another school. Behavioral science is the essence of management, say still others. Nonsense, says another group, the essence of managing will be found only in studying empirical evidence from which uniformities in functions between managers can be induced. To date no implacable reporter Stanley has plunged to the heart of the managerial theory jungle and produced the Dr. Livingstone for whom all apparently search. As one surveys the fray, a startling thought proposes itself.

Suppose there is no essence of management, only right or wrong choices by managers?

What might lead us to such a conclusion? First, we might logically presume that a general theory of management should be based on what the *successful* managers chose to do, and not include those things which describe the choices of unsuccessful managers. In developing our theory, do we presume that principles, systems, processes, and theories have been derived equally from companies that went bankrupt, or only from those that made a profit, provided a service, and met objectives? Do our principles of organization, planning, and control rest equally solid on armies that won, or on armies that were soundly thrashed and demoralized in battle?

In our quest for theories of management analogous to physics or mathematics, have we failed to note that the physicist discards theories that experiments indicate are inconclusive or false? In developing our metatheories of management from mathematics, statistics, or biology, we may overlook the fact that we are dealing with proposed explanations of what makes the successful manager successful. If this be the case, we might then well note that we must develop a correlative theory of why unsuccessful managers fail. Treating one of them as simply the absence of the other won't square, since often the unsuccessful one did the same things as the successful one—but it didn't work. It might even be—as was true with Henry Ford—that he continued to do the things that proved most successful in the past, and failed for doing so.

Still more persuasive for building theory only on the successful manager is the hard economic fact that those who don't succeed ordinarily don't exist as managers for long periods and accordingly may not be considered suitable subjects for protracted study. We certainly can't build theories of management on non-existent people. This leaves us with the conclusion which goes:

"Successful management is what successful managers do."

The scientific instincts of all of the hunters for essential management rebel at such a simplistic formulation. Why, this leaves us with the chaotic world of reality. We might even say it produces a tautology: "The successful manager is a manager who is successful." How can a science or a discipline be constructed of such obvious (if indisputable) stuff? Yet, if we start at such an apparently uncomplicated position, we find we have done something of more sophistication and worth than we may at first assume. For one thing, we have found a common ground for reconstruction of proposed explanations of excellence in management performance that can also explain managerial failure. We find it relatively easy to run up and down several abstraction ladders from this position. For example, if we can accept the self-evident nature of this statement, we must therefore accept a corresponding statement that "The successful manager is not a manager who is unsuccessful."

Good managers and bad managers

In the search for universals about management principles or theories we often overlook the quite obvious fact that there are good managers and bad ones; managers who succeed and those who fail. Over a decade, more fail than succeed. Of the 4½ million firms in the United States, over 450,-000 will go broke this year, and another 375,000 will go inactive, most of their owner-managers leaving to return to work as an employee for somebody else. The managerial crises in General Motors in the early twenties, at Ford in the forties, at Chrysler in the sixties, and numerous other instances show graphically how the men who hold managerial responsibility may fail. Their decisions proved wrong.

This experience which surrounds us constantly suggests that the real issue in management theory is not to find an essence of management itself, but rather to find *first* some proposed explanations (theories, if you please) which can explain the continued existence of the successful and the disappearance of the failures. Having assumed that the successful manager is the manager who is successful, we might proceed without undue stretching of our assumptions to propose that management theory then is nothing more than the finding of proposed distinctions between the existent successful and the soon non-existent failures. In short, it is a theory which deals exclusively with the existential nature of the successful manager, and the existential nature of the failing manager, which provides us with a means of discrimination between them. To be even more pointed, we could suggest that the only visible core for management theory is nothing but applied ontology—the science of existence. The successful manager made the right choices; the unsuccessful didn't.

Managerial ontology—is a theory possible?

Behavioral scientists, mathematical model makers, and even traditional or classical management theorists are likely to find themselves in a jungle because they thrash with their intellectual machetes in search of essence and determinate structure in managerial work. Meanwhile, out in the clearing, in innocent exposure, sits the manager himself, oblivious to the search being conducted for his essential determinants back in the underbrush. The world of the theory jungle is the world of the abstract. Such a world has a being of its own, and can be taught and learned exhaustively apart from factual existence. While the theorist is intuiting a new abstract essence with which to destroy his fellow determinant seekers, back in the clearing, where smoke stacks are belching, deals are made and checks are being written, the successful managers succeed, and the failing managers fail based upon choices made, decisions made. Why this apparent floundering in the dark when things are going on in such a concrete fashion? Perhaps it is because the existential manager and existential management is harder to understand and grasp with clarity than the shut-in world of management theory.

Let's hypothesize on the question, *What is management?* If we simply treat it as a discriminatory process between two existential managers, the successful and unsuccessful, we find that no definitive theoretical answer seems possible. That good managers exist as long as they succeed, and bad managers cease to exist as managers, is certain. This naked fact is the origin. Everything else comes after that. Existence is prior to essence. What do we mean, then, by existence?

Situational limits to decision theory

The existential manager operates in a world which defies definition of fixed essence or nature. His essence is to exist, to act. In the face of awesome unknowns *he is a collection of the choices he personally makes,* the acts he personally performs. Each one can be vital or trivial. Since we have carved out some ordered stockades of system in the protected confines of the larger corporations and institutions, and correspondingly have ignored in management theory the thousand-fold more small firms where managers work—usually to fail—we confine our attempts at finding a management theory to these sheltered environments. Almost all of the modern managerial theory taught in business school and management courses of whatever school might more properly be identified as "How to be a well-paid employee of one of the *Fortune* 500 list of corporations." Nobody proposes that the same principles apply in the 37,000 firms with 100-500 employees, nor the 4,300,000 firms from 1-99 employees. Local service industry, the small construction firm, where staffs are economically untenable, are unstable, having an average length of life for the firm of less than seven years. What possible management theory covers the chief executive of these firms?

The ordered explanation of the professional manager who is the subject of the theoretical warfare now current is most unlikely to survive if we apply careful questioning or even moderate widening of its application. The existential manager, removed from sheltered workshops, is alone in an economic world that is alien and remote from such theory about his traits, his functions, or even his behavior. The manager exists first, then makes himself. Psychology tries to reduce his behavior to the level of sub-human nature. Mathematics attempts to raise the level of chaotic nature to a system which expresses a spirit basically congenial and consistent with man. Modern decision theory ignores that the manager, like all men, is a conscious being with a chasm between him and sub-human things. This decision theory ignores the situational nature of the manager and his acts, only a few of which may be clearly revealed by abstract analysis.

Combatants in the jungle warfare about management theory attempt to win victories by showing how classical management principles, behavioral science, or mathematical management can provide static and fixed, or perhaps systematic determinants; all of them overlook this situationality. To face up to the sizable nature of this situationality of the existenial manager would be to abandon the present form of thought. Many of the situations which surround the existential manager resist theoretical analysis, are ever present, and insurmountable. Research to find universals ends up with "inconclusive evidence." In the words of Lawrence A. Appley regarding management science, "In many areas of management theory we are flying blind." These blind areas involve situations that limit us and hem us in. The decision theorist acknowledges their presence, but ignores the basic nature of what the situations are. We can neither plan for them, nor can we escape from them, only struggle against them and in the end be broken by them or divert ourselves toward destroying one another. What are these situations that defy theory?

1. The first boundary to any decision theory is the *situationality* of the manager himself. He no sooner escapes one situation than he is caught in another. The manager, like all men, is always in a dynamic case study, from which he can never escape. No sooner has he identified one problem and solved it than he discovers that his solution to the prior case has brought him in the last paragraph to a new case study different from the first one. Impatient with the lack of a clear solution, clearly a product of his past acts and choices, the manager cannot escape his own case. Choices which seem suitable today (good profit, fine growth) contain the seeds of tomorrow's stickler. The mythical Sisyphus was doomed for his offenses against the gods to pushing a giant stone to the top of the hill, only to find that exactly at the moment he reached the summit it would slip from his grasp and roll crashing to the bottom again. The existential manager voluntarily accepts as his own a similar assignment to keep pushing his giant rock upward again. This is his triumph and his joy, in the pushing upward and the long trudge down again after it eludes him and descends crashing to the bottom. The bright possibility held out by the various decision theories that this endless task can be changed into master's berth on a vast cruise ship, plowing serenely through smooth and well-charted seas with automatic pilots and well-marked courses, has vast appeal. Such an escape

from reality for the ultimately responsible manager is a delusion, however. Only employees can apparently enjoy such delusion for protracted periods.

2. The second situation for the existential manager is *luck*. Carefully skirted by most management theorists—except perhaps the statisticians and game theorists—it is ever present. Plans of the greatest importance may be demolished by a careless word, or the oxidation of a filament, sending his stone rumbling down into the chasm. Having assumed the management position, the manager is ever subject to this threat. The frantic efforts to eradicate risk, to insure the uninsurable, leave a residue larger than it controls, which make controls possible only in the smaller areas where order can be established and maintained.

In many circumscribed areas with which businesses concern themselves, the reduction of entities to logical constructions may do damage to both the logic and the entities. This extension of logical positivism to the work of the successful existent manager has many severe limitations. J. Bronowski points out that it is the right attitude in a science that is closed; it is hopelessly wrong where the science is still growing. The logical construction which has been made to contain only the existing facts cannot accommodate new relations.

3. The third situation is the fact of *struggle and conflict*. Complete agreement between humans is impossible. In its place we find forceful dominance, competition, subtle persuasion, clever manipulation in which competition without displays of hostility is the best which can be hoped for. If competition has been controlled by the state, it has only been transformed and muted, not eradicated.

The businessman exists in an economic world where the economic problem is the allocation of scarce resources among unlimited demands. This of itself is the root of a universal conflict. The resources being scarce, the demands being limitless, the result must be dissatisfaction, centered in the achievements of another. No amount of effort in conflict resolution rooted in the behavioral sciences, no bargaining model of mathematics, can do more than assist one of the parties temporarily to win or lose faster.

When economic equilibrium occurs, it merely indicates a stand-off in conflict, which can only occur when competition is free and its ravaging effects upon individual competitors is untrammeled by regulation. Companies come and go as the creative destruction of the inefficient works its ways upon the competitors. Under temporary conditions of price fixing, either by government or by firms which conspire among themselves (usually monopolies, duopolies, or oligopolies) the rationale is simply to simulate its effects while alleviating its uncertainties. If price competition is eliminated by some kind of arrangement that ostensibly eliminates this kind of conflict, a vigorous kind of non-price competition ensues, being a battle of copywriters and TV spectaculars to combat other businessmen. This may extend to the strategic use of scientific research brains to achieve temporary patent monopolies or cost reductions in process or product which give one firm leverage over another.

The literature of transactions and the studies of the enterprising man are ample evidence that the situation of the manager is irretrievably one of conflict, much of it unmeasurable and perhaps only partly describable.

4. The fourth situation for the existential manager which makes the general theory of decision making an unattainable chimera is *inescapable guilt*. Because he is forever doomed to pushing his personal stone up the uncharted hill only to lose it at times, he must experience some failure. Knowing failure while desiring everlasting success, he inevitably must, much of the time, be plagued with the sense of "If I had only done something else." If he pushes his burden to the peak of profit one year, only to have it elude him (through luck, competition, or other situational causes) in part the next, he must spend some time engaging in self-questioning: "How could that loss have been averted?" When the giant cake mix manufacturer finds 25 per cent of his market snatched from him by an impressive display of competitive energy by an unwatched competitor, such terms as "responsibility" and "blame" are employed internally by those in charge. To disguise these in terms of euphemisms is a form of maturity which indicates only that he can live with his guilt because he has experienced it before and intends to recover and carry on. It does not, however, remove guilt from the life of the manager, for his successes will merely trigger similar sophisticated expressions from his now crestfallen foes. Its effect on management theory is incalculable. Much of the quantitative study of market research is rooted in a hearty distaste for the guilt which accompanies failure. Yet the very success of one man's quantitative method can only lead to the rueful self-accusation by another of the wrong assumption, the improper judgment, around which the paucity of analysis is little protection.

5. Still another irreversible and unmanageable situation for the existential manager is *death*. His corporation is presumably an institution which has no theoretical death. (In fact, however, it is highly mortal, and the law which creates the fiction of its perpetuity ultimately presides over the division of assets when it expires.) The individual manager himself has no such assurance of immortality, and the thinly disguised limbo of retirement simply points up the more vividly the situationality of the manager. Removed by retirement from the site of compulsory choice and action, the manager becomes no longer the suitable subject of behavioral research and quantitative or empirical analysis. His weight of importance, his manners, his background, his opinions are no longer of interest except perhaps to social workers or trust officers.

While he is acting out his choices as an existential manager our man may constantly evade and supppress his mortal limit. If he is brought close to its brink while still engaged in pushing his stone, he will divert his attention with devices which would do justice to Tolstoi's *Ivan Ilyitch*. He can objectify the death of another manager, refer to his own approach to it in jocular analogy with vegetative organisms, and other abstract devices such as "executive replacement charts" or "tables of actuarial statistics." Since his date of death is indeterminate, his life is planned with a probabilistic certainty up to the retirement point. The present major forms of management theory have no way of accounting for this apparatus of objectifying, and theory accommodates itself to the real situation tangentially. Such terms as management succession, retirement, estate building, pension funding, deferred compensation, tax advantages and tax relief on present income, understudy, backstopping executives, executive health programs, and a host of others comprise the unrelenting need to accommodate to ultimate death of the existential manager. It would certainly be considered morbid, unmannerly, and in poor taste to develop a chapter or a text on Managerial Death. Yet as a limiting situation it pervades his life and in the search to avoid it management theory can assume "*certain sometimes, but not right away, so let's turn to theory as if it weren't there.*" How can a decision theory be constructed which accommodates itself to a statistical fact that the average chief executive who is sixty has five years to work and nine years to live? Is this decade irrelevant in studying the functions? No theory of mathematical, behavioral, or empirical nature can cope with it. Ultimately he will die alone. What effect this is having on his present acts and choices is imponderable. The brutal existence of this fact makes hash of logical theory of management which chooses to ignore it.

The imminence of death as part of a management theory based on ontology offers many explanations of the special ways in which the existential manager is circumscribed by *time*. The personal management of his time is one of the most often mentioned problems of executives. It has been noted that this search for authenticity characterizes the existential manager.

> Most executives work hard. Their lives are often organized to a point that routine activities are handled with machine-like precision. Such executives show a zeal for their work, typically backed up by great physical, mental and emotional energy. They are possessed by the job and the organization.

Time for the existential manager is not an ordinary continuum divided into the three parts of past, present, and future. Time is a matter close to his inner being. Unless he fills this moment with the significant content of final choice, he will lose himself in a welter of scattered fragments. Time, then, in the face of personal mortality, becomes a series of has-beens united to the future. The future for the existential manager is not an infinite series of *nows* but a finite boundary ultimately limited by his mortality. When he gives of his time it is of himself that he gives, and the future is controlling through the range of possible outcomes that present choices open to him.

SOME PATHS FROM THE MANAGEMENT THEORY JUNGLE?

There are many indications that a serious breakdown is present in management, business and decision theory in the Western world. At the very time there is a desperate need for sound and appealing explanations of the nature of administered capitalism, and the leaders in it, academic management theory seems to be at sea. There are no plausible syntheses, and the behavioral theories require a kind of salesman who entertains with the mental agility of the stand-up comedian to try to persuade managers that their wares are the tools of salvation. Quantitative models of management theory contribute obscure tautologies covering the least significant fraction of the business environment. The empirical searchers for uniformities, like the behavioralists, reach for ponderous principles that generalize into proof that which is merely indication taken from artifacts. Such studies, of course, have their place, but they have meaning only when they pervade the world of concrete experience as well as the special fields of science and theory.

From the viewpoint of the management scientist, the world of the manager often appears to be irresponsible and undisciplined. To treat the manager existentially, he will conclude, is a sheer bedlam of subjective observation in which no empirical verification is possible. "It gives us the hard choice between a description that is sure but teaches me nothing, and a hypothesis that claims to teach me but is not sure," says Camus. The existential manager does not provide a lack of empirical data, but rather *too much*. Generalization from unorganized and sparse observation has been the charge against the empirical schools to date. Only systematic organization of observation is meaningful, propose the quantitative and behavior theorists. In the process they have smelted and refined *too far*. The only alternative is to return to the existential manager in all his terrible complexity of acts and choices.

How then, the theorist will ask, can these data be organized? Surely we must concur that in his way each theorist may make a small contribution to ordering the phenomenon, if he will resist the impulse to generalize over-quickly, and continue to search for wisdom among the facts.

The discipline of ontology—the science of existence—is perhaps the most viable framework for organizing the existential manager. The reason for such a conclusion?

> *Ontology is the guiding, if unconscious, philosophy of the existential manager himself in his choices and acts.*

Astoundingly aloof from the prevailing jungle of management theory rooted in quantitative, behavioral, and classical schools, the movement of thought which is identified as existentialism is the de facto, if unrecognized, philosophy around which the successful manager organizes his life and work.

Of the schools of management theory it closest resembles that of the empirical school, without the latter's overzealousness in generalization from scant evidence.

The presumption of the theorist and academician that the most successful manager can be equated with the "thoughtful manager" is most certainly not borne out by much evidence. An even more persuasive case could be made that the successful manager is too busy succeeding (existing) to spend much time reflecting on theories which could explain his success. He is far too busy *staying* existent. He is like the trial lawyer who spurns the study of jurisprudence, the general practitioner who doesn't find time to do research, or the sailor operating his ship who is too busy sailing to study theories of velocity and marine engineering. This doesn't mean that principles aren't there, or aren't working. In the case of the manager, however, it becomes an increasingly plausible thought that the principles haven't yet been uncovered nor described.

Let's hypothesize for the moment that existentialism, the art of existing, is the only germane basis for theorizing about the manager. What kinds of evidence might be put forth for this anomalous position (anomalous because it starts off with the presumption that "no theory is possible, and that is my theory")?

1. The failure of organization to survive, and the attribution of that failure to unsuccessful management, make it amply evident that there are unsuccessful managers and that they outnumber the successful.

2. Existence comes first, then essence. The successful manager makes himself by his choices and his acts. He even chooses himself. He can quit existing as a manager or as a person any time he chooses. (Kreuger, the match king, did both at once.) Functions, systems, or processes, as well as theories which include unsuccessful managers must be considered suspect, since the unsuccessful ones don't exist as managers for long after their unsuccessful status is revealed.

3. The existence of the manager and the manager's choices are limited by his situational nature, and the facts of luck, conflict and struggle, guilt, and death (and time) which attend upon all, and are inescapable parts of his situation.

4. Today's manager is more likely to be attuned keenly to the existential nature of his managerial life than those who try to theorize about him, his work, and his functions. He is keenly aware of the values of survival to him and his firm. He turns his eyes to struggle and conflict, works closely with luck at his elbow, fends off the guilt of failure by any means and, knowing that death circumscribes his effect, plunges deeply into each present moment to make the most of it.

5. Where, then, is the place for decision theory? Remove the effects of situational differences between managers, conflict, luck, guilt and death, and management theory has smooth sailing. You have also removed the

real world in its inescapable facts, and the results are a somewhat sterile exercise in abstract logic.

SUMMARY

The proposal that we face a richer and far more complex field of study in management theory by turning our faces first more squarely toward the concrete is disheartening to those who would fit the discipline of management to the logics of inanimate or sub-human sciences. The human condition being what it is, small wonder we would escape it by treating man as a logic machine, or his work as a mathematical model, an input-out system, or by objectifying his behavior in rules of process or system. Unfortunately, truth lies in this segment of our condition only in part, and not the important and existent parts at that.

Building a science of management to date has been a continuing trend toward classifying management principles, processes, and theories along the lines of the Vienna circle of logicians. All propositions are to be classified as sense or nonsense. All propositions, other than analytic propositions, are significant if they can be empirically verified or falsified. Otherwise they are nonsense. "The meaning of a proposition is the method of its verification." Such a logic reduces to nonsense all moral and philosophical discourse. It also, it should be noted, reduces the scientists' own formulations of principles to nonsense as well. In the reconstruction of management theory, it may well prove worthwhile to return to the central core of the subject and reconstruct from the center outward. Such might be the contribution of an ontological approach.

In summary it might seem that this chapter has led to the conclusion that decision making, along with the rest of management theory, is a fruitless exercise. Quite the contrary is true. The trouble with decision theory is that it has been treated segmentally. It has developed mathematical, theoretical and systematic methods, at the same time it has denied that the problem of human acceptance of decision is important. The "creative management" school of group decision making has gone to the other extreme. It has concluded that quality, while important, is not significant as long as the decision is accepted by those who will be affected by it.

The assumption, then, isn't that systematic decision making is wrong, nor that consultative management is wrong. Both have much to offer, as does the practical mechanics of everyday choices.

The important point is that we should master all of the methods and synthesize them if we are to develop a useful guide to successful management. What is this successful management? It is assumed here that it goes beyond decision theory.

Successful management consists of setting good goals and following them to make the right choices. Those who do these things succeed (and survive). Those who fail these two tasks fail as managers. We can use a system for that small part which lends itself to systemizing. The rest is out of our hands.

Part III

The Tools of
Decision Making

The Search for Certainty

A cursory reading of the previous part of this book might have led the reader to the erroneous conclusion that logic and system in decision making are being discounted or their contribution minimized. This would be far from the intention here. The tools for rational decision making which are woven throughout the first part of this book are among the most important contributions to decision making of recent time.

It is suggested here that the new tools of applied mathematics offer insights and rationality of extraordinary power and value. No manager of the future will be able to ignore them, since the days of the purely intuitive manager are numbered.

In order that the basic tools may be defined, and explained in terms suitable for the non-mathematicians, the following chapters outline principles and applications of the new tools for decision making.

chapter 19

THE SEARCH
FOR CERTAINTY

Probability is the ratio of the number of favorable cases to that of all the cases possible.

—LAPLACE

Before you can become a better decision maker you must face one fact which may at first seem discouraging. You can never expect to be prefect in all decisions. The best you can do is improve your odds of being right more often than you are wrong.

The system that we've outlined in this book won't prevent wrong decisions. It will, however, improve the *probablility* of being right. But, you might protest, can't I do better than that? Isn't there some way I could learn to be right all of the time? Unfortunately there isn't, and anyone who proposes a system that guarantees it is some kind of charlatan. A system tries to reduce the amount of outcome which is left to mere chance by swaying events in your direction.

Chance, luck or random outcomes occur when the effect occurs without a cause. If no conscious will went into shaping the outcome of an event, it can be called blind chance that dictated the result. Under such circumstances we may try to attach cause to superstitious or unrelated events that happened at the same time as the result, after we have seen the outcome. Such things as blaming our failures on divine punishment for our past sins, or secret conspiracies which militate against us, or even the perversity of inanimate objects is pretty common stuff when we haven't planned a course based on analysis of the problem and conscious decisions.

The first step in seeking certainty (which you'll remember we won't ever find) is to make decisions to sway the odds in our favor. One way we may think of decision and problem solving is as a game played with fractions.

A   is the number of favorable outcomes of our decisions
___
B   is the total possible number of outcomes which could occur.

The whole purpose of our decision-making system is to make this fraction as high as possible.

For example, we have three billiard balls in a bowl—one red, one white and one blue. If you are blindfolded and reach into the box, the chance of pulling out a white one is $\frac{1}{3}$. If you could arrange the contents so that two of the balls were white and the third another color your chances of pulling a white one would be $\frac{2}{3}$. However, if by some arrangement you could plant three white ones in the box, the chances of selecting a white one would be $\frac{3}{3}$ on the first try. We'd call this latter probability one of complete certainty.

In the latter event, you'd have to have some information in advance before you could predict that outcome with complete certainty.

What has all of this got to do with your day-to-day decisions?

It means that much of our decision making is no more than the process of seeing the possible outcomes, and acting as if the most likely one would occur. What, you may ask, if it doesn't? Then you haven't lost anything beyond what you would have lost by just guessing randomly. Let's take an example.

Let's assume that you are an office manager who has been interviewing girls for a position as typist. You find that two applicants each type sixty words per minute. Each has passed the test with no errors. Each has excellent references from her school. Each has a neat appearance, and they both have plausible reasons for wanting the job. Which one is more likely to succeed?

... When to flip a coin to decide

The solution: Based on the evidence at hand you could choose either one. At this point you can do one of two things: You may choose one for *no cause* (flip a coin, pick the one that stands up first, or choose the one whose name begins with a letter closest to the letter A in the alphabet). Such a method assumes that the chances of success are exactly equal and that you will let some chance matter make your choice for you.

An alternative solution would be to continue pressing on in the interview until you had found some distinguishing feature that would be some indicator of greater probability of success. These indicators might include grades in school (although in the critical skill of typing they are alike), what other people in the office like or dislike about each (the one who is best liked may gain the greater cooperation from her fellows), or some other specific additional bit of factual information which can tip the probabilities judgments in one direction or another.

The search for certainty here has led you back to flipping a coin to make your decision. Does this mean that every decision should be made on flipping coins? Obviously not. For example, if you were to take the first ten girls who walked into the office and have all of them draw straws, then hire the first one to draw the shortest straw, you'd be using chance at a much lower level of certainty. You might have found by interviewing, performance testing, and fact gathering that two out of the ten are far more likely to have a good chance of being good secretaries than the other eight.

The kinds of tough decisions we make in life between a few alternatives which occur after extensive fact gathering and screening are far superior to those made by simply using blind chance without such screening and winnowing.

Decisions can thus be made by flipping coins if we have sorted out facts until we have found two or more possible choices, any of which would be equally probable of being right.

Such decisions are perfectly sound and logical provided either alternative would do, and neither choice has any factual advantage over the other as a selection. This willingness to move quickly once you know there is no difference is an essential part of making up your mind. It suggests this:

1. If you have some tangible reasons to believe one choice is likely to be better than another, follow the more likely one.

2. If you don't have such reasons and can't uncover them by further search and investigation, flip a coin.

... And when a flipped coin may fool you

If you toss a coin, the chances of heads coming up are ½ when you toss it the first time. The chances on the second toss are also ½. The chances of heads coming up on the third toss are likewise ½. The fact that the coin has been tossed previously doesn't increase the likelihood of its coming up tails the second time, nor the third time. Each toss is an independent one.

Now suppose that you must choose between two secretaries who have applied for a position. If they appear to be perfectly identical then a flipped coin (or even three out of five), will do. Yet, we know that such an assumption about any two women is a questionable one.

Even if we take two coins instead of one we see that the chances of matching by tossing is unlikely. Whereas the chances of coming up with heads is ½ for a single coin flip, the chances of coming up with two heads in a flipping of the two coins at once is only ¼.

Extending this to something as complex as an automobile, which has 10,000 parts, if the chances of each part being perfect are 999 out of 1,000, the whole car will be no more than 90 percent perfect. Imagine how much more complex individual differences in persons may be. The knowledge that this degradation of the outcomes is probable might mean that we should press on in our investigations and interviewing to get further information which might have a bearing upon qualifications of the applicant.

In choosing among people, for example, we might find that we have two persons who stand on a par with one another, even though they have some different qualities. Mary A, for example, may have a pleasant smile which will stand her in good stead in receptionist duties she must perform. Susie B may have a less pleasing smile, but on the other hand she has a nice telephone voice which equalizes her total asset value. In effect we trade off one asset against another in our decision.

In our search for certainty in decision making, we need to know one other thing about the way that probablility can work for us:

If we are trying to plan what to do when confronted with two events which are not independent of one another (such as our coin flip), we have a different kind of problem and probablility situation.

Let's take the same secretarial hiring situation and add into the case a personnel department which screens the applicants for us. We send a notice down to the employment manager to hire a girl who can type sixty words a minute, and who can be hired at a salary of $80 a week. The manager tells you that in his experience about half of the girls who come in can pass that rate in their typing test. He also reports that only half of the girls who can type that fast will accept pay as low as $80 a week; good typists can get more money. What are the chances of filling the position (this may have some effect on determining how long we must wait for a new typist to be proposed by the personnel department)?

The personnel department states that it has ten girls a day applying for a secretarial position. Here are the odds:

- The chances are 5/10 of finding a girl who has the required skill at typing.
- The chances are 5/10 of one of those who passed the skill tests being willing to work for $80 per week.

This means that the probability of finding such a girl is 5/10 times 5/10 or 25/100, or 1/4. Thus in two days we should be able to count on five potentially employable girls being referred.

The probablility of the final event isn't like flipping heads or tails on our coin, since the likelihood of the second event is dependent upon the likelihood of the first event. This means that the two probabilities must be multiplied, since the second decision is dependent upon the outcome of the first one.

In determining whether or not a final outcome is likely to occur we must decide whether or not the second event is dependent upon the outcome of the first one. If so, the probabilities are reduced by being multiplied, one with the other.

How do we know that the personnel department will get ten applicants a day? How do we know that half of them will be able to pass the typing test? How do we know that those who can pass the test will accept the job at our available pay? We are really predicting the future. The principle here is a simple one.

The probabilities of something happening in the future should be calculated from what has happened in the past, or from empirical data where they can be had.

The personnel department keeps records which show that 200 girls per month applied during the same month last year and for several years past. Does this make it certain that exactly ten will apply tomorrow? Not exactly, but unless some change in the labor market causes people not to apply or to apply elsewhere, it will probably occur.

As one philosopher pointed out, in the last 5,000 years since recorded history began, the sun has risen each day for a total of 1,826,213 times. Will it rise tomorrow? We can't be positive, but the odds are 1,826,213 to 1 that it will do so.

The binomial expansion and measurement of probabilities

Thus far we've seen three basic ideas of elementary probability. The first is the idea of probability as a ratio. The second is the addition of probabilities and the next is multiplication of probabilities. It is possible to express these ideas in a generalized fashion for use in working out the same results without working out the separate probabilities in detail. If there are two independent events the compound possibilities can be worked out by the expansion of the expression:

$$(p + q)^2$$

Suppose there are two independent events, with p and q equaling ½; we find the following derivation showing the probabilities:

$$(½ + ½)^2 = ⅛ + ⅜ + ⅜ + ⅛$$

Thus if we want to know the probable frequencies of the various outcomes of a given number of trials, these may be computed from the expression:

$$N (p + q)^n$$

The meaning of the symbols used in this expression are:

N represents the number of trials

p the probability of one outcome
q the probability of an alternative outcome
n the number of independent events

This can be illustrated by using a coin with a heads and tails on reverse sides. The possible outcomes can be represented as probabilities of ½ for each possible outcome. Thus in tossing the coin 200 times the probable frequencies are given by:

$$200 \ (p + q)^2 \qquad 200 \ (p^2 + 2pq + q^2)$$

This would figure out probable frequencies of two successes, one success and no successes for any single outcome out of 200 tosses. This example has been for a coin with two possible outcomes, heads or tails. Suppose there are three independent events? Then the binomial expansion would be used with these expressions:

$$N \ (p + q)^3$$

Thus when we know in advance the probabilities attached to similar but independent events, we may calculate the probable frequencies of any given number of successes or failures. This is true whether p and q are equal or unequal, as long as they remain constant.

Suppose you were induced into a crazy crap game with ten dice, all of them honest. You place all of the dice into a huge cup and throw them onto the table at once. You throw the ten dice from the cup 5,000 times. You have bet heavily that you can toss a 4, a 5 or a 6, and each time you do it would be marked down as a success. If, on the other hand, a 1, a 2 or a 3 comes up, each is a failure. The expression to calculate the theoretical frequencies of the various possible successes would be:

$$5,000 \ (½ + ½)^{10}$$

Since the number of successes would theoretically match the number of failures, the variance one way or another would be small. The mean number of successes would be:

$$M = np$$

and since we know n to be 10 and p to be ½, the mean number of successes per single cup thrown would be 5. The deviation from this average would be very slight, and would mean that your possible gains or losses would be small.

Marginal, conditional and joint probabilities

We've already noted that in probability theory events may be classified as dependent or independent. If they are independent the occurrence of one event will not affect the probability of the occurrence of the second event.

The first toss of an honest coin will have no effect upon the outcome of the second toss of the same coin.

Two events are dependent if the occurrence of one of the events will affect the probability of the occurrence of the second event. At this point a useful sequence of probability classification can be applied.

Marginal probability is the unconditional probability of an event occurring. This is the first toss of the coin, the first extraction of a bead from a bowl of beads.

Conditional probability means the probability of event 2 given that 1 has occurred. This is expressed by the symbol p (1|2). This vertical line doesn't mean "divided by," but a vertical line means "given that event 1 has occurred."

Joint probability refers to the probability of two identical events occurring. This can be expressed for independent events as P (AB) where A and B are independent events.

Example

Let's establish a game in which we have three bowls of beads which contain blue and white beads in the following number:

Bowl 1	. . . 20 white and 80 blue
Bowl 2 .	.. 60 white and 40 blue
Bowl 3	90 white and 10 blue

The rules of our game stipulate the following:
We draw a bead from bowl 1. If we draw a white bead, then draw a bead from bowl 2. If we draw a blue bead from bowl 1, then draw a bead from bowl 3.

What are the respective probabilities of drawing individual beads, and what are the possibilities of drawing different combinations of beads from these bowls by these rules?

1. The *marginal* probability of pulling a white bead is .20. The marginal probability of pulling a blue bead is .80, (the total of the two must equal 1.00).

2. If we draw a white bead from bowl 1, the probability of pulling a white bead from bowl 2 is:

$$P (W_2 \mid W_1) = \frac{P (W_1 W_2)}{P (W_1)}, \quad P (W_1) \neq 0$$

where, P is probability

W_1 is a white from bowl 1
W_2 is a white from bowl 2

$$\text{Thus, } P (W_2 \mid W_1) = \frac{.20 \times .60}{.20} \neq .60$$

3. This indicates that the conditional probability of drawing a white bead from bowl 2 is .60.

The *joint* probability of pulling a white bead from bowl 1 followed by a white from bowl 2 is determined:

$$P\ (W_1W_2) = P\ (W_2\ \quad W_1) \cdot P\ (W_1)$$
$$= .60 \times .20 \ \cdots\ .12$$

Thus, by setting forth all of the possible combinations we find the following:

Event		*Marginal*	$\times$		*Conditional*		$=$		*Joint*	
W_1W_2	$P\ (W_1)$	$= .20$		$P\ (W_2 \mid W_1)$	$= .60$			$P\ (W_1W_2)$	$= .12$
W_1B_2	$P\ (W_1)$	$= .20$		$P\ (B_2 \mid W_1)$	$= .40$			$P\ (W_1B_2)$	$= .08$
B_1W_2	$P\ (B_1)$	$= .80$		$P\ (B_2 \mid B_1)$	$= .90$			$P\ (B_1W_2)$	$= .72$
B_1B_2	$P\ (B_1)$	$= .80$		$P\ (W_2 \mid B_1)$	$= .10$			$P\ (B_1B_2)$	$= .08$
									$\overline{1.00}$

This can be visually presented by use of a tree diagram, a useful analytical tool in depicting probabilities. It is called a tree diagram because of its branching structure. It displays the possible outcomes of our bead game, and the probability of each final outcome. (See Figure 19-1.)

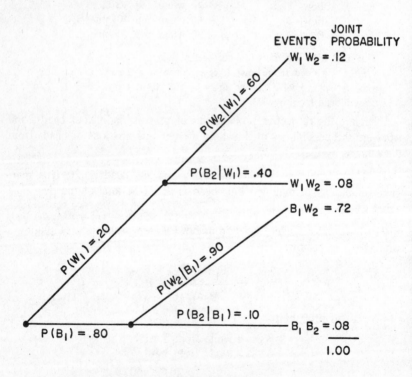

Figure 19-1

Time estimates or cost estimates are given more precision when the probabilities of the possible outcomes are defined with more rigor. In decision making we'd say that .72 is the highest "expected value," and would be our decision choice among the combined alternatives.

chapter 20

THE MANY USES OF SAMPLES

To control (guide) a process we must base our decisions on samples.
—ELLIS R. OTT

When we reach a decision the implication is that somebody is going to do something. He has chosen a specific act among the many available optional acts which might be taken. This naturally requires a vast amount of abstraction, or the decision will never be made. One of the most commonly used, and certainly most useful, tools is that of sampling.

The idea of a sample is that the sampler will row his boat out over the vast ocean of facts which surround him and will dip a little bucket here and there into this ocean. By closely examining the contents of the bucket he comes to some hard conclusions—not just about the content of the bucket—but about the entire ocean as well.

Mathematical statistical theory

Since our sampler intends to use the information he has collected in his smaller bucket to make decisions which lead to acts affecting something important, it's proper to note that he may be making decisions about the larger body based only on full knowledge of the smaller. Why can he make such a heroic leap? Consumer intentions to buy durable goods of 150 million people may be generalized from a sample report based on reports of 2,000 families, even though the decisions made assume that 40 million families will behave the same way that the 2,000 families indicate they intend to behave. A poll-taker in politics inquires about the political opinions of a few hundred to generalize and predict the outcome of the votes of millions of voters. Since he didn't actually test the millions, how can the sampler be certain that his decision is based upon knowledge of factual nature with regard to the many?

1. Early mathematicians demonstrated that all processes in nature exhibit variability. This variability is alike in that all data from processes in which only the laws of chance are at work will fit into patterns that can be depicted graphically as fitting under a "normal" or Gaussian curve. The shape of this bell-shaped curve is now commonly accepted by most rational people as being a natural condition of data into which all random distributions or measurements, or classifications will tend to fit (Figure 20-1).

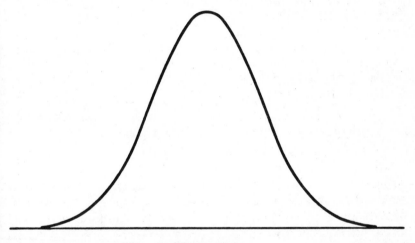

Figure 20-1

Such distributions are what we might expect to see when the laws of chance are the only influence affecting the distribution of outcomes. In real life not all distributions will be as smooth or symmetrical as the one shown above. There may be an awkward tail, or the distribution may be skewed with its peak to one side. Some distributions have two humps instead of one, others take a shape like a J. When such distortions of the normal curve occur, the observer then knows that some influence is at work other than pure chance alone.

2. There are two kinds of variability in measurements. The first kind is one which is based upon chance alone. This distribution according to chance permeates all processes, even when we try to control the process tightly, and believe it to be fixed. The second kind, which produces a non-normal distribution, is due to some cause or change that has disturbed the smooth curve and to some fundamental change in the process by which

the results were produced.

3. Using this basic information about data, we may reach some decisions about the nature of the process and changes which have occurred in it in samples. Behind this lies the impossibility of obtaining full and complete statistical description of the whole population. Economics bars us from asking all of the consumers, or all of the voters. Furthermore, it's possible to obtain reasonably reliable information from the sample. Samples have "risks" which wouldn't exist if we knew all of the facts, but the risks are sufficiently small that we can vastly improve certain kinds of decision by acting upon the basis of their being true. Much of the decision making in fixing insurance premiums, estimating national income, and numerous other important areas of decision are made on the basis of such sampling.

4. A further principle of sampling is that an average of a small sample is sensitive to any caused changes in the underlying nature of the whole population about which you want to generalize. It is generally not very reliable to try to estimate the nature of the whole population with a single example, but an average of several measurements will be much more reliable.

> *By taking several samplings and averaging them, then averaging the averages of several batches of samples, a very sensitive indicator of the prevailing trend or unobserved changes can be devised.*

5. The use of charts and graphics depicting the data adds to their usefulness. The array of data in their native state often leads only to confusion. Statistics provides some order and rationality to confusing information. It isn't that the data are a mess; the mess is in the mind of the observer. It takes a method of grouping and classifying data in such a way that all of the information is summarized in a few numbers or a curve. This process is often called *statistical description.*

6. Knowing that data will group themselves and fit under a normal curve, we have a useful tool for some decisions. We may then conclude that small samples drawn from this population will be predictable with respect to their statistical characteristics. This probability we call *a priori,* that is, we know in advance what the sample should look like because we have a picture of the larger population from which it is to be drawn.

7. The reverse of this is to dip into a population about which we know nothing; we pull out a sample about which we know everything. From the sample which we know for sure, we can reach conclusions about the larger population about which we know nothing. This process is called *inference.*

Before we can do this, however, we must be sure that the sample we took from the larger unknown population was really representative. If the bits we choose are random, then the inference is valid. If they were not random, it might be because we pulled them from the larger group in the wrong way, or perhaps because there wasn't an integrated large group at all Perhaps we were dealing with two populations or a dozen.

> *The problem of sampling at this stage is determining what model if any fits the situation. This means that to use sampling we must start at the bottom and work upward. First define the population, then the sample, then the inference, then the statistical description.*

There is plenty of working evidence to show that reasonably well behaved aggregations of data do exist in the world of science and nature. This means that data which can be quantified can be managed better if we can describe the average value, as well as the way all of the values are dispersed.

Probability calculations and the normal distribution

In the foregoing discussion, and in life generally, we are likely to find that the average reader is willing to rely on statistical laws on faith alone. If the experts say that data fill a bell-shaped curve, then I'll accept. This is the ordinary basis for the authority of the mathematical decision maker. But there is some value in seeing for ourselves. To take part in this elemental process, obtain a pair of dice which you presume to be honest. (Should the contrary be grossly true, you may learn something new about your own property.) Figure 20-2 is a chart on which you may record the outcomes from over 200 tosses of the dice.

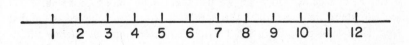

Figure 20-2

Let's assume that you know nothing about the dice, and wish to uncover their abilities to produce numbers.

As you make each individual toss (please bounce them against a side wall before they come to rest on the plane), record the outcome on the chart (or a similar one on scratch paper). Keep recording them in tally fashion ⧻⧻ until you have thrown and recorded 200. You may keep throwing as long as you like, but for purposes of illustration, let's pause here and look at the results. The outcome might look something like the Figure 20-1, or it might look something like the results of 200 tosses shown in Figure 20-3.

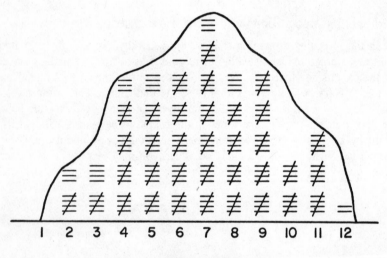

Figure 20-3

It is apparent that one number, the seven, occurs more often than any other number. That is, these things called dice produced numbers in this pattern. The numbers taper downward with the twelve and the deuce being the least frequent. This is a frequency distribution. Seven is also the arithmetic mean (or average) in a normal distribution. In the block form I've shown, this figure is called a *histogram,* which is used when the raw data are displayed. We can easily sketch a curve which will resemble the normal curve, and if we made enough throws, the results would come closer and closer to that curve. How can we use this in calculating probability? All we've done so far is a statistical description, which we've noted is the first step. How can we tap the useful methods of *a priori,* and of *inference* from this kind of arrangement?

In looking at the characteristics of the bell-shaped curve, we note several things. First, it is symmetric. By this we mean that if folded in the middle the left half matches the right half. Mathematically the area under the curve can be shown to be equal to one. For this reason, this distribution is often referred to as the distribution of percentages. This means that a random selection from the population will be seven or above in 50 per cent of the cases and seven or below in 50 per cent. We might cut the line at any point—for example, at the point where 25 per cent of the area under curve is included, and be confident that the probability of any sample throw fitting inside this area would be .25. This simple conclusion holds the key to probability calculations with the normal curve. But first we must change the scale of distribution from histogram, or normal curve showing distribution of raw data, into a *standard form*. By doing this we have changed the seven in our example to *zero* in order that we may use some laws of *central tendency*. The way this is done is shown in Figure 20-4.

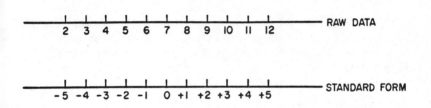

Figure 20-4

Draw a new scale directly below the original one on which you recorded your throws of the dice. You have converted the arithmetic mean into zero, and can now use the laws of probability upon the information you've collected more precisely. (The constant 7 is subtracted from each value.) With this standard form, you are permitted to use some of the laws of probability, especially the standard deviation.

The standard deviation and its uses

Knowing the average or typical value is of little use unless we also know the degree of variation of values around it. If we know the average (mean) of a population of data, and the way all of the bits deviate from that mean we can arrive at a measure of some practical value.

The standard deviation is the "root-mean-square of the deviations from the arithmetic mean." This is calculated for any collection of data by the formula expressed in Figure 20-5.

$$\sigma = \sqrt{\frac{\Sigma f(x^2)}{N}}$$

WHERE

σ STANDARD DEVIATION

x DEVIATION FROM THE ARITHMETIC MEAN

N IS THE TOTAL NUMBER OF ITEMS

Figure 20-5

Experienced statisticians have alternative methods of calculating this standard deviation, but the resultant product is what we are interested in here. Let's look once more at a normal curve which covers all of the data in a population where the distribution around the average is caused by chance alone. See Figure 20-6.

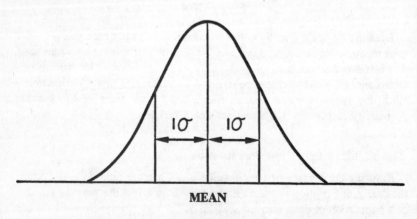

Figure 20-6

The standard deviation is important in analyzing data because in a normal curve 99.7 per cent of the data is included in the three standard deviations on either side of the mean. This shows the limits of fluctuations in results due to chance alone. When instances occur which do not fall within the three standard deviations we may assume with confidence that something in the population changed. For example, if we are using sampling from a population and find that an average of a small sample rests beyond the three standard deviation limits, we may conclude safely that something basic had changed within the entire process by which the data are produced.

● On an assembly line if the average dimension of a part is .750 inches, with an upper limit of .790 and a lower limit of .710 based on a calculation of standard deviations, what might we conclude if an average of five samples came out at .810? A single measurement of that size might indicate nothing. An average from a sample of five pieces would be definite indication that something had changed in the process which probably requires adjustment or repair. Often this sampling process can save losses in time and money which occur when long runs of improper dimension are produced before they are discovered.

● A businessman wants to know what his employees think of the benefits plans he has installed for them. One method of finding out, of course, would be to ask everyone. A more economical way would be to select a sample and ask them to rate the plans on a scale of 4 degrees of satisfaction from "I like them very much" down through "They are nig-

He takes five samples numbered 1-5

each sample consists of five persons named A to E etc.

		I		II		III		IV		V
						SAMPLE NUMBER				
PEOPLE	A	2	F	3	K	4	P	I	U	2
	B	3	G	I	L	4	Q	I	V	2
	C	I	H	2	M	2	R	2	W	3
	D	2	I	2	N	I	S	I	X	2
	E	4	J	2	O	2	T	2	Y	I
X (AVER)=		2.4		2.0		2.6		1.4		2.0

$= \bar{X} = \frac{10.4}{5}$ a

$\bar{X} = 2.08$

Figure 20-7

gardly and weak." If at a later time he wished to determine what the level is, and to ascertain any changes, he might sample again. If a solitary report were received that they now seem more favorable than in the past, he might be deluding himself. An average of a small sample, or several small samples, the averages of which are then themselves averaged, comprise a sharply sensitive indicator of any change. Let's suppose that he concentrates upon a particular question which is of greatest concern to him. His initial results indicate it is rated as shown in Figure 20-7.

He takes all of the numbers across the bottom, each of which represents the average of the five measurements found for five persons. The figure at the foot of the column thus represents the average response for that sample. Next he adds those averages and takes an average (arithmetic mean) of those averages.

Any subsequent actions he takes to remedy or change the attitudes of his people will be reflected accurately in this grand average, called $\overline{X}$ or Grand X. If this Grand X changes he may be confident that his program has succeeded or failed to the extent that he can see change in that $\overline{X}$.

As he looks at these results the manager faces the next logical problem: "So what? The attitude of my employees toward the benefit plan is 2.08 on this four-point scale, with 1 as the highest score and 4 as the lowest. Is this 2.08 good or bad?"

One way of judging this and of using the figure would be to try some programs to improve it, or communicate better its advantages to them, then resample again. If the $\overline{X}$ had moved higher, then his efforts were successful. If not, he had failed and could try something else.

This, of course, would be the standard deviation if only the laws of chance, a mass of floating chances, were not affected by anything causal in the situation. To determine if something is at work affecting the opinions, he now calculates the standard deviation for the actual survey results.

This leaves the way open for a statistician to go another step and calculate the theoretical frequency of outcomes as compared with the actual frequency. By referring to tables which show the area under a normal curve of error, he can determine whether or not the actual frequency as expressed in his standard varies by chance alone from the theoretical curve, or if some other causal force is at work. In his decision it may throw some light on which of the actual plant conditions gives rise to the emergence of the distribution.

Such analysis is most useful in decision making where the management of large numbers is cumbersome and calls for some precise simplification in order to ascertain what we have called, in our stages of decision making, the facts.

Is my sample representative?

One of the key problems in sampling is the selection of the sample not only with respect to its size, but to its character. It should fit the objective for which you are taking the sample. Just picking available people wouldn't be best. The population may not be homogeneous, in which case the conclusions arrived at would not be valid generalizations about the nature of the whole population. Various parts of the work force may have different attitudes and characteristics. The older people may be more approving of pensions than younger ones. The younger married people, rather than the older people, will approve the hospitalization plan with a pregnancy benefit. Some departments may want to take their money in cash, while others are concerned about the future. Fitting the sample to secure randomness requires that the plan fit the purposes of the study and the nature of the group being studied.

If the sampler is faced with several bowls into which he must dip, he may construct a *stratified sample*. That is, rather than one sample from which he generalizes, he may have several populations in mind and he selects samples from each, and makes separate generalizations for each of the differing populations.

Purposive sampling is another method of constructing sample plans. One of several control factors may be used in constructing the sample group. Sub-groups are employed rather than using the whole population. This would be a sample, for example, including only persons from 55 to 65 in the work force, or those living in the country as contrasted with those living in the city. When the data are punched onto IBM cards a number of classification questions at the beginning make such sorting easy, and the classifications can, in fact, be constructed after the fact by sorting according to different classification punches on the card.

Stratified purposive sampling is another distinct form of sampling plan. Thus if supervisors and non-supervisors were included in the sampling for opinion, some being in the office and others in the plant, several combinations of these variables could be used to make frequency distributions, show standard deviations and to work other analytical procedures.

All of this is useful in decision making because it permits the use of fairly scanty amounts of evidence upon which to generalize. In formal mathematical statistical sampling, several basic assumptions must be made about the veracity of the calculations. Normal, which is the base around which we note deviation of actual data, is a result of three general conditions:

1. There are numerous forces affecting each observation.

2. The forces affecting tne observation are reasonably independent of one another.

3. The chances of values above the mean are about the same as the chances of values being below the mean.

This, of course, is a never-never land in real life, and the statisticians indicate as much. Yet, the tools of frequency distributions and the measurement of deviations of means and standard deviations, tell us much about the characteristics of a distribution of the data in a case, and are worthwhile instruments for a decision maker.

chapter 21

PROBABILITY WITH A SLANT

Part of our knowledge we obtain direct: and part by argument. The theory of probability is concerned with that part which we obtain by argument.

—J. M. KEYNES

Most mathematicians and scientists, and the average person who is well informed, agree that the application of the calculus of probabilities is valuable. In decision making this means that we make our expectations consistent by those standards which are explained by the theory of probability.

Given dice or coins which are honest, we expect that the outcomes of tossing them will fit the patterns which the law of probability dictates. This doesn't mean that every toss will fit the mathematical possibility, but it means that the coin is likely, or the dice are likely by probability to fall in a certain way. Such expectations, however, are of a purely logical character. They relate to imaginary processes. These imaginary processes are believed by practically all rational people, and they comprise a realistic approximation of results achieved in the real world by coin tossers and dice throwers. It is almost always the way they work out when people with literal minds actually test the theory of probability by tossing coins for thousands of times.

Given a whole array of measurements, there is a tendency of most people to feel that the values will converge upon some measures of central tendency, and those who conduct measurements find that they often do. It isn't necesary, however, for us to do the experiments to use the theory.

Probability then is theoretical, yet it has great values in decision making.

A second decision which the decision maker must make may seem a trifle esoteric, but this question is being asked increasingly by decision makers and by statisticians themselves:

> How much reliance should I place on probability theory in the decision which confronts me?

For example, many rational people feel that probability theory is perfectly applicable with large numbers, but may not be a predictor for a single toss of a coin, or three or four tosses. Over the last ten or fifteen years there has emerged in the statistical profession a group of mathematicians and logicians who would bend statistics in a direction known as *subjective probability*.

According to these views, we should consider probabilities for two kinds of things. The first kind of outcome we might be concerned about is an *event*. The second is a *proposition*. The difference can be illustrated by a tourist entering a gambling den in California.

If he concerned himself only with the probability of *events* he would figure out the chances of the crap shooter in his little game throwing a seven, as opposed to a six or an eight, and realize he could bet even against the shooter and be ahead, once the initial toss had established a point. He'd also know that the odds against the shooter making his point, if it were a five or a nine, would justify his giving three-to-two odds, and if the shooter's point were a four or a ten, he could offer odds of two-to-one and still stand a good chance of winning. The events in this case are the appearance of a seven, six, eight, four or ten.

Another kind of probability might enter this scene, however, which would go beyond the mathematical probability of the events themselves. This would be the gambler's estimate of the probability of certain *propositions* being true. Among the propositions which he might weigh in his mind are these:

● Gambling is illegal in this town, and perhaps I shouldn't take a chance of entering the game at all. The probability of a raid is probably only one in twenty, or is it one in ten? If a raid occurs, I am sure to lose.

● Since this house is operating illegally, are there controls over the quality of the dice used? What is the likelihood or probability of the house being honest as compared with the probability of some dishonesty in method or devices?

● Since all of the others in the game are strangers, what is the probability that one, two or more of the other players are actually shills, working for the house to bid up the betting, with nothing to lose and all of my cash to gain?

Subjective probability doesn't deny the validity of probability theory, but goes further and suggests that we should apply the same degree of logic to the degrees of belief we have in propositions as we do to events. The subjective probability theorist also maintains that in their decision processes intelligent individuals should attach to prospective events some weights regardless of how their degrees of belief in these prospects were derived.

The entire apparatus of subjective probability is too cumbersome to present here. Most of it is found in the works of modern decision theorists, and some of the newer books on mathematical decision making are frankly subjectivist. The name most often used to describe the underlying theory is Bayesian statistics. Bayes lived over two centuries ago, but his disciples today are generally identified as a group of logicians, mathematicians and statisticians who have developed the subjective approach to statistics. They found their modern revival in Thomas Ramsey, a young English scholar at Cambridge during the thirties. The application of subjective statistics in modern decision making owes its origin to L. J. Savage of the University of Michigan, whose *Foundations of Statistics* probably did more to revive—if not create—Bayesian statistics than any other contributor. A list of references on subjective statistics or Bayesian statistics is included in Chapter 23 for those who have a deeper interest.

In its essence the Bayesian probability bends, modifies or slants mathematical probability by adding into the calculus of probability certain information which the decision maker knows to be probable, has a hunch on, his experience shows will work, or simply that his bones tell him and he can't push it aside.

The basic ideas of subjective probability

As it is used by the decision maker, the fundamental ideas of subjective probability might be stated as follows:

(1) Probability concepts as defined by Laplace which assume that the state of nature is one in which data occur as a *ratio* and that measures of dispersion of data tend to *converge* in a central tendency, are logical and imaginary. We describe the various degrees of rational belief about possible outcomes in terms of *probable* or *certain*.

(2) All propositions are either true or false, but in decision making we find that our knowledge of the facts is less than complete. This leads us to conclude that the calculus of probabilities for a given decision maker in a given decision must always be qualified by the limits of our knowledge. The *truth* is independent of opinion, but our decisions must be based on estimates of probability which are drawn from personal observations of part of the truth.

(3) At first glance this would seem to throw the whole matter of quantitative management of decisions up into a cloud of unscientific speculation, hunch and estimate. While this could be an outcome of being subjective, it

isn't wholly necessary. Subjective probability permits hunch and decision on incomplete information, but it asks that we heroically quantify all of our hunches and bits of evidence. It is finally determined by a willingness to act as if an estimate were true. This permits us to be precise about things we know for certain, and to treat the rest of our decision making with as much precision as the accuracy of the information allows.

(4) The ability to make perfect forecasts using the calculus of probability would be a wonderful thing, but subjective probability is more useful in making business decisions. Reliable objective evidence needed for perfect forecasts isn't available in business decision making, and personal experience may be substituted to fill in the gaps where the tools of statistics and calculus are powerless. (Will there be a depression? Will the President die while in office?)

(5) We still use many of the methods of probability of the objective style. We assume, for example, the probability of mutually exclusive states of a trial sum will be *one*. We assume that events may be dependent or independent. Independent events are those not affecting nor being affected by the occurrence of another; dependent events are those in which the occurrence of A affects the probability of B.

(6) The decision maker then can formalize his hunches into prior probabilities which need not be distributed uniformly among the various possibilities. Managerial judgment and experience can be used to arbitrarily

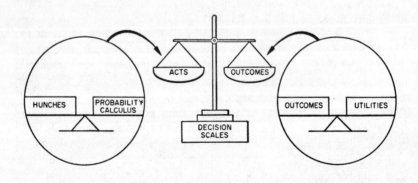

Figure 21-1

estimate probabilities. This can be combined with *utility* estimates. The reasonable decision maker then maximizes the mathematical expectation of the consequences of the acts he is considering.

A simplified sketch of this process would look like Figure 21-1 for the use of subjective probability in decision making.

In the scale of decision making we are likely to weigh the possible actions we might take against the possible outcomes of those actions. In the figure we note that in calculating the probability of the action we not only apply mathematical statistics, but because our information is less than perfect we must weigh these probabilities against inside dope we might have about the probabilities. This subjective counterbalancing of probability assigns numerical weights to such things as our experiences, small cues which crop up in our study of the evidence, even hunches, or biases. On the other side in weighing the possible outcomes we size up the worth of each of the possible outcomes by our utility for each of the possible results.

> The possibility of earning a dollar to a millionaire is less attractive than it is to the flat-broke man who wants to buy a meal or a drink.

Since there is an application (oversimplified) of the Bayes decision rule in Chapter 3 (the case of the dubious outing) you might refer back to it for an example. In operation, the Bayes decision aids the decision maker when he must act on imperfect information.

1. The first step is to list all of the possible outcomes.
2. List next to each the possible outcomes—its utilities.
3. Assign a subjective probability (weight) to each outcome, using evidence, subjectively observed, to determine the weight of each probability.
4. Figure the consequences of each act in terms of utility.
5. Multiply outcomes times probability times utility to obtain the expected values.

It's quite obvious that the Bayes rule incorporates subjective judgment into its decisions. It does so when the objective is being determined to begin with. It requires subjective judgment to estimate the probabilities of certain outcomes in the face of imperfect information. Personal feelings undoubtedly affect the measures of the consequences which will result from a certain state of nature with a given act.

Some guides to using probability tools in decision making

What are some guides to getting started in using probability in decision making? Its usefulness as a tool of decision making might be enhanced by application of some of the following rules:

● If you have no reasons whatsoever for supposing that anything but the law of chance (the theory of probability) is at work in your case, act as if it were true. This can be done by flipping a coin (a randomization device), which sets aside any subjective biases.

● If experience shows this to be unreliable, return to hunch and bias, or experience. When applying hunch, however, place a numerical weight to make the effect of the subjective judgment felt in making the choice.

● As the number of instances increases, the bias of the results can move away from hunch to reflect the actual condition.

The case of the unsafe grinder

We've seen one example of how this method might be used in an unquantified form in Chapter 7, where we worked through the selection of options for preventing the little old lady from barking her shins. Let's take another safety problem and see how decisions required can be made with somewhat more precision through use of a table of expected values, which calls for some determination of probability estimates with subjective judgments being used to estimate the probabilities.

Suppose three methods of making a grinding wheel safe for operation by a wide range of different users are being considered. The machine is a rotary grinder which is used by a dozen or more machinists for miscellaneous chores such as removing burrs, sharpening small tools, smoothing welded surfaces, and similar small tasks. It stands in a corner of the department, is maintained by a general mechanic who services many other machines, and has several wheels which are interchangeable on the same hub by removing a nut, changing the wheel and replacing the nut. A number of small injuries, sparks and dust in the eyes of the users, have occurred and a few years back a wheel broke in pieces while in use and blinded one man in one eye. This apparently has been forgotten by the crew, however, and it is now common practice for men to grind without goggles. An accident frequency of .10 per million man hours is noted. After some consultation with various experts, three choices emerge as being most likely.

1. Affixing to the machine a transparent shield which must be in place or the machine will not run. A limit switch turns the machine off when the transparent shield is raised.

2. Issuance to each individual in the department of a pair of safety goggles to wear when he is using the grinder. The chances of their being needed at other times is small.

3. Hanging single pair of goggles on a hook on the machine, with an instruction sign, stating that goggles must be worn while grinding, placed above the machine.

Figure 21-2 indicates how this might be presented visually.

BENEFITS / RELATIVE IMPORTANCE / CHOICES	SAFETY RECORD 0.8	COST 0.2	EXPECTED VALUE
TRANSPARENT SHIELD	.01 P/MMH	$550	
INDIVIDUAL GOGGLES	.03 P/MMH	$95	
COMMON GOGGLES	.05 P/MMH	$10	

Figure 21-2

Across the horizontal line are the two major benefits or criteria which will be used in judging among the three alternative choices. For purposes of illustration, cost and safety record will be used. The manager of the department wants to achieve safety as expressed in a low accident rate per million man hours worked. He also must bear costs in mind, although this isn't nearly so important as the safety of employees.

1. *Benefits:* Includes safety in lost-time accidents per million man hours. Also includes costs as expressed in dollars. The determination of these criteria grow out of the desires of the supervisor, and the objectives set for him by higher plant management. He *must* show an improvement.

2. *Relative Importance:* Since the two may be mutually exclusive, the manager now attached a weight (relative importance) to each and quantifies it. This quantification should be equal to 1.00 in total. The choice which the manager makes is that safety rate 0.8, whereas cost is weighted at 0.2. This doesn't necessarily mean that the manager only rates human factors four times greater than money, but rather that he hopes to avert fantastically high costs for little or no incremental gain.

As is shown in Figure 21-2, the supervisor is able to complete the grid, using industry statistics, his own judgment and experience in managing factory operations. He might draw on factory statistics for relative safety performance, plus some experienced judgments of the safety director who assists him in making his estimates. Their calculations go about as follows:

● Actually any of the three has a theoretical accident frequency of zero, but to make such an assumption would be unrealistic. People are likely to follow the path of least resistance—or behave in a way which has the most favorable consequences for them in terms of immediate ease, convenience, comfort, and simplicity, as well as in overall safety.

● The transparent shield practically bars anyone from grinding without a guard unless he deliberately fixed the switches so that he could do so. This might occur if the shield became pitted or scarred, so that the man grinding couldn't see his work if he used the shield. Other kinds of real possibilities for accidents include things which even the shield can't prevent. Thus, the estimate of accident level with the shield and limit switch is calculated at .01. A hard estimate from the machine shop and electrical estimator show that the cost of installation will be $500 with an estimated added $50 for periodic replacement of the glass when it became pitted through use.

● Individual goggles would serve a similar function and if everyone used them every time, would achieve accident-free operation. The supervisor and the safety director, being experienced, know what will actually happen, however, which isn't full use of the goggles. Men will forget them, and unless supervised may "just grind this little corner off" without going to the trouble of fishing through their tool box to find "those damned goggles." Since they would be worn only for that task, they would be lost more easily, and the man who grinds infrequently would be the least likely to use them. As a result they choose a somewhat higher accident frequency as being the probable outcome. A catalogue of safety supplies fixed the price for one set of goggles per man, plus replacements, during the year at $95.

● Hanging a single pair of goggles on the side of the machine so that anyone might use them when he grinds is the third option. If there were a pair there, and everyone who came to the grinder put them on, the effects would be excellent. Theoretically the accident rate would be zero, and the costs would be only $10. However, the supervisor and the safety director know that from common experience they would be carried away, would become broken or in disrepair, some people wouldn't wear goggles worn by others ("I don't want to wear goggles after that sweaty slob has worn them"). A small minority of people might even lift them; some people would swipe anything that wasn't tied down. If they became stained or scarred, they wouldn't be used. As a result the improvement in accident rate would be at a minimal acceptable rate.

Calculating expected value

How can these two diverse things be combined into a common unit? How can you add dollars and accidents together to get a meaningful sum?

It is like adding bananas and apples. The need is to find a common unit. In the case of bananas and apples the common unit might be pounds, ounces, or even dozens. They have the same common properties.

The common property in this case is called *utility*, which is an arbitrary scale devised for the purpose of measuring what seems unmeasurable. We simply adopt a scale of 1 to 100, just as the teacher does in school. Anything below 70 on that scale is unacceptable, and 100 is perfect. Since so few things are perfect, it is ordinarily accepted practice to use 90 as the highest level of utility. Everything which rates below 70 is excluded. How this looks in the next stage of calculation is shown in Figure 21-3.

BOUNDARIES	SAFETY RECORD	COST	
HIGHEST PRACTICAL	.01	¢ 10	
LOWEST ACCEPTABLE	.05	¢ 550	
* RANGE OF CHOICE	-.04	-¢ 540	
* NEGATIVE READINGS MEANS THE LINE ON THE GRAPH WILL SLOPE DOWNWARD			

Figure 21-3

In this chart the data are arrayed showing what the highest practical value for both safety and cost would be (in this case a safety record of .01 at a cost of $10) and then the lowest acceptable limits for each is posted (in this case .05 safety frequency and $550 cost).

The next step is to convert the various benefits into utility, which puts the raw numbers into positive form and transfers them to a chart shown in Figure 21-4, which shows the cost being transferred to a utility scale which ranges from 70 to 90. This is a schedule of the amounts of utility which are produced at a corresponding schedule of prices. Remember, utility is a scale which reduces the unlike to measurable likeness so that we can make decisions.

Remember too, that the only modification being performed is to trans-

Converting Cost into Utility

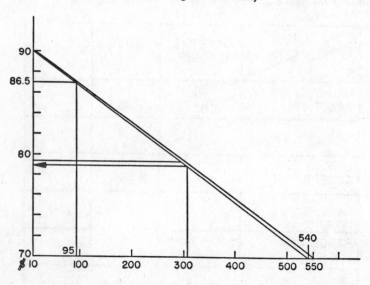

Figure 21-4

pose cost onto a neutral measuring scale called utility. Across the bottom are the range of available choices in dollars. Utility, ranging from 70 to 90, runs up the side axis. This chart shows that in terms of cost $10 has a "utility value" of 90. The sloping line shows that at the utility level of 70 the cost would be $550 (or another way, the utility value of a $550 cost is 70 on the utility scale). Using this scale we can calculate the utility value of $95 cost which is the third remaining cost option available to us. This equals a utility rate of 87.

A similar conversion is needed for our other benefit, which is the safety record. This is shown in Figure 21-5. We note that the same utility scale,

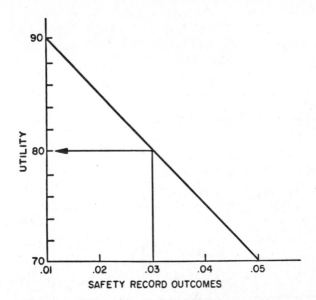

CONVERTING SAFETY RECORD INTO UTILITY

Figure 21-5

from 70 to 90 is used on the vertical axis. The horizontal axis is divided to show the available ranges of safety record outcomes which would be acceptable. By managerial directive we note that .05 is the worst outcome permissible or acceptable, so we equate this to 70, which is the lowest passing utility. The highest expected utility is 90, at which the safety record would be .01. Having plotted this on the graph we may now calculate on that same graph what the utility would be for a safety record of .03, which is the third possible outcome. This comes out at a utility rating of 80. Notice if you will that we have calculated the utility of each benefit separately. We happen to have two listed benefits in this example, but there might be many more. Note also that the curves or lines for these benefit-utility lines all are straight, and all slope downward. This might not be the case in every instance, but for purposes of illustration we've kept it simple to demonstrate the principle.

At this point we've found the "utility"—or common denominator—to compare the three options for two criteria. To determine expected value we post these to a master chart which will produce the decision. *Expected value* is the combined index or calculated figure which reflects the highest combinations of all the values. Thus, the highest expected value is the best choice among the options. In effect, in finding the expected value we make our decision.

We find the expected values in this case by posting the utilities for each option onto a chart which RCA calls a "combinex" chart, used in values analysis work in purchasing by Mr. Carlos Faloon, manager of value analysis. This is shown in Figure 21-6.

RELATIVE IMPORTANCE	SAFETY RECORD	COST	EXPECTED VALUE
	0.8	0.2	
TRANSPARENT SHIELD	90　　72	70　　14	86
INDIVIDUAL GOGGLES	80　　64	87　　17	81
COMMON GOGGLES	70　　56	90　　18	74

Figure 21-6

Expected values are calculated by posting utilities for each option and each benefit in the upper left hand corner of the chart. See Figure 21-7.

Having posted these utilities, the utility is then multiplied by the fraction which reflects the weighted importance for each option. This product is posted in the lower right-hand corner of the square. This calculation is performed for all squares in the grid. The totals for each square are added across and posted in the expected value column on the right. This figure represents the expected value for each optional course of action.

The expected values for each are shown as follows:

1. Transparent shield—86
2. Individual goggles—81

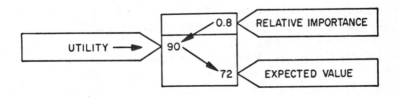

Figure 21-7

3. Common goggles—74

Thus the selection of method would be that of installation of a transparent shield, which would be the best combination of all the expressed desires of the management for safety at acceptable cost. This happens to be the best outcome in this firm at this time; at another time or in another environment one of the others might be best.

One word of caution about the method hinges upon the calculation method. Since the expected value is based upon a multiplication of relative importance times utility, it is apparent that you can't work with the system if any utility or any relative importance figure is zero. (0 × 0 equals zero.) This scrubs the whole exercise, and you must preserve the additive function.

SUMMARY

The point of this illustration, of course, hasn't been how to safeguard a grinder. Rather it has aimed at demonstrating how expected values can be used to aid decision making, combining the major values you want to include in the decision, and showing how experienced judgment and objectives can be included in decisions.

It should also be noted that while we've used this method in evaluating criteria, it also has some use, often unnoticed in decision theory, when you are choosing objectives. You might even conclude that making the transparent shield work is now an objective and that the supervisor now has a specific target against which he can supervise his dozen machinists. If his rate falls below the safety record, or goes above the cost which he has projected for that activity, he should begin taking preventive or curative action.

One ingredient of the process which is also overlooked is the side effect of commitment on somebody's part that the estimates of outcome comprise guides to his behavior, and for lesser levels of management commitments to manage in a way which causes this goal to be achieved.

The practical supervisor might quite sensibly ask, "What if the supervisor runs into different circumstances or gross carelessness?" This could cause the results he has projected to vary from his estimates. Unlike the situation where he had not made the estimates and projected outcomes, he now has committed the company to a course of action, and has likewise committed himself. He must now supervise in a way to control the outcome, training and disciplining people who fail to use the guard as stipulated.

Of the categories of problems we noted earlier, this decision is a decision about a systems problem. It assumes that supervision will be adequate to make the system work, and the affected people know the system because they have been trained in its operation.

Many systems are perfectly designed, such as the well-known program budgeting system of the Defense Department and the United States Bureau of the Budget, but fail to work as well as hoped for because the higher echelon officials assumed that the systems alone would control all factors which could affect their outcome. Having failed to train all affected persons—as is true with the Defense Department and other major departments —they obtain only partial return on the systems. The fact that a system pays handsome returns may be relatively small compared with its potential.

chapter 22

OPERATIONS RESEARCH TOOLS

*It is no longer a question of whether or not
scientific principles can be applied to the
management process.*
— WALTER W. FINKE

Operations research has been described by Dean E. Woolridge as the
scientists' invasion of the business world. Originating during World War II
to solve complex problems of military strategy and tactics, it found its way
into business decision making through mathematicians, mathematical
economists and engineers. As scientists, they brought to business certain
qualities and training which had been conspicuously absent in many quar-
ters. Their objectivity in managing data was facilitated by their ability
to handle quantitative data at a high level of complexity using scientific
methods.

The model as the key

The general processes of decision making in operations research include
the establishment of criterion to be used, devising or choosing the model
to be used, and which decision optimizes—comes up with the most efficient
answer—in the existing situation. This making of models begins with a
process of abstraction. It faces squarely the necessity of ignoring some
aspects of the problem and abstracting from all of the facts those which
comprise the essential parts.

The model itself is a counterpart of the empirical problem in all of its glorious complexity. The model duplicates the essential behavior without reproducing all of it. A good model will include all of the essentials in such a way that adding details would add nothing to the knowledge of essential behavior. Such a model might fall into one of several major types.

1. It might be a physical model. A wind tunnel or wave tank simulates the environnment of a jet plane or a ship under way. The small plane which fits into the wind tunnel is a more conventional idea of a model. It is a pilot replica of the larger one proposed for construction. It can be tested in small scale and the mistakes in design can be corrected in small scale, this being economical in costs.

2. It may be an abstraction. Kurt Lewin describes the "life space of an individual" in such terms. Economists construct supply-demand curves, indifference curves, or break-even charts to represent a process symbolically. Verbal descriptions of processes are often abstractions as well.

3. Mathematical models. Although mathematical models could be considered abstractions, there are also abstractions which are not mathematical. Mathematical models use the symbols of mathematics to depict the underlying processes. In their use by applied mathematicians they are tied inextricably to the real world and he is constantly checking his model against reality, and his predictions against the actual results obtained in application. Statistical models are a kind of mathematical model, but the kinds of mathematics used in model making extend from simple arithmetic through algebra, geometry, calculus and finite mathematics. It is in the latter grouping of analytical tools that complex problems can be reduced to manageable proportions and managed by the logic of mathematics, which is far more highly developed and rigorous than intuition. Most models used in operations research are mathematical restatements of the actual problem.

The advantages of the model are many. By abstraction it permits the human mind to grasp the essential features of the situation. Relationships between variables are clarified. It suggests places where more empirical data should be collected. The model requires that measures of effectiveness be developed. It leads to explanations of cause and effect which might have remained obscure. A model permits treatment of the whole problem rather than segments of it. It may be treated as a whole, or its parts may be managed as sub-systems of the larger model. It permits the management of situations where large numbers or vast complexity appear to make clarity and order impossible. The model itself can be modified and the essential changes in the process seen and predicted without disturbing the real-life situation in a way that might be unremediable.

> The presumption in model making is that the conclusion in decision making derived by pure logic serves as a solution to the empirical problem.

The two major possible errors in the use of models lie in possible errors in logic, and the wrong choice of variables to be abstracted for inclusion in the model.

Model-building technique

It isn't always necessary to design a model to make a business or personal decision. The choice of a luncheon spot, such as Sardi's for eggs benedict or a joint on Eight Avenue for a beer and a corned beef sandwich can be made without a model. Countless other decisions of similar scope are perfectly well achieved without the precision of model construction prior to action, in which case you don't use a model.

In those complex situations where models promise to clarify and aid in improving the decision, there are four stages which are ordinarily accepted as being suitable for most situations.

1. *General formulation.* Dig into the situation deeply and be briefed on its characteristics, including most of the available facts. Look for factors that influence outcome, and note relationships among these contributors. Flow charts and diagrams, schema and other representations in rough form may be of assistance here. Then convert the generalized data into a mathematical model.

2. *Empirical data collection.* Go back to the real-life situation or to records which reflect it and collect empirical data to be used as parameters indicated in the model.

3. *Work the data.* Using the empirical data collected, run them through the model and see how it would work for planning and control.

4. *Check and correct.* The first run through of the data is a test of the accuracy and sufficiency of the model. Its reliability and the validity of choice in abstraction can be tested here. For example, if you established a model, and tried it using last year's factual data, the model should predict the actual outcome. If it does so, you might then tentatively try it in real life using this year's data to predict this year's outcome, for example. If it doesn't, you revise the abstraction, the model or amend the design. The first model isn't cast in concrete, but is subject to proof.

The bulk of operations research model-making process is found in equations which express relationships. These may be classified as being one of the following:

● *Physical relationships.* These are equations which abstract from reality the basic relationship between two physical phenomena such as manpower hours and labor costs, input of raw materials and output of product yield, or income being equal to consumption plus investment.

● *Human behavior equations.* These relate one cluster of human activity to another or to a specific result. The economic idea that expenditure for luxury items increases as incomes rise above a certain minimum level would be an example. The fact that savings as a percentage of total income rises as the family income rises would be another. The idea is made more precise by fleshing out the model with actual data from consumption and savings records, more so than simply noting the relationship in verbal form.

● *Organizational equations.* Such equations express the behavior of organizations and the relationships of one kind of organization behavior upon output, or its relationship to another kind of behavior. The hog-corn cycle used in agriculture is an example of how the farming community might react to price changes in corn.

Unlike real life, the model can be adjusted to produce the data backward, which is useful in finding causes of a single effect, or imputing weight to causes. Models may also permit side conditions to be expressed, showing some conditional variables. More complex problems may not lend themselves to the foregoing kinds of equations and may call for the use of inequalities as a method of expression. Mathematicians are often cited as being guilty of proving that things are equal to themselves—which is an often justified accusation. Many operations researchers, however, are equally adept at building models which show inequalities and the art of mathematics is equally facile in dealing with this murky area as well.

Granted that much of the final result rests on the faith of the non-mathematician in the ability of the specialist, there is also much of the model itself which aids the layman in his decsion making.

1. It forces someone to dig deeply into the obvious and clarify the problem. This process itself can have some invaluable fall-out effects for the manager.

2. Inchoate assumptions are made explicit, since they must be expressed as part of the model. They may force decisions which previously had been left to accident or intuition.

3. It reveals contradictions and self-canceling logic in the process through abstraction and display of the underlying nature of the process.

4. The questions of interpretation and study are made simpler, since the main ingredients of the situations are isolated and made obvious to the decision maker.

Specific tools of operations research

The characteristics of models in general are made more meaningful when we look at the actual models employed in applying operations research to the problems of business, engineering and management. Some of the tools are merely applications of probability processes and statistics of an objective or subjective nature. Others have been more narrowly confined to operations research and are perhaps more characteristic of OR as a distinct field. The operations researcher doesn't limit his calculations to these models, but has shown great ingenuity in applying the scientific method and systems generally to the development of optimal solutions to actual problems.

Queuing Theory deals with the nature of waiting lines. A long roster of individual units may be bottlenecked behind a single productive facility, or may have a choice among several kinds of bottlenecks. Which hours will incur the greatest lines at the toll booth? If this question could be answered with any degree of accuracy the management of the facility might arrange the hours of employees to permit maximum flow of traffic with the minimum cost of labor in collecting tolls, and prevent traffic tie-up. Queuing theory can provide such optimal answers. It can also aid in defining optimal levels of storage of spare parts, can bring about cost effectiveness in military and civilian parts supply, storage and inventory. It can be used in supermarkets for optimal staffing of check-out counters, and similar avoidance of "hurry up and wait" situations wherever queues occur.

Game Theory, first developed by two mathematicians Morgenstern and Von Neumann, has been applied in working out simplified strategies, competitive bidding models and bargaining theory.

Inventory Control Theory entails the use of models for the establishment of economic lot sizes, and for the determination of optimal inventory levels by type of commodity to permit the optimal level of inventory to be maintained for continuous supply without excessive tying up of capital in stock.

Information Theory was used originally in the design of electronic and telephonic communication systems, design of communications systems, and design of computer information systems. Some recent applications have been in the design of social communication systems.

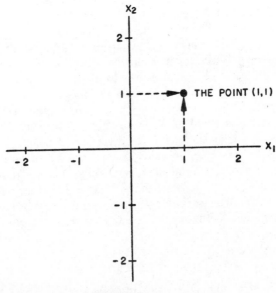

Figure 22-1

In addition to the basic tools noted here, others which are sometimes subsumed under the operations research function induce dynamic programming, which uses probability theory outlined in the other chapters, statistical decision theory as it is used in market research and quality control, and time series and econometrics, used in sales forecasting, marketing analysis, capital budgeting, and other types of long-range planning.

Linear Programming uses linear equation models to manage quantitatively such practical problems as optimal blending of gasolines, scheduling transportation systems, making production scheduling models for most effective use of available manpower and equipment, investment scheduling, and location of warehouses and service centers.

Just as a refresher for some of you oldtimers who took high school math so long ago you draw a complete blank on graphing, the exploded diagram (Figure 22–1) shows the intersection and a couple of points on the graph scale used in linear programming. (Don't be abashed at not recalling . . . people who don't use something they've learned don't retain it, and most businessmen haven't had to use their algebra since they were graduated, except perhaps some who worked in engineering.)

The two lines represent two variables which trade off or relate to one another. Line X_1 is usually the horizontal line. It is divided into numerical segments. The numbers to the right are positive numbers on X_1. The numbers to the left are negative (minus) values. The vertical line X_2 shows how much of another variable we have. The points on the line above the zero are positive numbers. The points below the zero are negative (minus) values. This graph permits us to show as a single point the value of one variable in terms of the values of another variable. Look at Figure 22-1. Suppose that the X line represents dollars and the vertical line represents hours of work. We note that the wages for a particular job are $1.00 an hour. We could graph this point in the square to the right of X_2 above zero and above the horizontal line X_1 to the right of zero. The dot shown on the graph would indicate this value for labor per hour (the point 1,1). Just as an easy refresher, you might want to try plotting these points with a pencil on the enlarged graph. Note that the value for X_1 is expressed first when describing the point. For example, the point (.5, 2) is plotted by finding the .5 position on the X_1 line to the right of zero (because it is a positive number), and running a vertical line upward from it. You then find the value 2 on the X_2 scale above the zero and to the right (since it is positive) and draw a horizontal line to the right. The point at which the two lines intersect is the point (.5, 2). Practice with these:

$$(2, 2)$$
$$(-1, -1)$$
$$(-1, 2)$$

In linear programming we don't just plot single numbers, but equations.

By taking the mathematic model and displaying it geometrically we can see more variables at once.

Let's turn to equations.

The mathematical key in linear programming is the linear equation. This is an equation which is drawn on a graph. Let's look a little more closely. In this example we won't go any deeper than graphing a straight line. (In other models the experts use computers and it clearly calls for mathematical training.) The basic ideas don't require such training. It merely requires that you know what your problem is and be able to state it in a way that the experts can shape the model.

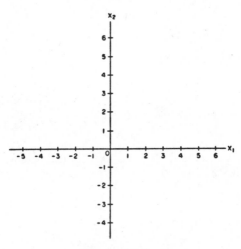

Figure 22-2

You'll recall from your high school math that this graph provides us a way of plotting (graphically) visually the way an equation or a number would look. The horizontal line we identify as X_1, the vertical line we identify as X_2. The point where they intersect is point 0 (zero). We denote minus numbers to the left of zero on the X_1 scale, or below zero on the X_2 scale.

Onto this graph can be fitted equations, and once fitted they spell out relationships which might not be obvious if they were not couched in this form. Let's take the equation:

(1) $4X_1$ plus $2X_2$ equals 6

We transfer this to our graph by finding all the points in the plane which satisfy the equation. All that's necessary in this case is to find two points on the line and we've satisfied the equation.

To determine the points in the most useful fashion we can solve the equation for one of the variables, say $4X_1$, thus:

(2) $2X_2$ equals 6 minus $4X_1$

or even more simply we can solve it to find what the slope of the line is.

(3) X_2 equals 6/2 minus $4/2X_1$

Although these equations are in different forms, they are all represented by the same line on the graph. Here's how these equations look on the graph as a straight line:

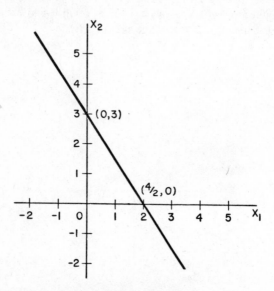

Figure 22-3

Every point on the line in Figure 22-3 now satisfies the equation. But in real life we may find situations which can't be handled by equations. These are called *inequalities* and consist of all of the points which don't satisfy equation (1) but rather, satisfy something else. We might then express the equation as:

(4) $4X_1 + 2X_2 < 6$

The sign $<$ in the equation you'll recall means "less than." If it is drawn the other way around $>$ it means "more than." In Figure 22-3 this would represent everything to the left of and below the line. This means that the points satisfying equation (4) lie below it.

You might express the various possible equations in these ways:

equation	*which means*
(5) $4X_1 + 2X_2 \leq 6$	All of the points on the line in Figure 22-3 or below that line.

(6) $4X_1 + 2X_2 \geqq 6$ All the points above the line or on the line.
(7) $4X_1 + 2X_2 > 6$ All of the points above the line.

These inequalities are important in linear programming to solve managerial problems because they are the means by which we express limiting conditions or side conditions. For example, we may not know the exact equation for a product mix or a bargaining strategy, but we do know that we have some upper and lower limits which we simply cannot go beyond. These inequalities help us to describe these limiting conditions.

Let's see how this would look in a simple case as it might be analyzed for decision by linear programming.

The tin can factory

To illustrate, let's look at a simple model of a tin can factory. This small plant manufactures two styles of tin cans. The first is an I style, which has rectangular shape (like a furniture polish can) and has both ends affixed at the can plant, plus a nozzle for pouring. The second line of cans produced is the O style which is closer to square in shape (like an olive oil can). This can has two ends plus a spout-type nozzle. To operate on one line of product or the other, change-over of the presses for ends and nozzles, and changes of fixtures, dies and tools for assembly are necessary. In other words, we can produce either I style or O style, but not both at the same time.

For purposes of illustration we'll set aside some of the complexities of the real plant such as time lost during change-over, differences in annual

Table 1

DAILY CAPACITIES

	Production	
Department	O Style	I Style
Ends	30,000	70,000
Nozzles	16,000	34,000
I Style Assembly	——	32,000
O Style Assembly	14,000	——

Figure 22-4

peaks, and try to uncover one solution: What would be the ideal mix of production for the two lines in all three departments—ends, nozzles, and assembly, for each of the two lines?

In Table I we chart the daily capacities of the three departments under the conditions of producing each of the two kinds of products. We note, for instance, that in the end department we can produce 30,000 O style ends, or 70,000 I style ends. Similar figures are shown for nozzles and for assembly.

Making tin cans is the activity, the output being a single tin can. If we let,

X_1 = the number of style I cans produced per day
X_2 = the number of style O cans produced per day

we can readily write the following series of restrictions, utilizing the data in Table I, for our operation.

$$\frac{(2\ ends/can)\ (X_1\ cans)}{70,000\ ends/day} + \frac{(2\ ends/can)\ (X_2\ cans)}{30,000\ ends/day} \leqq 1\ day[1]$$

(NOTE: There are two ends per can)

$$\frac{(1\ nozzle/can)\ (X_1\ cans)}{34,000\ nozzles/day} + \frac{(1\ nozzle/can)\ (X_2\ cans)}{16,000\ nozzles/day} \leqq 1\ day$$

$$\frac{X_1\ cans}{32,000\ cans/day} \leqq 1\ day$$

$$\frac{X_2\ cans}{14,000\ cans/day} \leqq 1\ day$$

$$X_1 \geqq 0$$
$$X_2 \leqq 0$$

Our cost accountants have accumulated some appropriate cost figures and reveal the following:

Can Style	Profit per Can
I	$.05
O	$.15

We can express this profitability in equation form. Our goal, of course, is to maximize profit from our operations. We therefore write this as follows:

$$Maximize\ (P = .05X_1 + .15X_2)$$

In graphing this series of equations in Figure 22-5 we obtain a visual representation of our problem. From this we can answer our decision problem, namely, to find the optimal combination of can styles to produce.

[1] The reader should note that the units on both sides of the inequalities above are the same, i.e. days < days.

The cross-hatched area represents all of the possible combinations of I style and O style production. The term "possible combinations" refers to all those that satisfy the restrictions of the problem. The broken line represents the line of profit, which is assumed to be constant and not subject to fluctuation for level, since we are using standard costs. Look for a moment at this profitability line which is an expression of various values of the equation:

$P = .05X_1$ plus $.15X_2$, and solving the problem on the graph means that we wish to move this broken line as far up and to the right as possible and still intersect a point in the shaded (or feasibility) region. This is possible because the slope of the line representing an equation always remains the same as long as we don't change the coefficients of X_1 and X_2. Thus if we keep the two coefficients in the equation as .05 and .15 for the unit profits for I style and for O style respectively, we can then keep moving the line to the right and upward until it fits the highest intersection with the feasibility area. This ability to move the line without causing it to fail to satisfy the equation is expressed in the general expression: $P = .05X_1 + .15X_2$. To put it another way, you move the profitability line on the graph to the right by enlarging the figure assumed for profit (P), or lower it by reducing the number. The lines are parallel on the graph.

From Figure 22–5 we see that the profit line intersects the feasibility region at $X_1 = 2333$ and at $X_2 = 14,000$ for a maximum profit, P, of $2,216.65. In other words, we find that our production per day should be as follows (assuming we can sell all we produce):

> 2333 style I cans
> 14,000 style O cans

We therefore require:

> 4666 style I ends
> 2333 style I nozzle
> 2333 style I assemblies

> 28,000 style O ends
> 14,000 style O nozzles
> 14,000 style O assemblies

Comments on linear programming

In real life the making of tin cans is much more complex than we've shown here. You might want to figure out the balance of the products by days, weeks or even months if the business came in with seasonal spurts. You might run extra shifts to backlog, and have a bank of ends and nozzles. You would allow for down-time. You might have to include many more variables. The point, of course, is that the illustration is not how to make

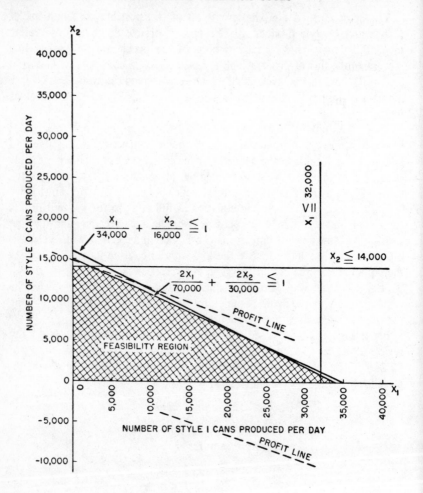

Figure 22-5

tin cans profitably. Rather, it's to illustrate the key elements in linear programming as a method.

● Many of the calculations are lengthy in real problems and are best handled on a computer, which can be programmed to handle all of the operations rapidly and accurately, although a persistent analyst could, I guess, work them out on hand calculators.

● The main advantage of linear programming is that it requires close attention to all of the variables, and the forcing of some choices. The model used deals quickly with these variables and shows the decision maker the possibilities in the situation.

● At this stage you aren't equipped to perform any really complex linear programming problems, nor was it intended that you should be. Rather, you know all of the *major* principles involved, and should be better equipped to talk intelligently with an operations researcher when he asks you questions about your operations in order to assist you in your decision making.

Heuristic problem solving

Heuristic problem solving means the use of reasoning that is plausible, but is lacking in rigorous proof. It is used for problems which do not appear to lend themselves to a highly programmed approach. The thought processes don't proceed in a straight line from start to finish. It is the maze-solving ability of the mouse, and indeed, some persons are "maze-bright" and others are "maze-dull." It involves searching, learning, appraisal, searching once more, relearning, and reappraisal. The results of trial and error, and past experiences in the same or identical situations, are stocked and fed back to apply to new situations.

The search in heuristic reasoning is as much a hunt for the processes of discovery as it is for the solution to a specific problem. The stages of heuristic problem solving could be identified as follows:

1. *The tabula rasa.* The problem solver starts out with a problem for which apparently there is no solution, or for which his past experience gives him few clues as to general guides to solution. The old riddle:

> An employer has three candidates for a position. All three appear equally qualified. The employer decides upon a test of thinking ability. He puts them in a room and instructs them as follows: "I have placed a mark on the forehead of each of you, which naturally you cannot see, although you can see the mark on the forehead of the other two. The mark on your forehead is either black or white. Your instructions are as follows: when you see a white mark on anybody else's forehead, raise your hand. When you know what color the mark on your head is get up and walk into my office. The first one there gets the job." He then got up and left. The three removed their blindfolds. Each raised his hand. Nobody moved for several minutes. Mr. A noted that the other two had white marks. He got up and walked into the office. "Mine is white." Mr. A was correct and got the job.
> How could Mr. A know that the mark on his forehead was white?

After running through the regular pattern of searches for tricks, mirrors, signals and the like, heuristic logic can begin. At this stage the slate is clean and the problem solver must search his mind for some key to find a wedge which will lead to solution.

2. *A first wedge.* The beginning of solution begins when a possible wedge toward cracking the problem appears. The problem solver notes some evidence that is found in the hands raised and the white spots. He may flounder a bit here trying out false starts such as "A saw the two

hands and knew they were looking at his forehead." He rejected this however, when he realizes they might have been looking at each other.

3. *Relationships.* A then thinks through some further relationships between the people. B and C could be looking at A himself, or at one another. A's hand is raised for either one or both of the other contestants. He structures this relationship in his mind.

4. *Abstraction ladder.* He then hypothesizes the various possibilities and explores each until it logically must be exploded. For example, he may think, "Suppose mine were black, what would the outcome be?"

5. *Insight.* By trial and error of the black hypotheses and persistent visualizing of the outcome of that supposition being true he comes to this conclusion. "If the mark on my forehead were black, then all three of us would have raised our hands, since I would have seen two whites and each of the others would have seen one white apiece. Then a light strikes. IF MINE HAD BEEN BLACK THE OTHERS WOULD HAVE KNOWN. Therefore mine must also be white."

Since the others would have looked at A's forehead and at the other person's raised hand, they would have known that their own mark was white, and would have rushed for the door. The fact that they all sat there puzzled indicated that black on A's brow must be excluded.

This rather simple example illustrates how the process of problem solving may call for experience in problem solving until the individual has acquired some facility in discovery. The method in this case happened to be an abstraction ladder, but other forms of syllogistic logic would apply in others. This is most often developed in a combination of studying logic and practice in dealing with such problems.

On one occasion the writer actually tried this mark-forehead experiment with three students. No sooner had the bandage been removed than one contestant snapped the answer, "My mark is white." I enquired into his reasoning and received a very sensible reply:

"I've heard this puzzle before."

Heuristic problem solving may often require experience.

Decision tree for decision making

This is a tool of operations research used for decision making where a sequence of decisions must be made, and the outcome of today's decision sets the stage for tomorrow's decision. The theoretical origins of this method lie in the mathematics of joint, conditional, and marginal probabilities discussed in Chapter 19. The enlargement of this simple model into operating management decision and analysis starts with the concept of tree diagrams as illustrations of sequential decisions. It calls upon estimates of probabilities for each of the branches following the initial decision, and it extends these in terms of added financial data extremely meaningful to the executive. For example, the costs of each alternative may be calculated, using the estimated probabilities for that outcome, and the revenues or income may also be calculated using the same probabilities as a base.

Three basic symbols are used in constructing the tree diagram:

1. ☐   Key decision point.

2. ◯   Chance or competitive event.

3. ☐   Course of action or decision.

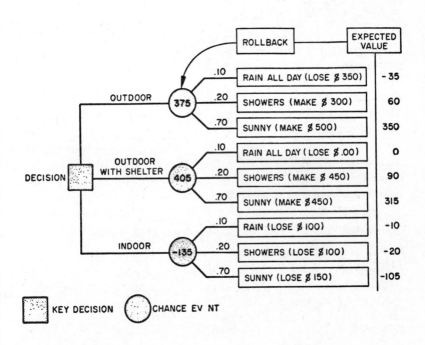

Figure 22-0

The nodes shown here indicate key decisions and the branches or lines between nodes are indicators of time elapsed between decisions or chance events.

How these might look in a simple tree diagram are shown in Figure 22-6.

For purposes of illustration we have constructed a tree diagram for the same outing which we made a decision upon in Chapter 3. The first step is to construct a payoff table for the respective choices which you might make about the picnic.

PAYOFF TABLE—EVENTS AND RESULTS

Choices	all-day rain	showers cloudy	sunny
1. commit to outdoor picnic all day	−$350	$300	$500
2. plan outdoors but inside cover for showers	—	$450	$450
3. plan for an inside outing and rain	−$100	−$100	−$150

Figure 22-7

At the basic decision point on Figure 22-6 we choose among the three alternatives which are the branches—outdoors, outdoors with shelter for a short time, and indoor and no provision for outdoors. Three possible outcomes are seen, and their consequence in budgetary terms.

1. If we commit ourselves to an outdoor picni nere are three possible financial outcomes.
   - If it rains we lose $350.
   - If we have showers we still make' $300.
   - If it is sunny all day we may make $500.

2. If we commit ourselves to an outdoor picnic but provide a temporary shelter and a movie we lay out another $50, but we face these outcomes.
   - If it rains all day we break even because people leave early, but our basic costs are covered.
   - If we have showers then our emergency plan goes into operation and we make $450
   - If it is sunny we stil make $450, having spent the safeguard funds for nothing.

3. If we schedule an indoor outing we can see the following outcomes.

- If it rains we lose $100, due to low attendance and high promotion and general expenses.
- If we have showers we still lose $100.
- If it is sunny we lose $150 since many people who promised to come won't show up, since the weather is so nice they'll find personal pursuits that take them outside.

Calculating expected values for each outcome

The weighting of each of these financial outcomes against the probabilities of each of the three kinds of weather helps clarify the decision-making process. It would look something like the tabulation at the right of the tree diagram. The probabilities have been posted against the possible outcomes for each of the three choices available, and this has been multiplied by the budgeted financial outcomes.

In terms of budget alone the choice of running an outdoor picnic with the expectation of sunny weather would be the best budgetary choice. Yet, the total of the expected values for any single outcome of weather, leads us to conclude that the highest collection of expected values lies in running the outing outdoors, but with shelter provided. The expected values are applied to the decision itself rather than to the final outcomes of the chance events.

The choice here of where to select the site of the picnic is what is being evaluated, and where the risk lies. The risk is not simply one of budgets, to be sure. There are risks of funds, of personal reputations, and of other variables. There is the risk to the members that they may waste a valuable summer day when they might be doing things more interesting or profitable.

It is now apparent that the use of tree diagrams is but another—very useful—method of presenting information for purposes of making up one's mind. The use of expected values, of probability, and of arraying the choices and the outcome was seen in the earlier calculations, and in PERT, and runs through most of operations research. Decision trees are simply a means of laying out in a clearer fashion what we might figure out the hard way on tables, charts and graphs of other types.

Much of its value lies in making the abstract seem concrete.

chapter 23

GUIDES FOR
FURTHER DEVELOPMENT

*Part of the feeling of dissatisfaction with the
mathematical treatment of economic theory
derives largely from the fact that one is
offered not proofs but mere assertions which
are really no better than the same assertions
given in literary form.*
—VON NEUMANN and MORGENSTERN

If you have gone this far, you have undoubtedly developed some interest
in decision making, and might be interested in a more complete treatment
of the various subjects which have been covered here in laymen's language.

First, let's summarize the approach to decision making which has been
taken in this book.

1. There's no doubt that many conflicting opinions of decision theory
exist. Since this book has attempted to merge several, it will find many in
sharp disagreement with many of the ideas proposed, or theories explained.
That's because there are as many ideas about the proper form for decisions
as there are writers and scholars in the field.

2. Each approach, the mathematical, the behavioral, the intuitive and
the empirical, has its own sub-school, all of which are apparently confident
of their grasp of the ultimate explanations. Naturally, all of the best features
of most of them have been included here, a statement certain to arouse
disputatious replies.

Rather than rush to defense before an attack has emerged, it might be
wiser at this point to abstract some of the better known books in the field

of decision making. This list isn't intended to be exhaustive, but to span the field and provide the reader with a suggested guide for further study if he's so inclined. Many excellent journal articles could also be cited, but limitations of space and time don't permit their inclusion.

I. *Books which are in general agreement with the approach here.*

Juran, Joseph, *Managerial Breakthrough.* New York, N.Y.: McGraw-Hill Book Company, Inc., 1965.

A book for the operating manager and staff analyst presenting an analytical scheme and system for moving a situation from controlled equilibrium to new levels of excellence through making "breakthroughs." Loaded with original insights and an orderly system for altering the present level or condition to new levels.

Drucker, Peter, *Managing for Results.* New York, N.Y.: Harper & Row, 1966.

One of the best written and most insightful of the popular books on management decision making and problem solving. This book agrees with Juran that problem solving merely restores normality. An award winner in the McKinsey books award program, this volume is widely applauded by critics and practicioners alike.

Kepner, Charles, and Benjamin B. Tregoe, *The Rational Manager.* New York, N.Y.: McGraw-Hill Book Company, Inc., 1965.

A systematic approach to problem solving and decision making, used as a text for their widely used management training simulation course. It has been used widely to train managers in America's leading corporations. It draws heavily upon the basic concepts of Herbert Simon in defining problems and causes. Numerous case studies.

Simon, Herbert A., *The New Science of Management Decisions.* New York. N.Y.: Harper & Row, 1960.

A germinal work in the application of systems to decision making. In the opinion of this author all decision-making theory in management will be dated "before Simon" or "after Simon" in the future. Simon defines the problem as a deviation from a standard (like Kepner and Tregoe, who add that the deviation must be important enough for somebody to want to close the gap). This book suggests that in addition to the deviation, it is solved when somebody is committed to its solution (thus the title of this book). Simon also suggests that causes of problems are changes which caused the problem to exist. Juran would add that where you can't see the change or find when it occurred you may use Pareto's law to make a breakthrough. Simon's work is based upon many years of research into computer processes which simulate human thought

II. *Books which amplify some materials covered partially in this book.*

Bursk, Edward C. and John F. Chapman, *New Decision Making Tools for Managers.* Cambridge, Mass.: Harvard University Press, 1963.

This is a series of articles originally published in Harvard Business Review, and is an excellent introduction into the use of mathematical tools for managerial decision making. Undoubtedly the manager of the future must be conversant with these tools, and this book is a fine reference point to make him a talented amateur. The major limitation here is that it usually assumes that the problem and objective are already defined, and that in some instances all that's left is mathematical ways of choosing among alternatives. It doesn't get into specifying a problem, defining an objective, or implementing the decision once it has been made.

The Irwin Series in Mathematical Analysis for Business is a series for the would-be professional in the field of operations research and mathematical analysis for business decisions. Among the leading general decision-making volumes in this series are the following (all are published by Irwin, Homewood):

Bowman and Fetter, *Analysis for Production Management* (rev. ed.). Homewood, Ill.: Richard D. Irwin, 1961.

Deals especially with mathematical techniques for analysis of production problems. The techniques and tools are almost the same as used in other functional areas, but are applied to manufacturing decisions.

Bierman, Bonini, Fouraker and Jaedicke, *Quantitative Analysis for Business Decisions* (rev. ed.). Homewood, Ill.: Richard D. Irwin, 1965.

For students with much business course work, plus some college math. It is almost half filled with applications of probability theory, plus some applications of game theory, linear programming, and simulation. The latter part of the book is the application of these techniques to such problems as waiting lines, investment decisions, pricing decisions, and merchandizing decisions.

Howell and Teicheroew, *Mathematical Analysis for Business Decisions*. Homewood, Ill.: Richard D. Irwin, 1963.

A more general mathematical decision-making book, it draws on more advanced mathematics including algebra, calculus, and probability to structure decisions. Presents models for decision in finance, accounting, and organization.

III. *Other current mathematically oriented decision books.*

Hein, Leonard, *The Quantitative Approach to Managerial Decisions.* Englewood Cliffs, N.J.: Prentice-Hall, 1967.

This book is cited as being one for non-mathematicians, but if you can't understand or get baffled by math, you'll find it rugged going. It covers deterministic and stochastic managerial decision models. It starts with some basic definitions, moves quickly into the computer and its uses. It covers mathematical probability and shows how it works on waiting line problems, work sampling, control charts, and linear programming. It also explains PERT, PACE, learning curve critical path method, and line of balance. Like most such books, it mixes managerial and technical problems. It also deals mainly with how to make choices among alternatives, or to display those alternatives and their consequences. It doesn't deal with how to decide whether or not you have a problem, or to spell out an objective. It presumes that objectives are given, and that decisions are similar to what Kepner and Tregoe would call solution of problems, restoring norms, or preventing less than normal outcome from occurring.

Shuchman, Abe, *Scientific Decision Making in Business.* New York, N.Y.: Holt, Rinehart & Winston, Inc., 1963.

This is another book for non-mathematicians which consists of readings by a variety of authors on operations research. It tells what operations research is, what its methods are. The research tools for dealing with complexity, lack of information, are discussed. It concludes with examples of applications to inventory, production scheduling, sales and promotion, accounting, budgeting and mergers and acquisitions. Very readable and clear explanation of OR.

Morris, William T., *Management Science: A Bayesian Introduction.* Englewood Cliffs, N.J.: Prentice Hall, 1968.

As we've noted in this book, the old-fashioned kind of "frequent" statistics are now passé among the advanced decision makers. The works of Savage are frankly too deep-dish for most managers who haven't kept up with their math. A recent book, *Probability and Profit*, by Professor Fellner of Yale (Irwin, 1965) is good but doesn't include busir   decisions and is aimed more at the economist. Bayesian statistics in practice appear in many other newer texts, but this new one pulls together a loose collection of models, techniques and ideas in management science and ties them together based on Bayesian decision theory. The author tries to tie together intuition, experience, judgment staff analysis. A tough assignment, as this author can testify. Again, it says it's not for mathematicians and, in fact, you can skip over the calculus if you choose. It's a lot more mathematical than this book, for example.

IV. *Books about behavioral aspects of decision making.*

Maier and Hayes, *Creative Management.* New York, N.Y.: John Wiley & Sons, Inc., 1961, and Maier, Norman F., *Problem-Solving Discussions and Conferences.* New York, N.Y.: McGraw-Hill Book Company, Inc., 1963.

Professor Maier, a one-time noted experimentalist, nas of late concentrated on the decision-making and problem-solving process as faced by managers. His concern is with democratic principles in authoritarian institutions. He proposes that authoritarian methods of problem solving stifle creativity, and reduce the quality as well as the acceptance of the decision. The group which participates in the identification of the problem, or the establishment of the objective will move with more creativity toward its solution and certainty will accept the decision more readily. His definition of the problem is like Kepner-Tregoe's or Simon's, but his approach is less centered in analysis than in acceptance and group conferences.

McGregor, Douglas, *The Human Side of Enterprise.* New York, N.Y.: McGraw-Hill Book Company, Inc., 1960.

Already a classic, this work by the leading behavioral scientist dealing with management probably has had more impact on the way decisions are made than any other. His style of management, noted in this text, proposes an assumption about people called Theory Y. The average person, this theory goes, finds work as natural and pleasant as rest or play, and therefore can be relied upon to be creative and productive when he knows the goal. Decision making can be autocratic or democratic, and he proposes that decisions which are the former will result in less overall effectiveness in the organization than the latter. A book dealing with a specific system for decision making, it presents a philosophy around which a whole management system could be constructed.

It has some rather jaundiced views of many of the conventional tools of managerial decision making, which would include tight technical organization and tight discipline, enforced by scientific management tools. Clearly a humanistic approach, with a strong following.

Odiorne, George S., *Management by Objectives*. New York, N.Y.: Pitman Publishing Corp., 1965.

A book for managers which tells how the system of management called "management by objectives" operates. Not mainly philosophy but a system, the book has been described as moderately behavioral, but "more Skinnerian than McGregorian" in emphasis. It proposes that commitment between manager and subordinates is more important in getting organization objectives achieved than any single ingredient in management practice. It proposes that objectives, whether set from top down or bottom up, should be clearly understood by superior and subordinate. It proposes that breaking these job objectives down into three major categories is a key step in defining goals: regular, problem solving, and creative. This present book is an expansion of the earlier work and deals with management of one category of objectives, the problem-solving objective.

SUMMARY

Clearly this listing is incomplete, but its purpose isn't intended to exhaust the literature, but to provide some further suggested references for those interested in added work and study of the fascinating idea of decision making and problem solving. A few significant omissions should be noted, especially Jay Forrester's *Industrial Dynamics*, Rensis Likert's *New Patterns of Management*, and Ed Schleh's *Managing for Results*. Beyond these are numerous other texts and a plethora of journal articles. Time and space prohibit their inclusion.

INDEX